Baseball in Chillicothe

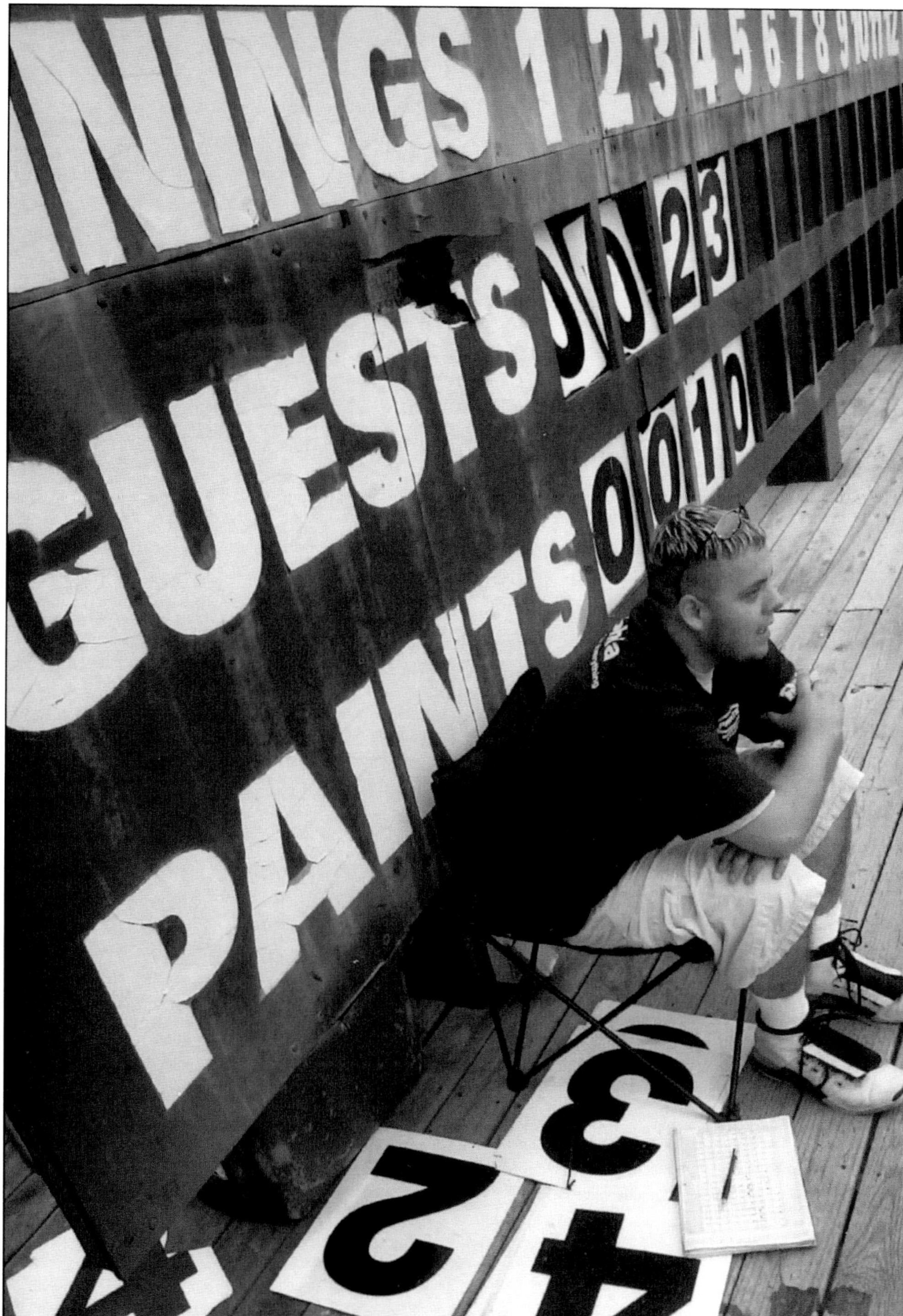

V.A. Memorial Stadium has a modern electronic scoreboard, but in a nod to the nostalgic past the team retains the old-fashioned manual version. Travis Hill does the honors here. (Courtesy of Scott Osborne.)

BASEBALL IN CHILLICOTHE

Mike Shannon

ARCADIA
PUBLISHING

ISBN 978-0-7385-3356-8

Published by Arcadia Publishing
Charleston, South Carolina

Printed in the United States of America

Library of Congress Catalog Card Number: 2004116415

For all general information contact Arcadia Publishing at:
Telephone 843-853-2070
Fax 843-853-0044
E-mail sales@arcadiapublishing.com
For customer service and orders:
Toll-Free 1-888-313-2665

Visit us on the Internet at www.arcadiapublishing.com

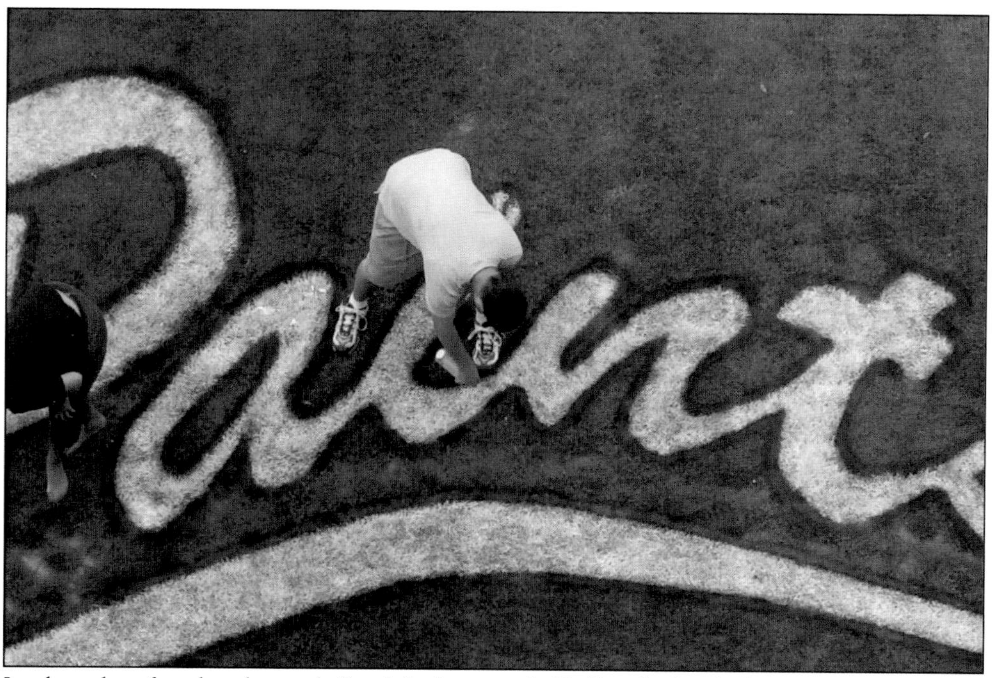

It takes a lot of work to keep a ballpark looking good. Chillicothe baseball fans are lucky that the Paints' organization takes so much pride in making V.A. Memorial such a beautiful place to spend a summer evening watching gallant young men chase their dreams. (Courtesy of Scott Osborne.)

Contents

Acknowledgments

As the photographs are the heart of a book of this kind, my first thanks must go to those who made photographs available to me. The Chillicothe Paints' organization is at the top of that list. I wish to thank owner Chris Hanners, President Shirley Bandy, and General Manager Bryan Wickline for permission to use the photos owned by the Paints and for making them freely available to me, in both senses of the word. My additional thanks to Bryan for producing some especially helpful pictures; and to field manager Jamie Keefe and John Wend, the team's Director of Sales and Marketing—as well as the best damn P.A. man in the business—for help in identifying the players in many photos and for information about the players. Jamie and John must have wondered why I made so many trips to Chillicothe to research the book and to hunt down photos, and I don't mind saying here that it was partly because I could always count on a warm welcome from them and a fun time joking and reminiscing at the Paints' offices. The majority of photos in this book have been supplied by the Paints, and all unattributed photos are courtesy of the team.

I am also grateful to Maleine Davis, who trusted me with her big box of Paints' photos for several months; to Harry Chenault, who lent me Paints' baseball cards and programs; to amiable shutterbugs and loyal Paints' fans Tim Reiter and Tom Wonderleigh for sharing their pictures; to Robert J. Moorhead who supplied some of the first-class photos he took for the *Chillicothe Gazette*; and to Scott Osborne, who generously offered me use of his outstanding photos. (Some of Scott's other brilliant work can be seen at www.sportshooter.com/scottosborne.) The Ross County Historical Society was also very helpful, and I wish to thank in particular Lisa Hess and Pat Medert.

The *Chillicothe Gazette* has always provided excellent coverage of the Paints, and I tip my cap to their writers whose stories preserved the exploits of the team as they happened: Jeff DiVeronica, Brent Neal, Bob Barnhart, Theoden James, Mark Sonka, Scott Hennen, Bill Broderick, James Johnson, Paul Warner, Mike Griffin, and, most of all, the talented Phil Gray.

Doug Kimsey is the official historian of the Chillicothe Paints, and I thank him for graciously allowing me access to the Paints' statistical record he has maintained since the beginning. I also thank Dan Ramey, one of the two original Paints' broadcasters (along with John Rose), for a photo I was unfortunately not able to squeeze into the book; Matt Andrews for a great photo of Chief Krazy Horse; the fine people at Mears Photography in downtown Chillicothe; my friend Jim Walsh who pinch-printed a number of photos for me; Andrew Smiley for creating my website (mikeshannonbooks.com); Commissioner Bill Lee for my Frontier League press pass; umpires Max McLeary and Jim Schaly for always making me feel at home in their world; all the folks at Arcadia who helped create this book, especially editor Jeff Ruetsche; and Paints' fans everywhere, the best baseball fans anywhere.

Finally, as always, my deepest gratitude must go to my father and mother, John and Willie Shannon; to my sisters and brothers, Laura, Susie, John, and Tim; and to my loving wife, Derms, and our five wonderful children, Meg, Casey, Mick, Babe, and Nollie Boy.

INTRODUCTION

Minor league baseball was made for a city like Chillicothe, Ohio, where the love of the National Pastime runs as deep as the heritage of the native American Indians who first settled the area. After Chillicothe lost its last entry in the old Class D Ohio State League in 1916, it seemed that the friendly southern Ohio city that was the first capital of the Buckeye State would never again have a professional team to call its own. But the revival of independent pro baseball gave Chillicothe another chance.

It was the Chillicothe-Ross County Chamber of Commerce that first expressed interest in obtaining an original Frontier League franchise for Chillicothe in 1992. When the cost of doing so proved to be prohibitive, Chris Hanners, a local dentist identified in the newspaper as an "optometrist," stepped up to the plate, paying the $3,000 franchise fee and pledging another $40,000 in start-up costs. "It's my way of trying to do something for the area," said Hanners. "The area has been very good to me."

The Paints' organization hit the ground running, and with the help of numerous volunteers they readied V.A. Memorial Stadium for professional baseball. The first league tryout and draft was held in Chillicothe, and both *Baseball Weekly* and *Baseball America* took note of the event, recognition that put Chillicothe on the baseball map. Hanners' leadership not only made the Paints' the rock of the league, but was also instrumental in seeing the league itself through its shaky first season of existence. The Frontier League has gone into bigger and bigger markets and is now recognized as an unqualified success. The Chillicothe Paints, one of the league's bigger markets in the beginning, is now it's smallest; nevertheless, the Paints remain a model of how to run a professional baseball franchise. The Paints are strongly supported by the Chillicothe-Ross County business community, and there exists between the team and its fans a love affair that is truly heartwarming in this era of cynicism and self-aggrandizement.

On the field the Paints have battled hard and have earned a reputation for being, year-in and year-out, fierce competitors. In the 12 years of the Frontier League's existence, the Paints have twice compiled the best overall record in the league. They have qualified for the playoffs six times and have reached the finals four times. The organization has sent 27 players into affiliated ball; placed eight players on the Frontier League 10th Season All-Star Team (Scott Pinoni, Mitch House, Mike Cervenak, Gator McBride, Rick Blanc, Bob Spears, Brian Tollberg, and Bobby Chandler); and was the first to graduate a Frontier League player to the major leagues. The only thing missing is that elusive victory in the finals, which would give the Paints their first Frontier League Championship. However, as Roger Hanners, the manager with the most victories in Frontier League history, would say, "That day is coming."

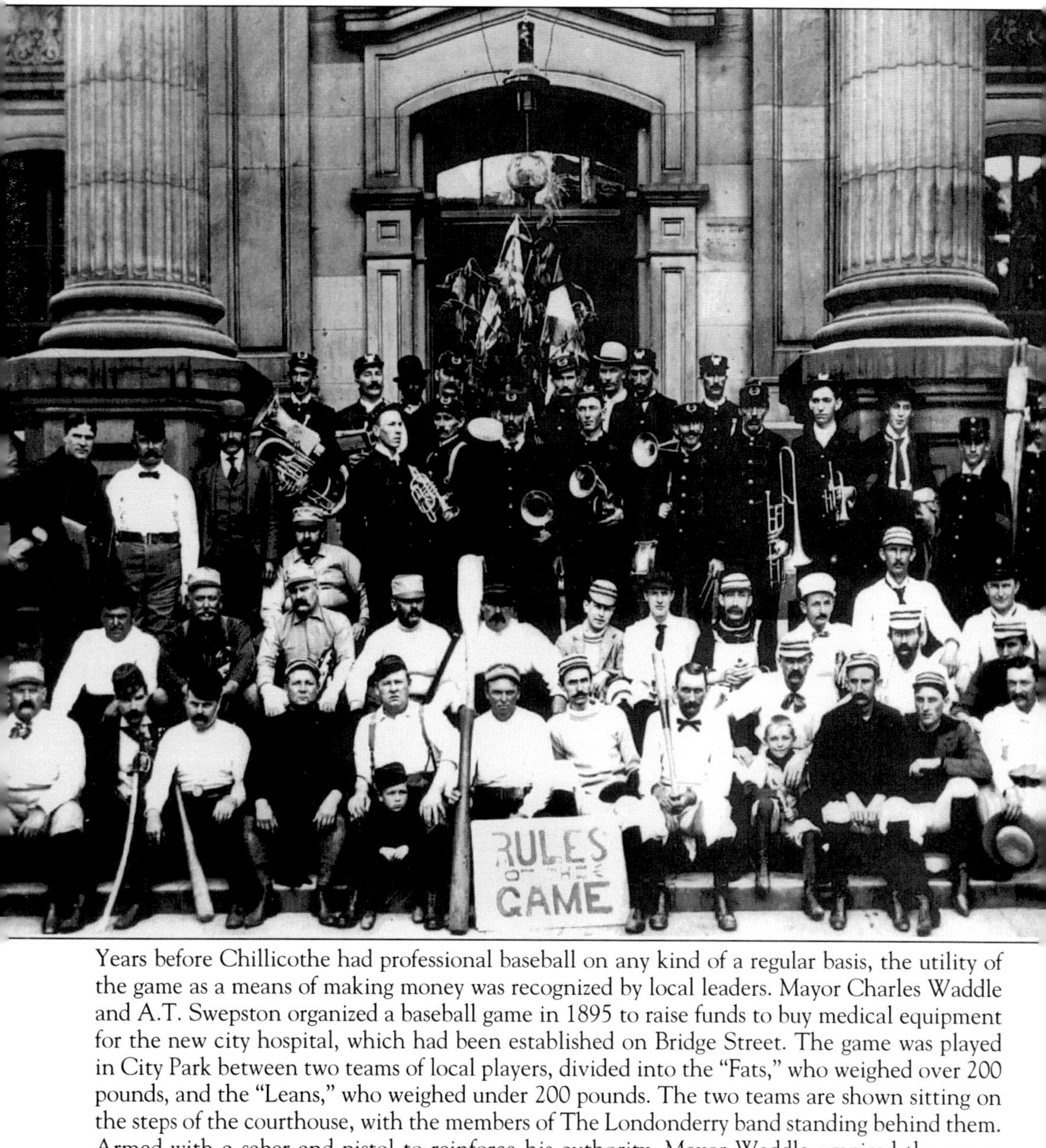

Years before Chillicothe had professional baseball on any kind of a regular basis, the utility of the game as a means of making money was recognized by local leaders. Mayor Charles Waddle and A.T. Swepston organized a baseball game in 1895 to raise funds to buy medical equipment for the new city hospital, which had been established on Bridge Street. The game was played in City Park between two teams of local players, divided into the "Fats," who weighed over 200 pounds, and the "Leans," who weighed under 200 pounds. The two teams are shown sitting on the steps of the courthouse, with the members of The Londonderry band standing behind them. Armed with a saber and pistol to reinforce his authority, Mayor Waddle umpired the game, which was won by the Leans. (Courtesy of Ross County Historical Society.)

ONE

Beginnings

Almost certainly, baseball in some form was played in Chillicothe even prior to the War Between the States. The earliest record we have of organized ball dates back to 1866 when a town team from Chillicothe defeated the Circleville Eurekas, 25-2.

Professional baseball came to Chillicothe amazingly early, although it did not last very long. In 1884 the Chillicothe Logans were founded as charter members of the Ohio State Association, but they disbanded when the Association folded at the end of the season. Ten years later another professional outfit was formed in Chillicothe as members of the Tri-State League. This team suffered the same fate as the Logans, disbanding along with their league after the inaugural season.

The formation of the Ohio State League, a Class D circuit, in 1908 gave Chillicothe another shot at the professional game, and the Chillicothe Infants joined the league as a new franchise in 1910. The Infants, or Babes as they were also called, finished last in their first season, behind Lancaster, Newark, Marion, Lima, and champion Portsmouth. Oddly enough, three of the Infants' opponents (Lancaster, Newark, and Portsmouth) represented cities that would join the Chillicothe Paints in the Frontier League eight decades later. Chillicothe improved to fourth place (with the league expanded to eight teams) with a 76-62 record in 1911, but dropped to last again in 1912.

In 1913 the Babes (83-49) won Chillicothe's first professional baseball title when they finished in a virtual tie for first with Charleston (84-50). Chillicothe's Frank Nesser led the league in hits with 178. The Ohio State League fell into disarray in 1914, as four of its eight teams withdrew in mid-season. Chillicothe won the first half championship, but finished third overall with a composite record of 72-65. Chillicothe withdrew from the league after the first half of the 1915 season, and the franchise was moved to Maysville, Kentucky, where the team was renamed the Angels. Chillicothe rejoined the Ohio State League for the start of the second half of the 1916 season. Six games later the league disbanded, and Chillicothe would not have a pro baseball team to call their own again until the independent Frontier League came to town.

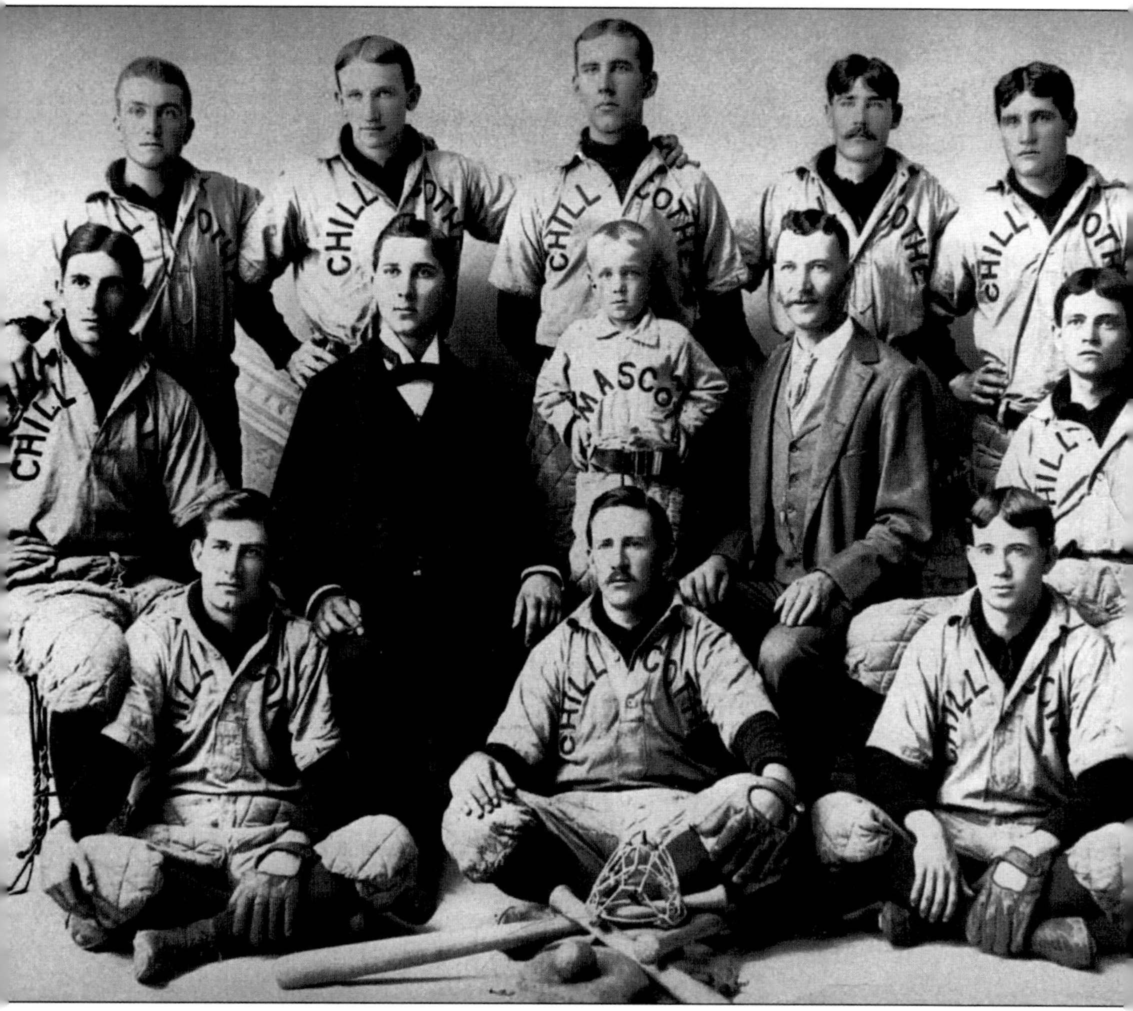

Before the turn of the century almost every town worthy of the name had an amateur baseball team that represented the community. One such "town team" was this aggregate of Chillicothe players organized by Johnny Hamm; they played games on the present site of Mt. Logan School. Hamm's Nine of 1896 played exhibition games against two National League clubs, the Cincinnati Reds and the Baltimore Orioles. Both teams had future Hall of Famers in uniform: Orioles Ned Hanlon, Hughie Jennings, Willie Keeler, Joe Kelly, and Wilbert Robinson; and Reds Buck Ewing and Bid McPhee. The two men not in uniform in this photo were managers of the team, Henry Hamm and George Hamm, Sr (George Hamm, Jr. was the mascot). Not pictured: Johnny Hamm. (Courtesy of Ross Historical Society.)

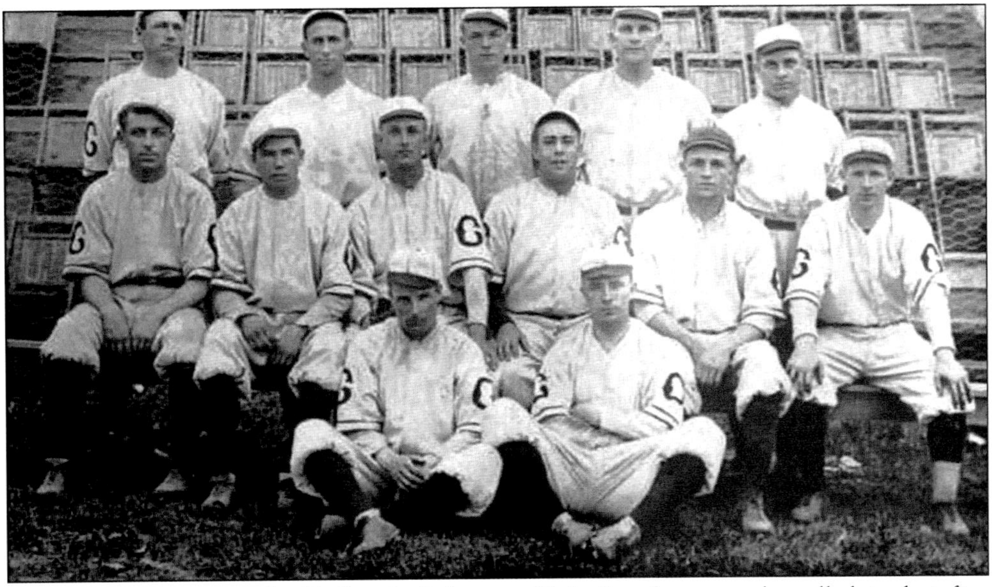

This is a team picture of the Chillicothe Infants, or "Babes" as they were also called, in their first year of existence, 1910. Chillicothe was a member of the Ohio State League (for at least parts of each season) until the league disbanded a week into the second half of the 1916 campaign. This photo appeared in the July 29th issue of the *Scioto Gazette*. Pictured from left to right are: (front row) Ware (C), and DeWitt (CF); (middle row) Irwin (1B), Wilkie (P), Harrison (P), Hiram Grandel (P), Cooperrider (P), and Whalen (2B); (back row) Lohr (LF), Kebler (3B), Purtell (SS), Haley (C), and Potts (RF). (Courtesy Ross County Historical Society.)

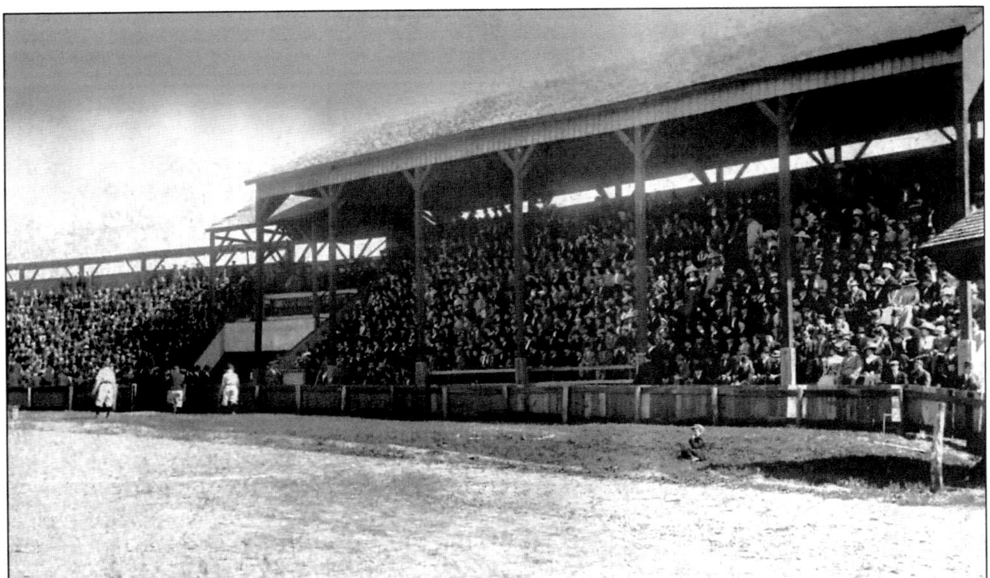

May 5, 1910, turned out to be an unforgettable Opening Day for Chillicothe's new minor league team. Not for anything the team did on the field but because the grandstands at League Park caught fire and burned. This is the scene moments before the ballpark caught fire. (Courtesy of Ross County Historical Society.)

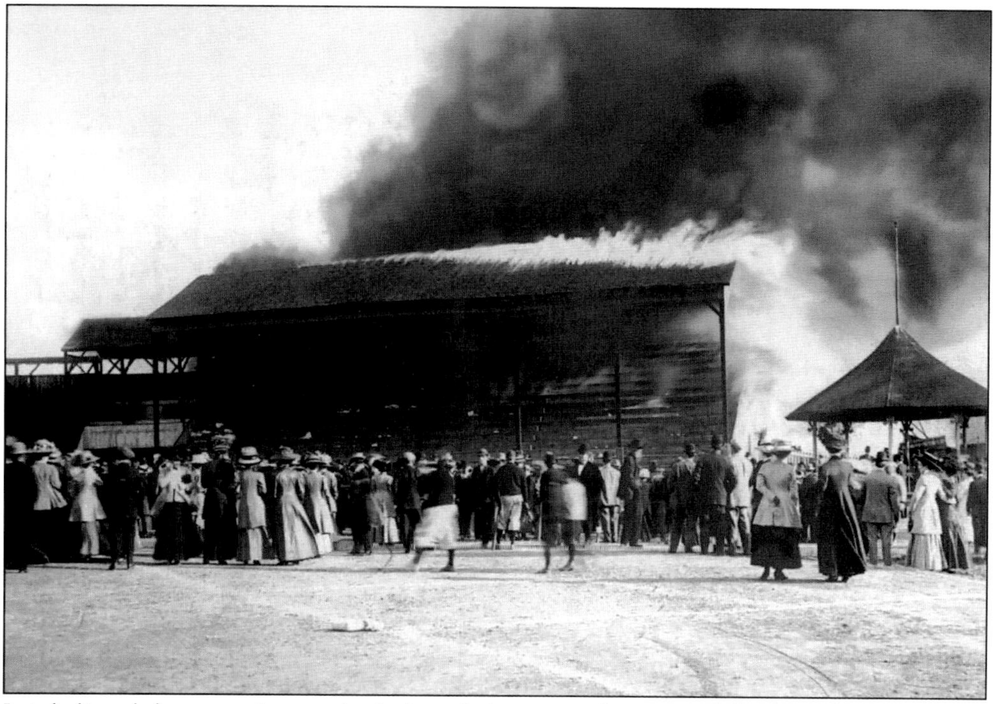

It is believed that a careless smoker's discarded cigarette butt caused the fire, which started in the grandstand and spread to the bleachers within five minutes. Although the ballpark was a total ($3,000) loss, no one was injured, as cool heads prevailed and directed an orderly emptying of the grandstands packed with fans. The *Scioto Gazette* reported that the Chillicothe team's games would be moved to the Kite track. (Courtesy of Ross County Historical Society.)

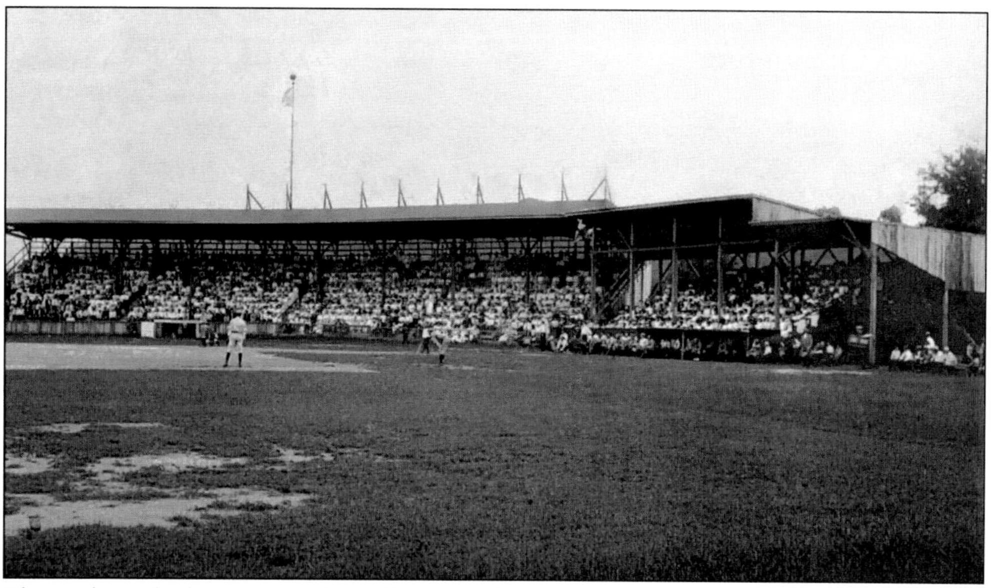

This is the re-built League Park on "Hospital Day" in 1911. According to state law, the new structure had to be built of concrete or iron, and the cost of re-building was estimated at $5,000. (Courtesy of Ross County Historical Society.)

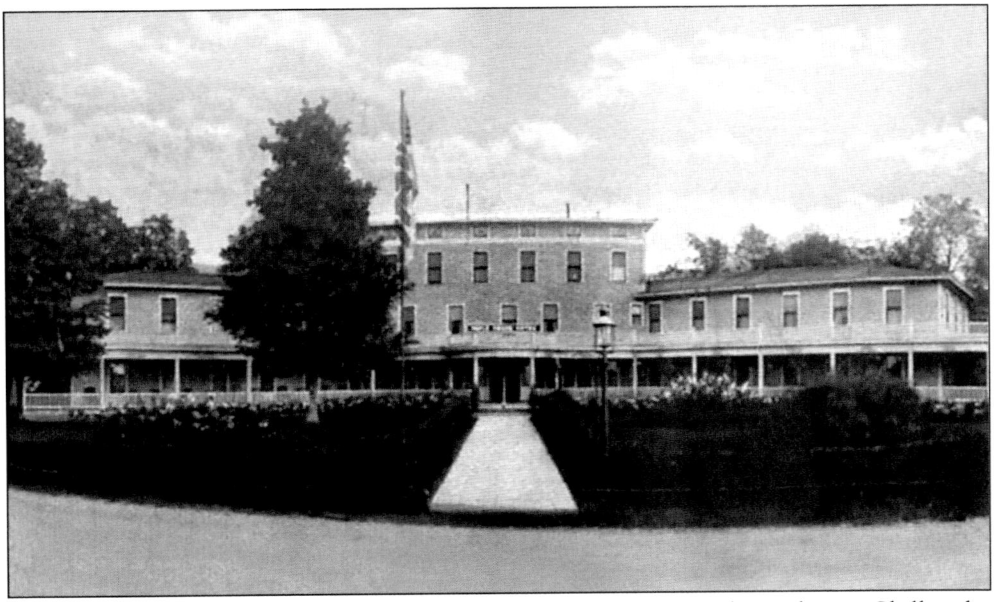

The Maple Grove Hotel, a popular luxury health resort that was located near Chillicothe in Union Township on the Frankfort Pike, was pretty as a postcard. The main attraction of the 100-room Hotel, which opened in 1908, was the mineral spring on the property that was advertised as a cure for a variety of common ailments and diseases. To meet the exercise needs of the guests the Hotel offered croquet, a bowling alley, a pool, a billiard room, a dance pavilion, and a baseball diamond. In 1910 and 1911 the Columbus Senators Baseball Club held their spring training at the Maple Grove Hotel. The resort fell on hard times during the depression and never recovered. Only a small portion of the original hotel still stands, and it survives as a private residence. (Courtesy of Ross County Historical Society.)

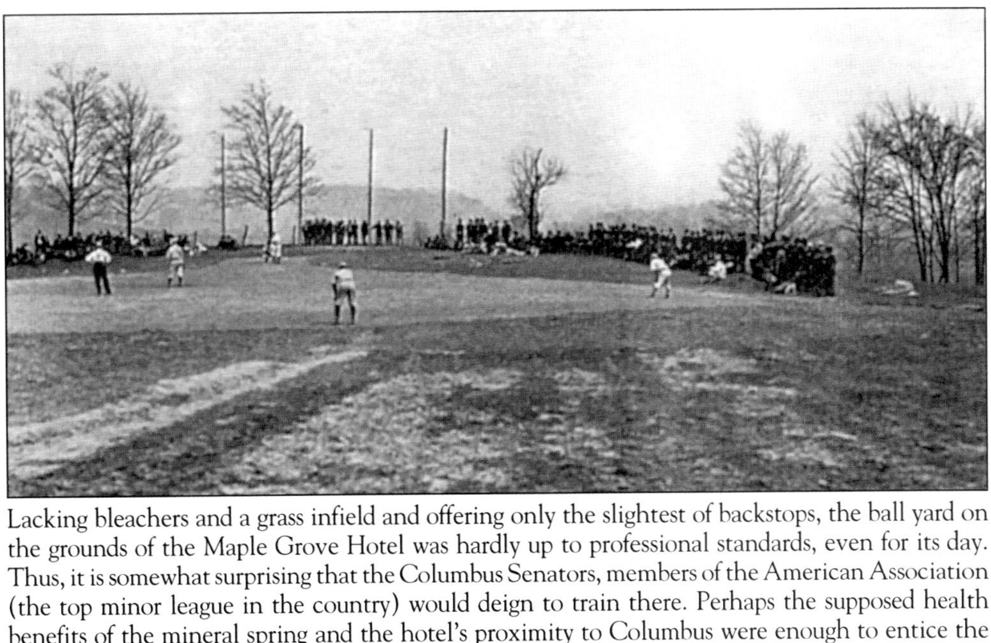

Lacking bleachers and a grass infield and offering only the slightest of backstops, the ball yard on the grounds of the Maple Grove Hotel was hardly up to professional standards, even for its day. Thus, it is somewhat surprising that the Columbus Senators, members of the American Association (the top minor league in the country) would deign to train there. Perhaps the supposed health benefits of the mineral spring and the hotel's proximity to Columbus were enough to entice the Senators to the Maple Grove. (Courtesy of Ross County Historical Society.)

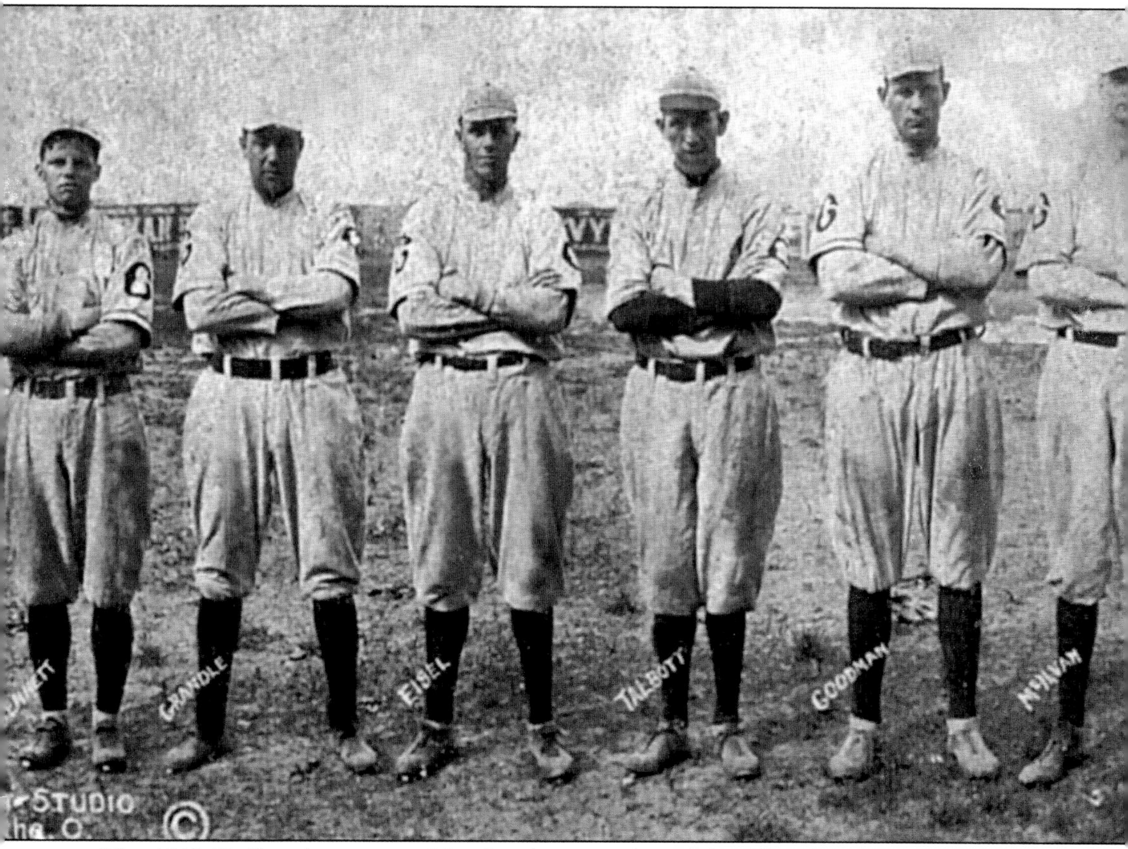

The 1913 Chillicothe team tied for the championship of the Ohio State League with a record of 83-49. Pictured from left to right are Bennett, Grandle, Eisel, Talbott, Goodman, McIlvan,

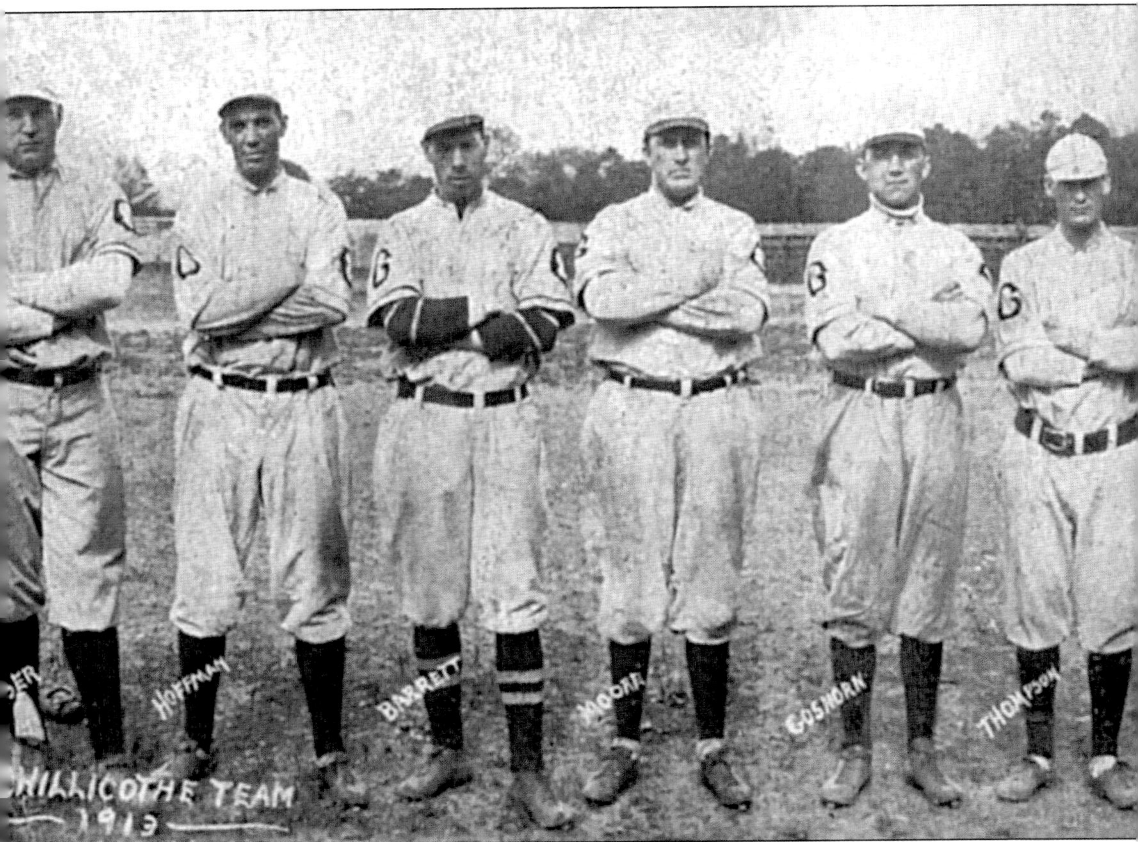

Nesser, Hoffman, Barrett, Moore, Goshorn, and Thompson. Frank Nesser led the league in hits with 178. (Courtesy of Ross County Historical Society.)

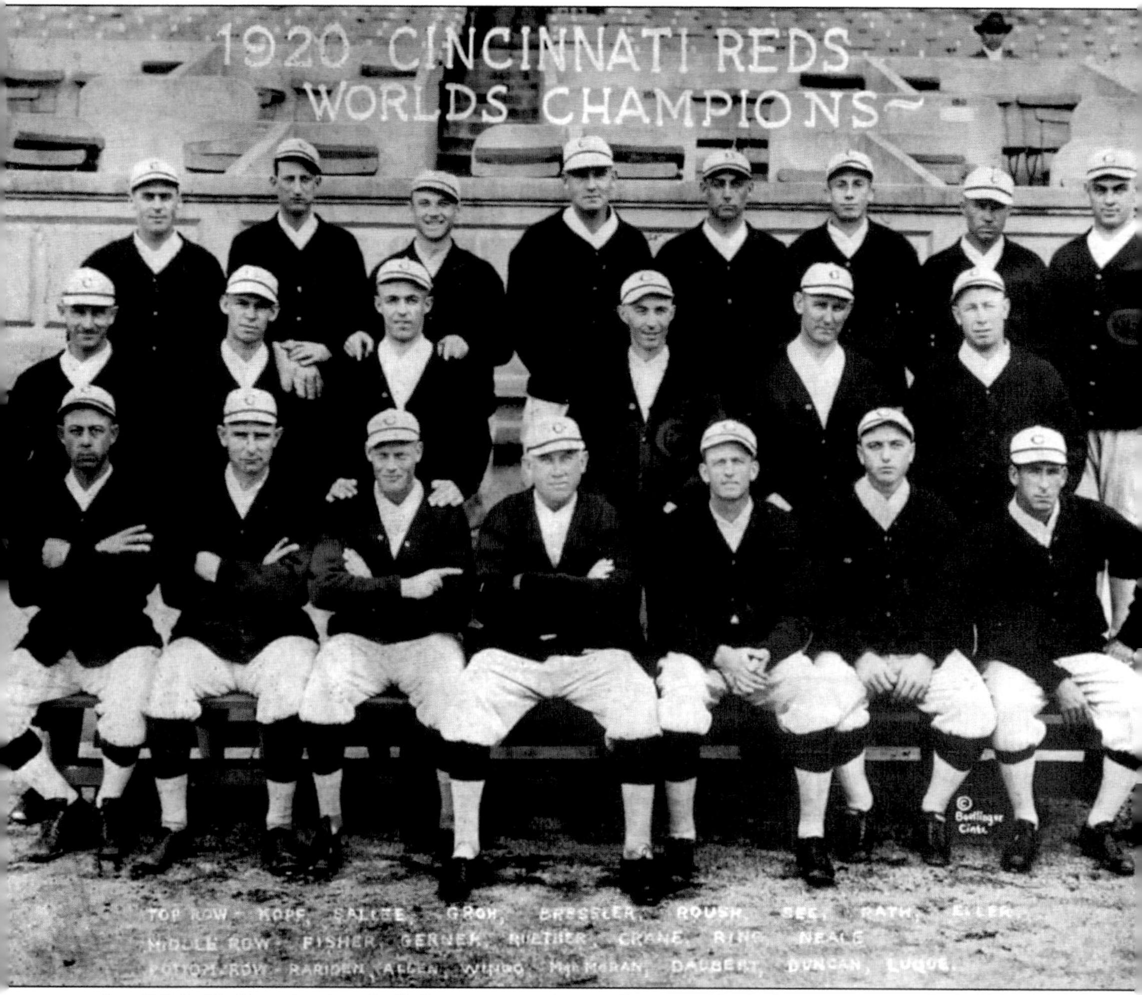

In 1920 Chillicothe baseball fans received a real treat when the reigning World Champion Cincinnati Reds came to town for an exhibition game at Meaco Park. The previous fall the Reds had upset the Chicago Black Sox in the most infamous World Series ever played. These Reds, who believed they would have beaten the White Sox even if the Sox had not fallen in with gamblers, took on a local all-star team. The Reds' Hod Eller struck out 17 batters in the game. Pictured from left to right are : (front row) Bill Rariden, Nick Allen, Ivy Wingo, Pat Moran, Jake Daubert, Pat Duncan, and Dolph Luque; (middle row) Ray Fisher, Ed Gerner, Dutch Ruether, Sam Crane, Jimmy Ring, and Greasy Neale; (back row) Larry Kopf, Slim Sallee, Heinie Groh, Rube Bressler, Edd Roush, Charlie See, Morrie Rath, and Hod Eller. (Courtesy of Ross County Historical Society.)

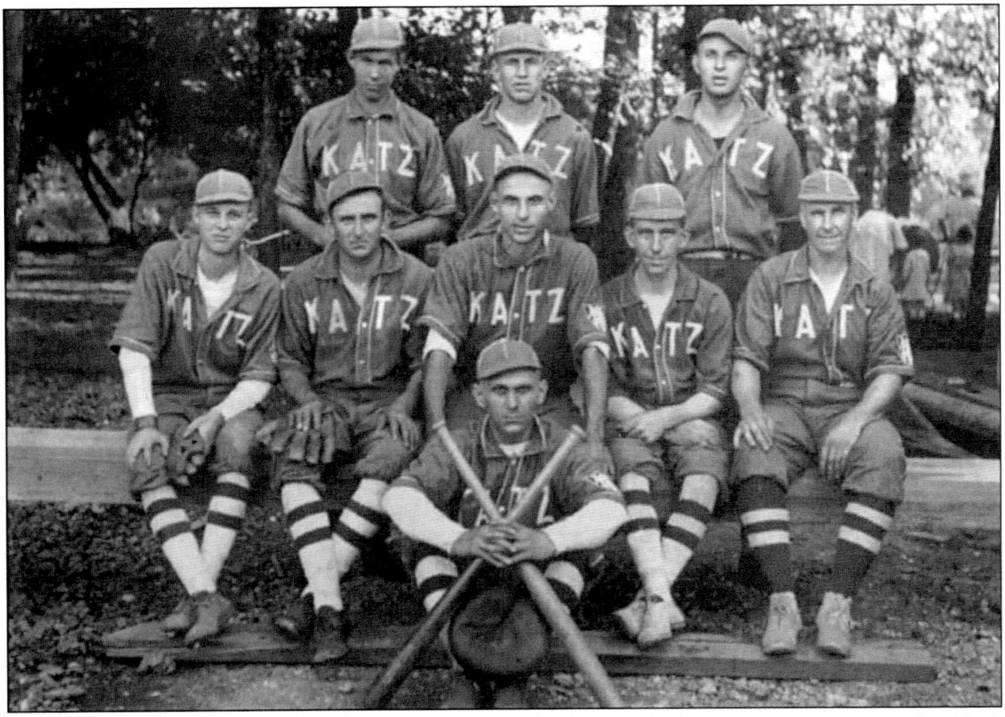

The Mead Paper Company has long been one of Chillicothe's best corporate citizens. In 1919 Mead organized an intramural baseball league for company employees. The league consisted of four teams, and their uniforms were supplied by the Katz and Katz Men's Clothing Store. (Courtesy of Ross County Historical Society.)

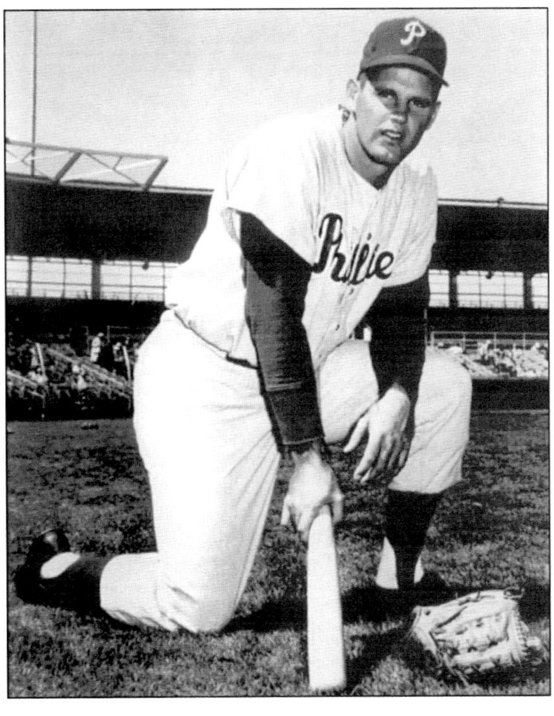

The best baseball player to ever come out of Chillicothe High School, John Herrnstein (Class of 1955), was one of the 16 original inductees into the Chillicothe High School Sports Hall of Fame in 1993 (along with Greg Cook,1965, a first round draft choice of the Cincinnati Bengals and the AFL Rookie of the Year in 1969, and Neil Johnston, 1946, whose eight-year career with the Philadelphia Warriors also landed him in the NBA Hall of Fame). An outfielder-first baseman, Herrnstein played parts of five seasons with the Philadelphia Phillies and briefly with the Chicago Cubs and Atlanta Braves, as well. He hit six home runs in 1964, the year the Phillies lost a seemingly clinched pennant by blowing a 61/2-game lead with 12 games left to play. (Courtesy of Ross County Historical Society.)

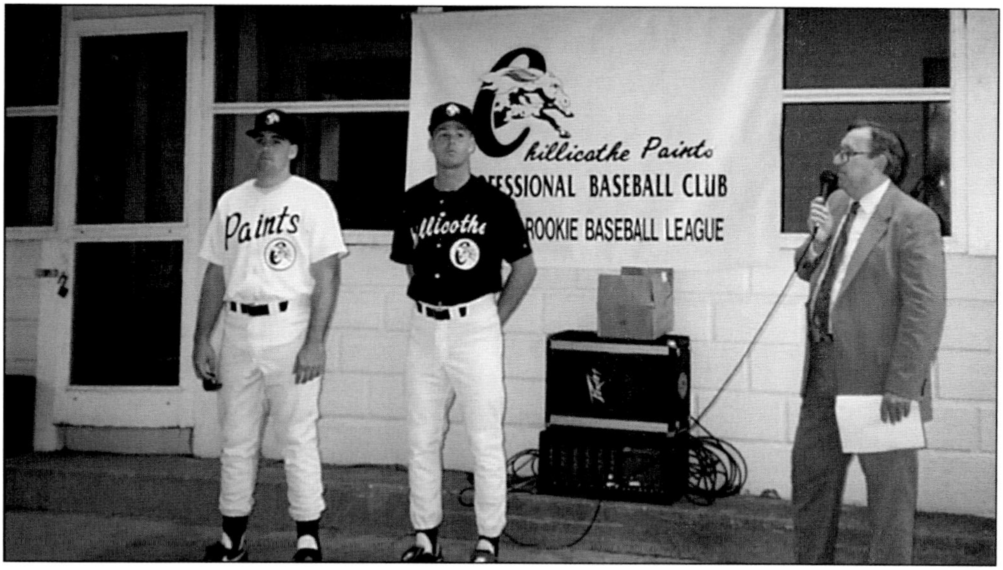

At a press conference before the first season in Paints' history, GM Terry Barthelmas introduces players showing off the new team's original uniforms. A former football player at the University of Miami (FL), Barthelmas had worked in the front offices of the Reds, Cubs, and Indians and had helped begin the Toronto Blue Jays organization. On Monday, July 12, with the Paints standing at 6-4 in second place, Barthelmas abruptly announced his resignation, citing "philosophical differences" with the ballclub. Two weeks earlier, however, Chris Hanners had acknowledged in the *Chillicothe Gazette* Barthelmas' contribution to getting the organization up and running in such a hurry: "Terry is probably one of the only guys in the United States who could have pulled off what we did in one hundred days. Unless you've seen the day-to-day stuff, it would be hard to understand." (Courtesy of Maleine Davis.)

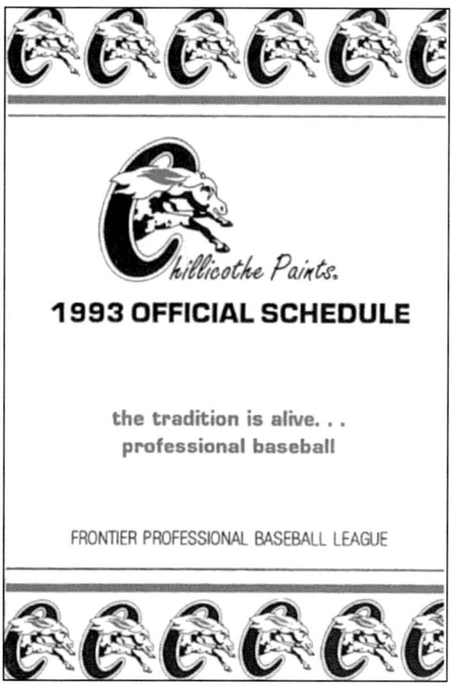

The Paints' pocket schedule for 1993 contains a few retrospective clues to the vicissitudes inherent in the inaugural season of an independent baseball league. The Paints were originally scheduled to play 28 home games and only 24 road games, an imbalance that would normally not be tolerated by teams disadvantaged by it. The folding of the Tri-State Tomahawks and the West Virginia Coal Sox two weeks into the season threw the schedule into total disarray and resulted in the decisions to shift the Portsmouth Explorers from the Western to the Eastern Division, to adopt a split season format, and to hold an All-Star Game between the first and second halves of the season.

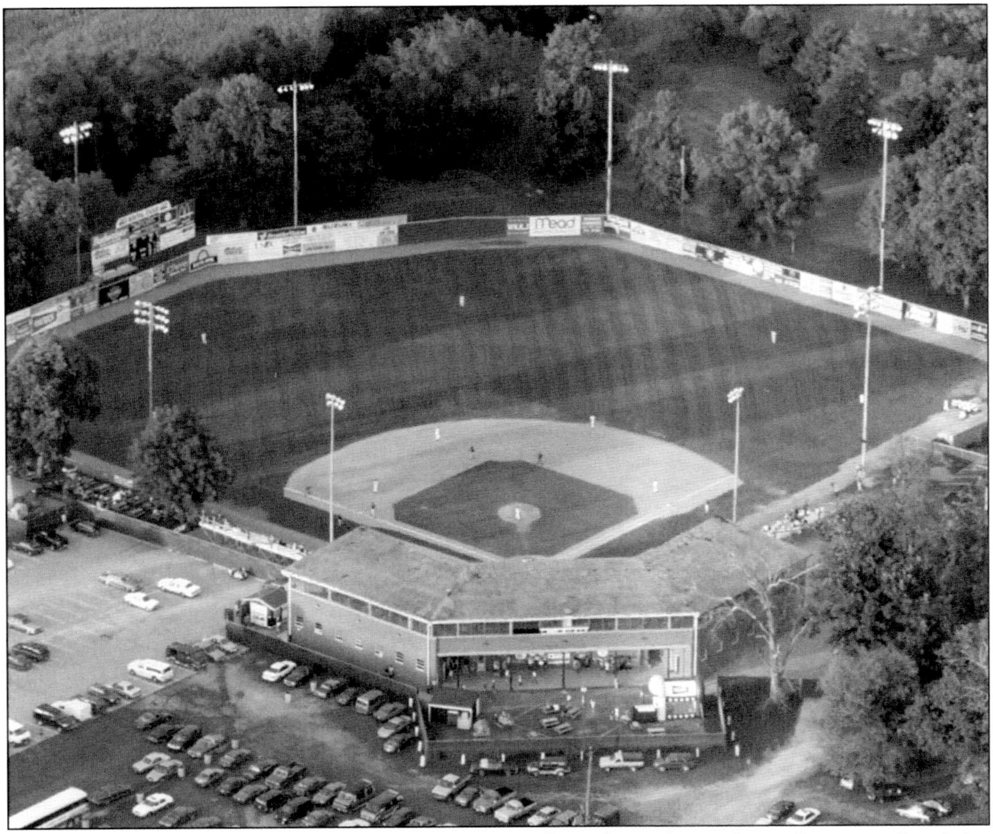

The Paints' first and only home is V.A. Memorial Stadium, located on the grounds of the Veterans Administration Medical Center. Built in 1954 by the Blue Star Mothers of America, an organization of mothers of Navy servicemen, the ballpark is owned by the Federal Government and leased to the Paints for a nominal fee. The Paints poured a lot of money and volunteer labor into the renovations necessary to bring the Stadium up to professional baseball standards. When the Frontier League began in 1993, V.A. Memorial was the best overall facility in the league. As the league moved into the suburbs of major cities, the new multi-million dollar state-of-the-art ballparks built for the new teams overshadowed V.A. Memorial; yet the Paints' home continued to offer a charm and authenticity that the new ballparks do not.

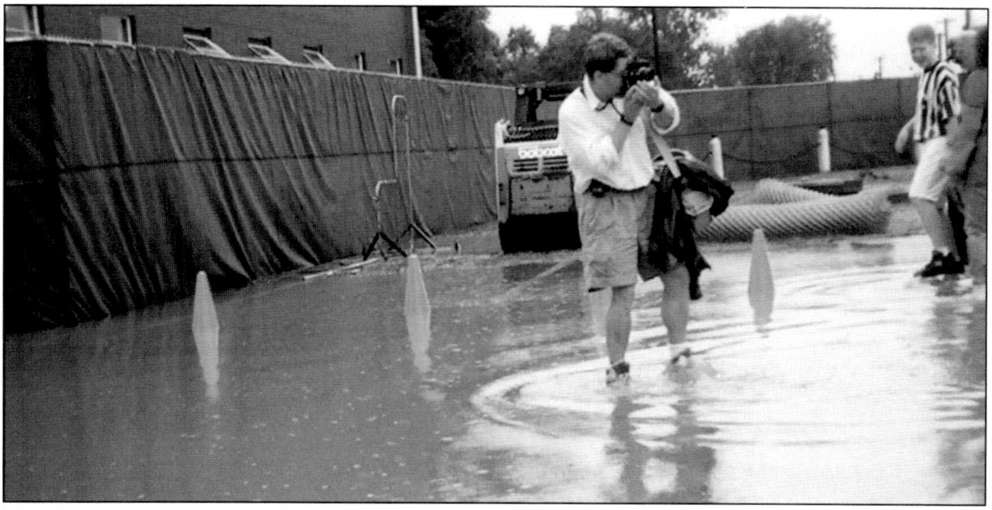

The first game in Paints' history, set for Wednesday June 30, 1993, did go off on schedule but not on time. A heavy thunderstorm went through Chillicothe and delayed the start of the game. Rain water swamped the field, but the Paints' organization was determined to get the game in. The heroic, frantic efforts of the grounds crew paid off, and the first pitch was delivered by Marty Gentry at 9:05 p.m., an hour and a half late. The rain also flooded the parking lot behind the ballpark, but local fans, eager to welcome professional baseball back to town, were as determined as the ballclub and made their way around and through the parking lot lake. (Courtesy of Maleine Davis.)

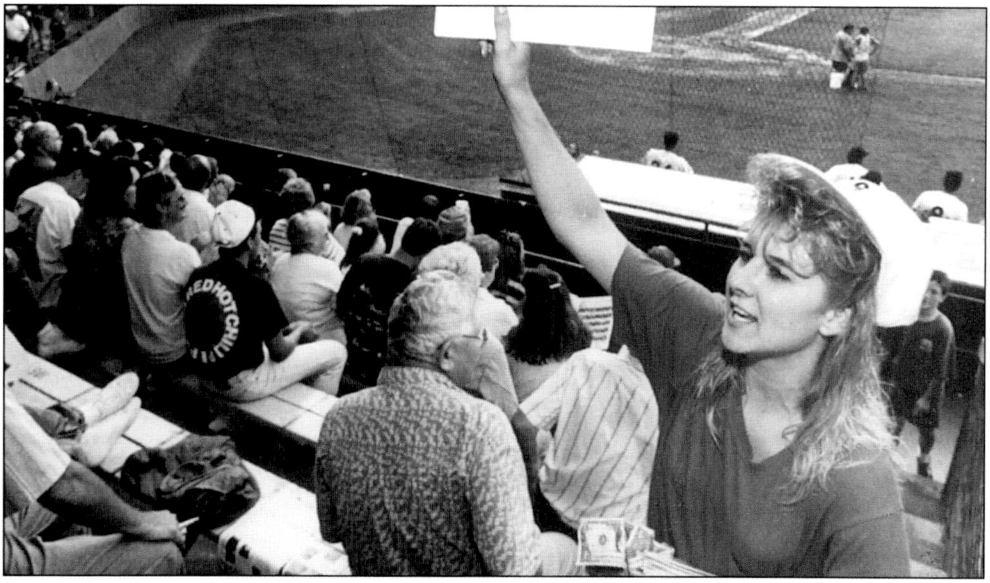

On Opening Night 1993, fans and players on both teams (the Paints and the Portsmouth Explorers) intently watched the grounds crew do their thing and waited patiently for the start of the Frontier League. A crowd of 2,154 showed up to welcome the Paints and the first season in Frontier League history. A stoic Chris Hanners told a *Chillicothe Gazette* reporter: "I prayed for good weather last night. Very seldom do I ask Jesus for little dinky favors, but I said, 'We labored for one hundred days to get ready for this day. Please give us this one day.' ... I guess He's testing us a bit."

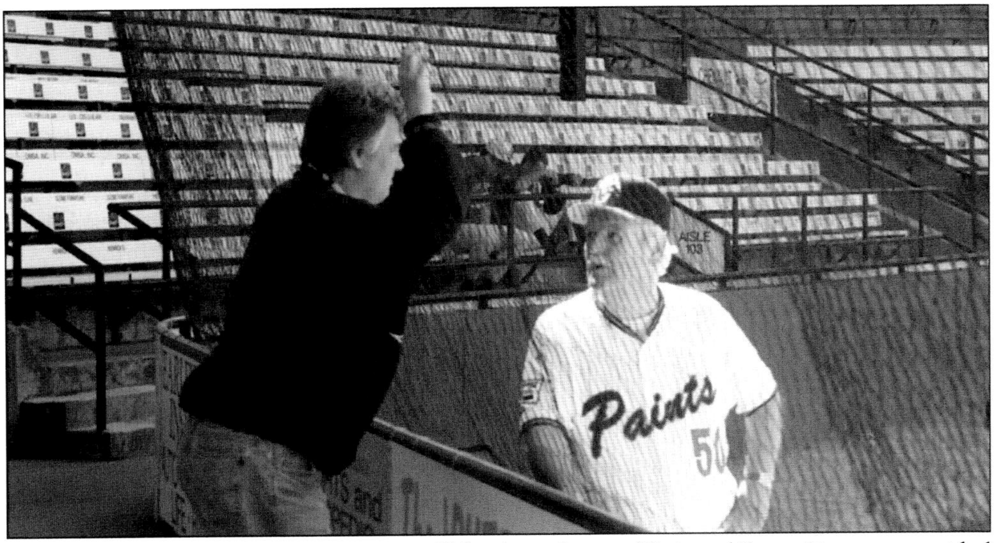

As the Paints and the Frontier League itself slowly took root, Chris and Roger Hanners provided the integrity, stability, and leadership that made Chillicothe the most respected franchise in the league. Outsiders often assumed a role reversal for the two men: that the father was the team owner and the son the team's manager. The team's first GM, Roger Hanners, stepped aside for Terry Barthelmas and became Director of Operations and pitching coach. He became the Paints' second field manager when Mark Jones was fired after the first 21 games of the 1993 season, and he remained at the helm until poor health forced him to retire midway through the 2000 season. (Courtesy of Maleine Davis.)

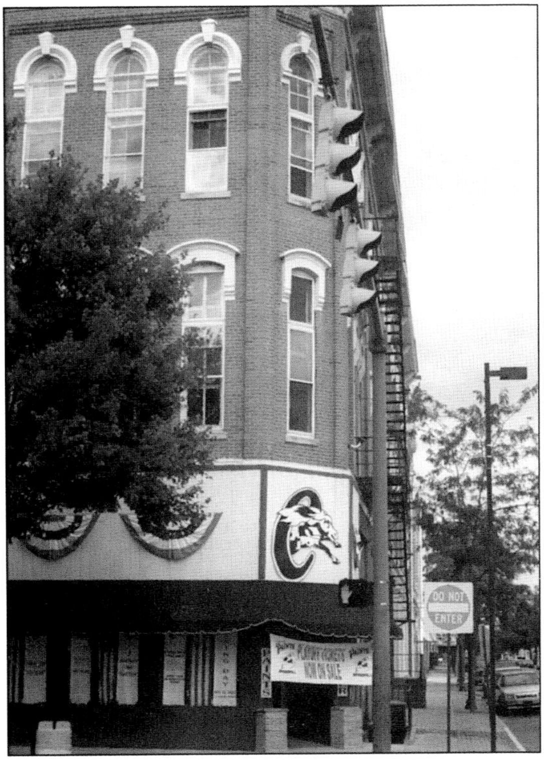

The biggest drawbacks to V.A. Memorial, besides its isolated location on State route 104 about two miles outside of Chillicothe, are the cramped locker rooms and public restrooms, all located beneath the grandstands. The space shortage forced the Paints to locate the team offices in town, and the Nipgen Block Building on the corner of Paint and Second Streets was chosen to serve the purpose. Burst water pipes during the winter of 2003 did extensive damage to "Paints Corner," as the offices came to be known, but the resilient Paints stayed put and rebuilt, ending up with better accommodations than before. (Courtesy of the author.)

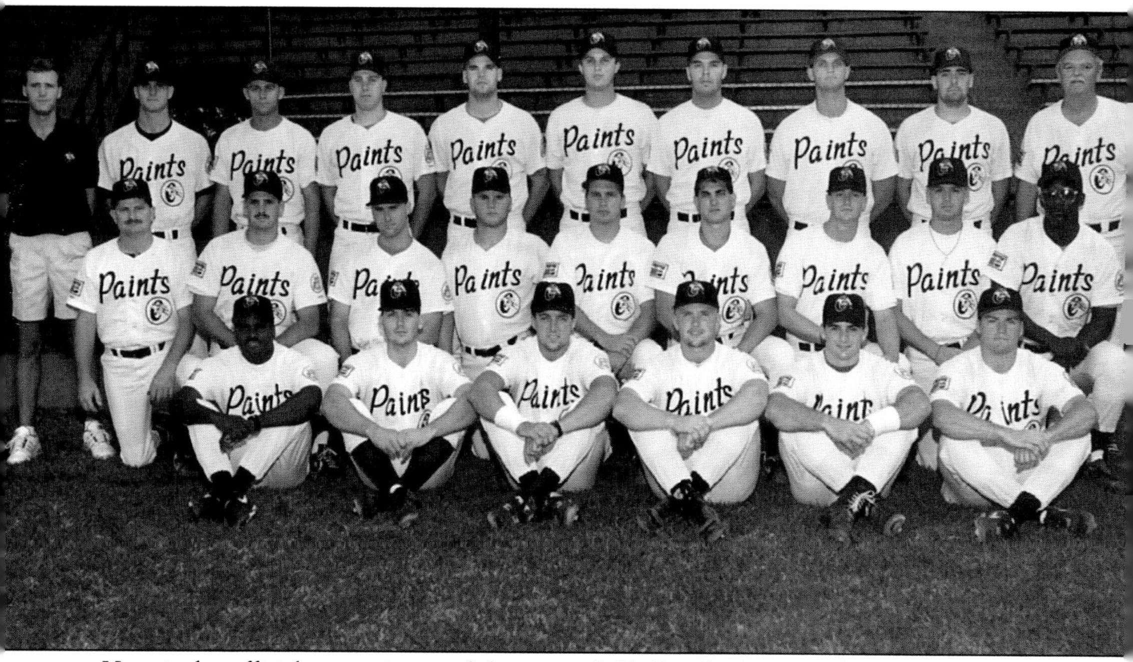

Here is the official team picture of the original Chillicothe Paints, taken in August of 1993. Pictured from left to right are : (front row) Marty Dunn (coach), Jeff Anderson, unidentified, Mark Gabbard, Jack Scholz, and Damon Treadway; (middle row) Jeff Noble (coach), Cory Pate, Tony Bellinato, Greg Wittman, unidentified, Rich Moffo, Robert Meyer, Mike Strausbaugh, and Ron Royster; (back row) Mike Ramsey (trainer), Marty Gentry, unidentified, Mike Hickle, Scott Larkin, Steve Gassler, Jayson Smith, Robert Davis, Aaron Crabtree, and Roger Hanners (manager). Outfielder Tony Bellinato was signed August 6 and replaced pitcher David Nunn. Tony hit .299 with three homers in 67 at bats. As a starter and a reliever Richard Moffo posted a 5-5 record and an ERA of 3.71. Larkin (in 23 games) worked mostly as a set-up man and went 2-2 with a team-high four saves and a 4.22 ERA. Used mostly as the closer, Hickle appeared in 25 games and went 1-2 with three saves and an ERA of 3.80. (Courtesy of Maleine Davis.)

Two

Growing Pain(t)s 1993–1995

To no one's surprise, the Frontier League of independent professional baseball teams struggled in 1993, its first year of operation. Two teams (the West Virginia Coal Sox and the Tri-State Tomahawks) folded two weeks into the season, and the Portsmouth Explorers were moved from the West Division to the East to achieve balance. In addition, a split season format and the first Frontier League All-Star Game (played at V.A. Memorial Stadium in Chillicothe) both happened as afterthoughts. The League did survive its initial go-round, as did the Chillicothe Paints, but it wasn't easy.

The Paints won the first opener in team history and completed the first home stand with a winning (4-2) record, but an inability to beat the Zanesville Greys, who won both halves of the West Division, relegated Chillicothe (25-27 on the year) to also-ran status in 1993. The first Paints' GM resigned on July 12, and the first field manager was fired on July 26. Owner Chris Hanners pulled no punches in the explanation for the dismissal. "We are not going to play unaggressive, .500 baseball and go through the motions. We're not just going to throw the lineup on the board and let the kids play." After the Paints' started the second half 0-5, new manager Roger Hanners offered to step down, but the players rallied to his defense and Hanners would go on to manage the team successfully until poor health forced him to retire in 2000.

Chris Hanners' emphasis on striving to win, not just compete, quickly became a hallmark of the entire Paints' organization and was borne out by the composition of the 1994 team, as only three of the eight players invited to return to Chillicothe made the final cut: pitcher Marty Gentry, and infielders Greg Wittman and Damon Treadway. All three made significant contributions, as did several newcomers: catcher-first baseman-DH Mark Avery, catcher Jason Moore, outfielders Steve Grandizio, Kurt Venneman and Mark Tangen, and pitcher Brian Tollberg.

By winning both halves of the Southern Division, despite a losing composite record of 33-34, the Paints qualified for their first participation in the Frontier League playoffs. They were eliminated by the Lancaster Scouts in the first round, two games to one. The lone win came in Game Two at V.A. Memorial and was accomplished due to the strong pitching of Tollberg and reliever Brad Roser and a bottom of the ninth inning rally that produced three runs after the Paints were down to their final strike.

After taking one step forward in 1994, the Paints took several steps backwards in their third year of existence. Chillicothe finished last in the Frontier League in batting (.256), last in fielding (.947), sixth (out of eight teams) in pitching (with an ERA of 4.69), and last in the standings with a 21-48 record—a dismal seven games behind the seventh place Portsmouth Explorers. The best individual efforts were turned in by Gabby Angulo, who batted .320, and starting pitcher Matt Copp, whose ERA of 2.88 was sixth best in the league. The Paints have never sunk as low again as they did in 1995; in fact, a complete reversal was right around the corner.

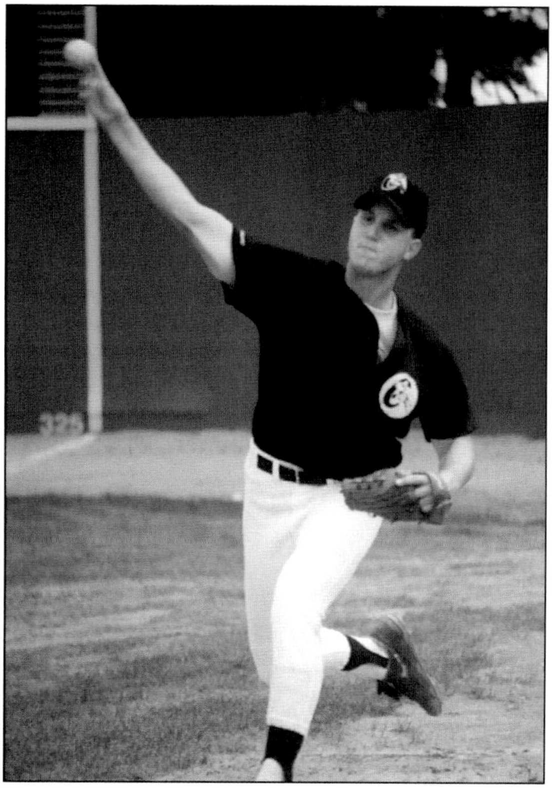

Steve Gassler was the Paints' number one pick (seventh overall) in the draft of players participating in the first Frontier League tryout. The Paints' coaching staff described the big (6' 5", 210 lbs.) right-hander out of Iona College as "fast for this league" and thought that he also possessed a sharp curve and excellent control. Working out of the number two slot in the starting rotation, Gassler lost something off his fastball and struggled the first month of the season. Roger Hanners helped him regain his speed—instructing him to follow through more and to quit throwing across his body—and he pitched more effectively the rest of the season. The highlights of his season were a six-hit complete-game victory against the Portsmouth Explorers on August 13 and another complete-game win a week later over the Lancaster Scouts when the lone run scored against him was unearned. He went 3-5 on the year with an ERA of 4.81.

Along with Mike Strausbaugh, Aaron Crabtree was the first local boy to sign with the Paints. Crabtree was also the first graduate of Chillicothe High School (class of 1989) to play for the team. A catcher during his career at Marietta College and Ohio Dominican, Crabtree was the back-up to Rob Davis behind the plate and wound up playing some first base after Beck Wells left the team for affiliated ball. While catching the second game of a double-header at Portsmouth on July 6, Aaron went 2-3; his bases-loaded single in the top of the seventh snapping a 1-1 tie and propelled the Paints to a 5-1 win. Crabtree's most unusual accomplishment was stealing home against the Kentucky Rifles on August 10 (he pilfered another base in the same game on a double-steal play). He also threw out four would-be base stealers in one game on August 16.

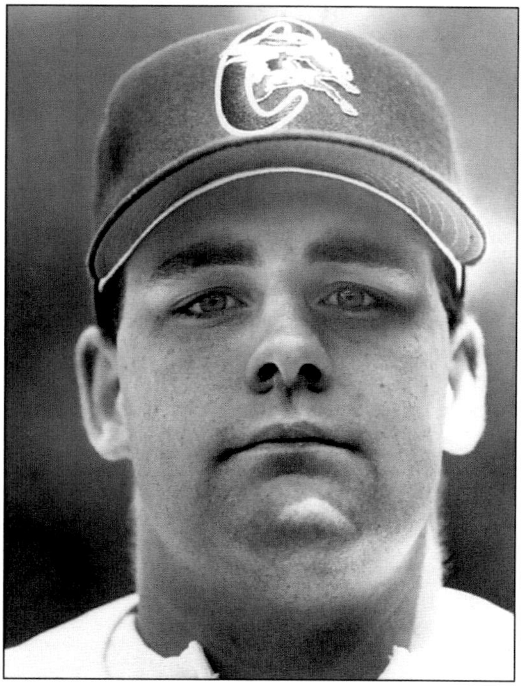

A graduate of Southeastern High School, Mike Strausbaugh came to the Paints out of Ohio University-Chillicothe, for whom he had played baseball and basketball. He was the first local player to appear in a Paints' game, pinch-hitting in Chillicothe's second game ever on July 1, 1993. The speedy Strausbaugh played sparingly at the beginning of the 1993 season, but he took over center field and the leadoff spot in the batting order after Joe Robinson got hurt. Given his chance, he took advantage of it, racking up at least five multiple-hit games. His bases-loaded hit in the sixth inning knocked in the winning run against the Kentucky Rifles on August 17, and his base knock on August 21—the Paints' lone safety in the game—kept Chillicothe from being no-hit by Zanesville Greys' pitchers Eddie Neo and Jeff Townsley. Mike hit .270 for the season.

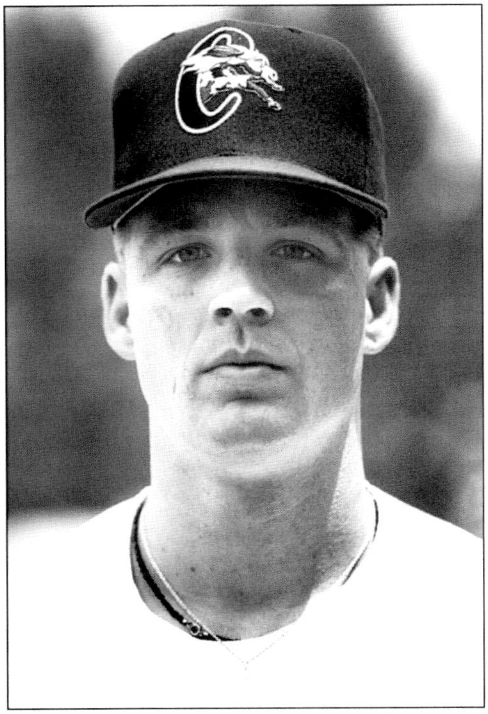

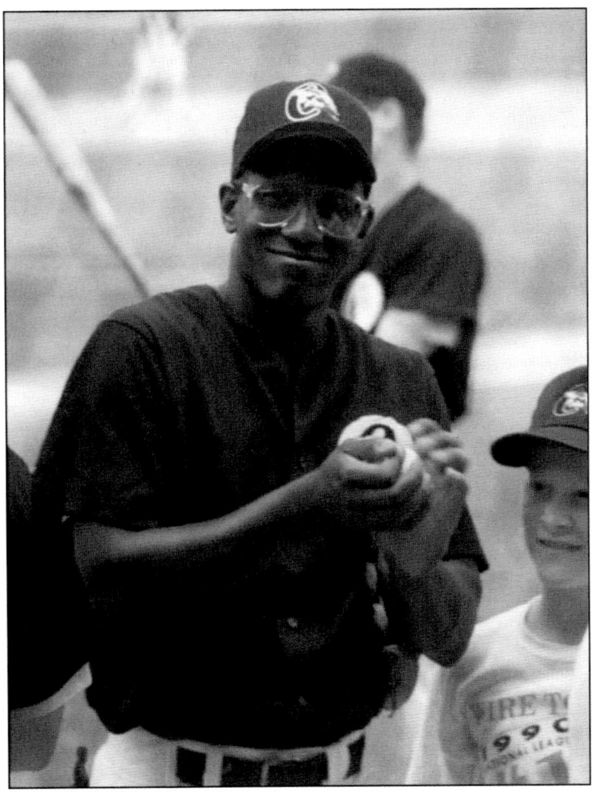

Ron Royster, Jr. out of Quinnipiac (NY) College was the fifth player selected by Chillicothe in the pre-season draft of 1993, and he thus holds the distinction of being the first black player signed by the ballclub. Ron got two hits in the first Paints' game ever and settled in as the regular right fielder. On July 17 he became the first Paints' player to hit a grand slam home run, as his first-inning blast helped visiting Chillicothe blow out the Lancaster Scouts, 12-3. Royster lost his starting job to newcomer Tony Bellinato in early August, but he went 2-4 with 3 RBI while subbing for Bellinato on August 20. He also enjoyed a last hurrah in the final home game of the season. With the Paints down 4-0 in the bottom of the ninth, Royster delivered a clutch pinch-hit, RBI double; unfortunately, he died at second representing the tying run as the Paints' comeback fizzled out.

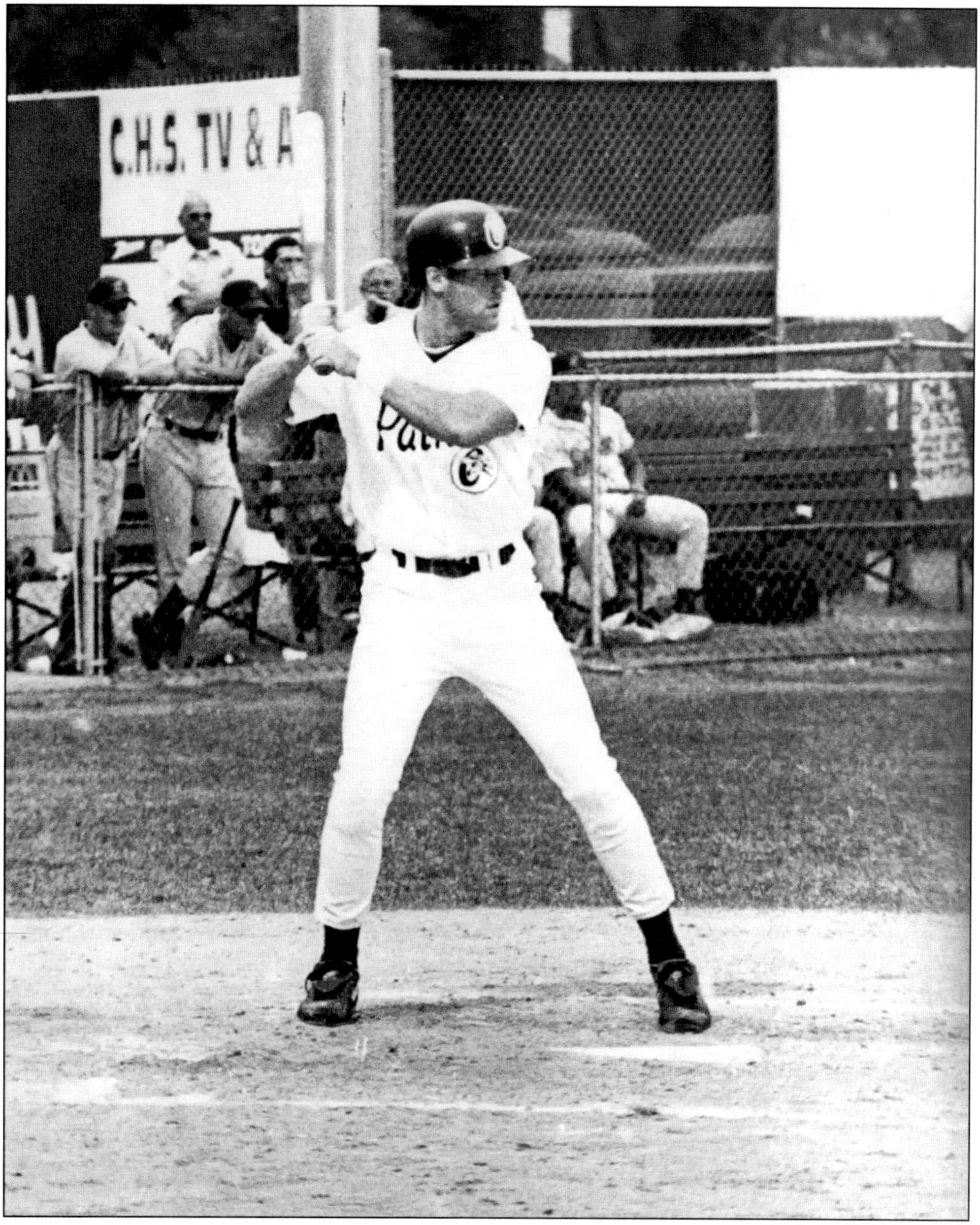

An All-American for first Paints' manager Mark Jones at Howard Payne University, Beck Wells grew up in Brownwood, Texas, where he and Damon Treadway played junior and senior high school baseball together. Equally adept at playing either corner or catching, Wells began the inaugural Paints' season as the regular first baseman. Batting cleanup, he got the first base hit and RBI in Paints' history, a two-out single that knocked in Artie Schmitt, Jr., who had drawn a walk. After 21 games, Wells became the first Paints' and second Frontier League player to sign with a major league organization. At the time of his signing, Wells led the FL in RBI with 20. He reported to the Texas Rangers' Class A club in Charleston, South Carolina, where he batted .247 in 77 games with 4 HRs and 20 RBI.

Left-handed starting pitcher Cory Pate out of E. Texas Baptist College turned in a fine year for Chillicothe during the Paints' inaugural season. Pate was second on the team in wins with five (against three losses), and his 3.01 ERA was third best in the league. He was named to the West Division All-Star team and pitched a perfect inning in the Frontier League's first All-Star Game, held at V.A. Memorial Stadium. Cory was a good hitter too. On August 16 Roger Hanners let him bat in the bottom of the ninth inning with the Paints trailing 1-0. Pate singled to put runners on first and third, and moments later on Mike Mulligan's hit he scored the winning run to seal his own complete-game victory. He was nominated for the All-Time Paints' 10th Anniversary Dream Team.

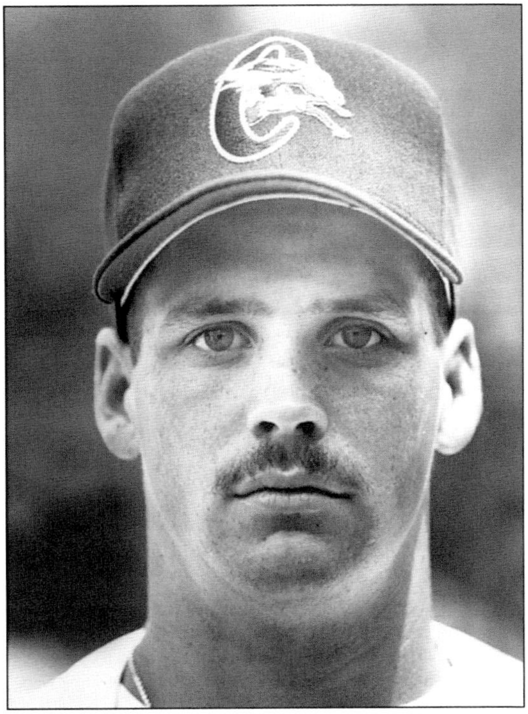

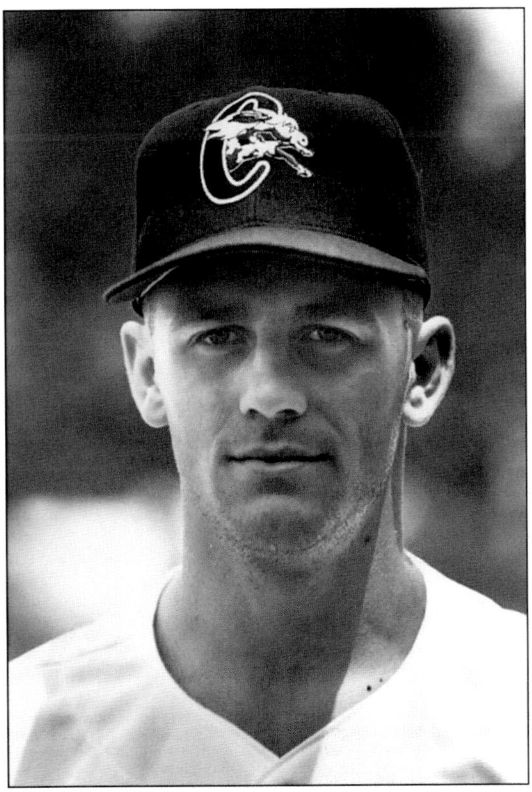

Signed as a shortstop out of the University of Cincinnati, Robert "Bob" Meyer started the season sharing third base with Eric Hagen, who was released on July 20. When Greg Wittman was knocked out of the lineup due to a pulled quadriceps, Meyer filled in for him at short, but Bobby too was hampered by injury (a bad heel). In 1993, before the Host Family program was set up, Paints' players lived in the Veterans Administration housing facility behind V.A. Memorial Stadium. When asked how he liked the arrangements, Meyer said, "It's like living in a dorm, except here we don't have to study." For the season Meyer hit .245.

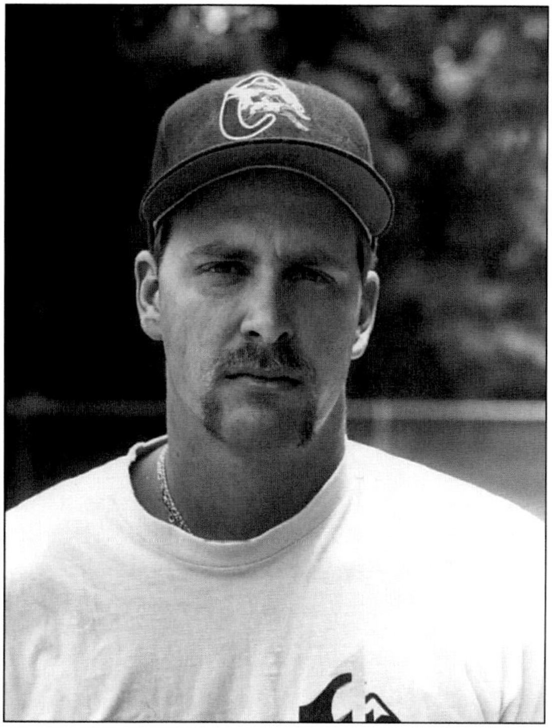

Dave Dorish was a left-handed pitcher who came to the Paints in a supplemental draft of West Virginia Coal Sox and Tri-State Tomahawks players after the Coal Sox and Tomahawks folded on July 15. (The Paints also drafted pitcher Tony Susino and second baseman Jack Scholz from the Coal Sox and pitcher Camen Moon from the Tomahawks.) After he took over for Mark Jones, manager Roger Hanners put the Paints' bullpen in order, establishing Dorish as the set-up man and designating Mike Hickle as the closer. Dorish did a fine job, often dousing rallies by the opposing team and bridging the gap between starter and closer. Dorish appeared in 16 games, and his 2.52 ERA was best on the team.

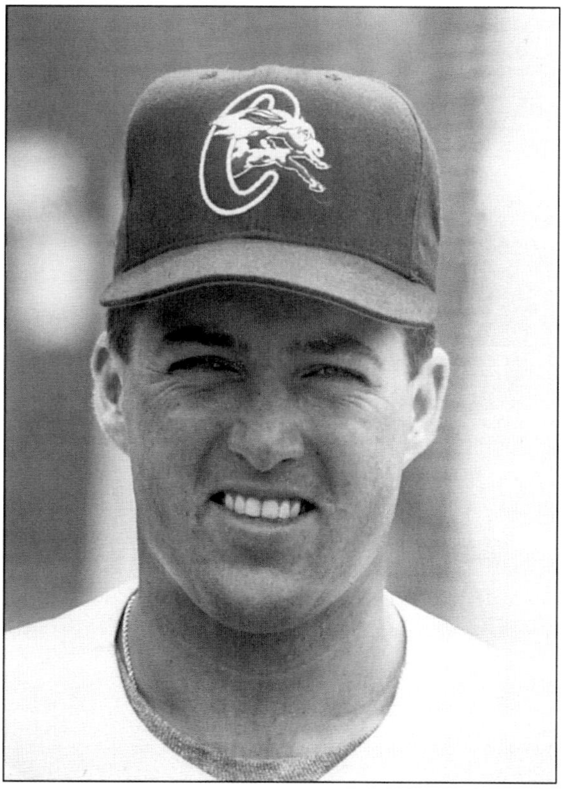

Outfielder-first baseman Mike Mulligan joined the Paints halfway through the 1993 season after he worked out a deal with his employer that allowed him to play for Chillicothe. The former Ohio State Buckeye was hot right from the start. He went 3-4 with two RBI in his first game on August 5, went 4-5 a couple of games later, and finished off his first week in pro baseball with a grand slam against Portsmouth, earning him Frontier League Player of the Week honors. The day the honor was announced he celebrated by having another 3-4 day that included a two-run home run and three RBI. Mulligan lead the team in batting with a .342 average and RBI with 26.

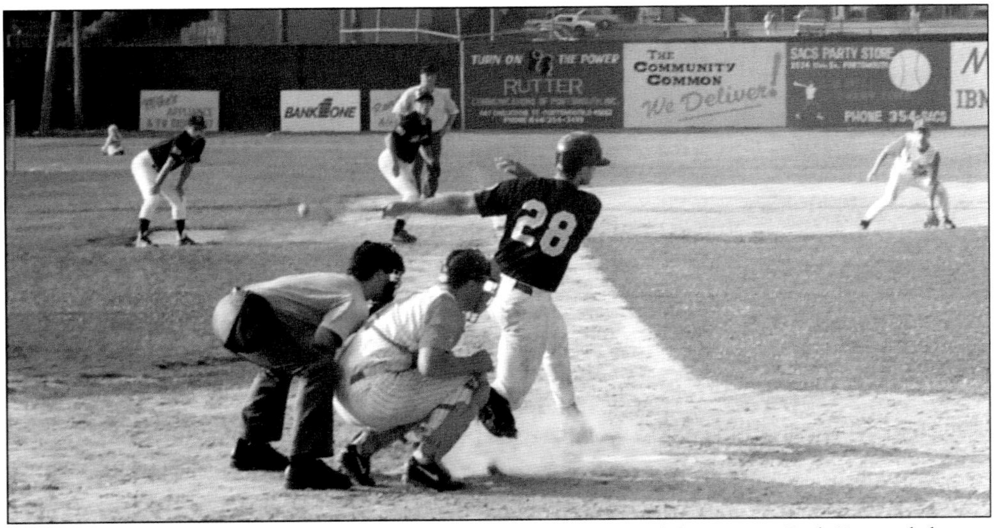

Nicknamed "Sarge" because of his military-like appearance and demeanor, Rob Davis did most of the catching for the 1993 Paints. The well-put-together young man out of Central Missouri State College was credited with hitting the first home run in Paints' history on July 5, on a ball that actually never left the yard. Although Davis' drive into right-center field actually one-hopped the fence, the base umpire ruled it a two-run home run. The call infuriated Lancaster Scouts' manager Scott Sims (who was ejected from the game after bumping the base umpire) and helped the Paints break a 3-3 tie and go on to win the game, 6-3. Davis, shown here batting against the Portsmouth Explorers at Branch Rickey Park, was named to the West Division All-Star team and got one hit in the first Frontier League All-Star Game. Davis' stats on the year were .240-15-3.

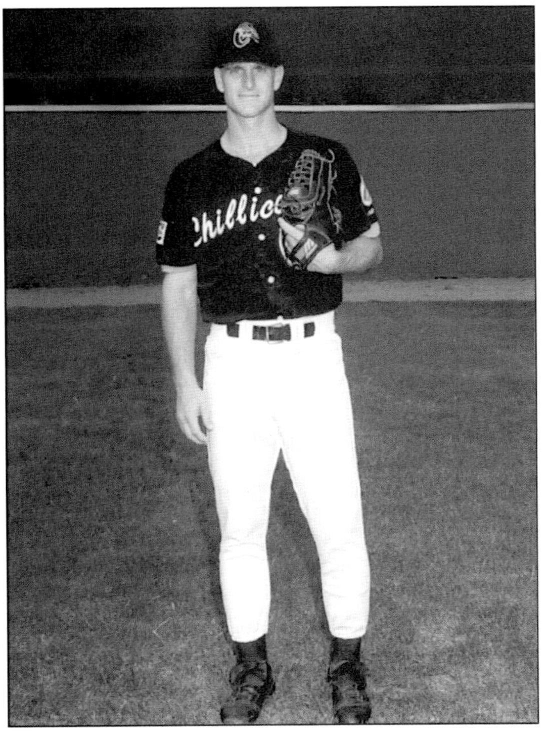

The honor of being the starting pitcher for the first game in Chillicothe Paints history went to this young man, Marty Gentry of Mason, Ohio. Gentry got the job done, scattering three hits and allowing a single run in seven innings to lead the Paints to a 6-2 win over the visiting Portsmouth Explorers. He went on to have a fine year, posting a 6-3 record with a 3.49 ERA. The day after Gentry worked a scoreless inning in the inaugural Frontier League All-Star Game, Roger Hanners became so frustrated with the relief pitching during a 4-3 loss to the Kentucky Rifles that he had Marty warm up in the bottom of the ninth. Unfortunately, the game ended with Gentry still getting loose in the bullpen. Gentry was named the Paints' Most Valuable Pitcher for 1993.

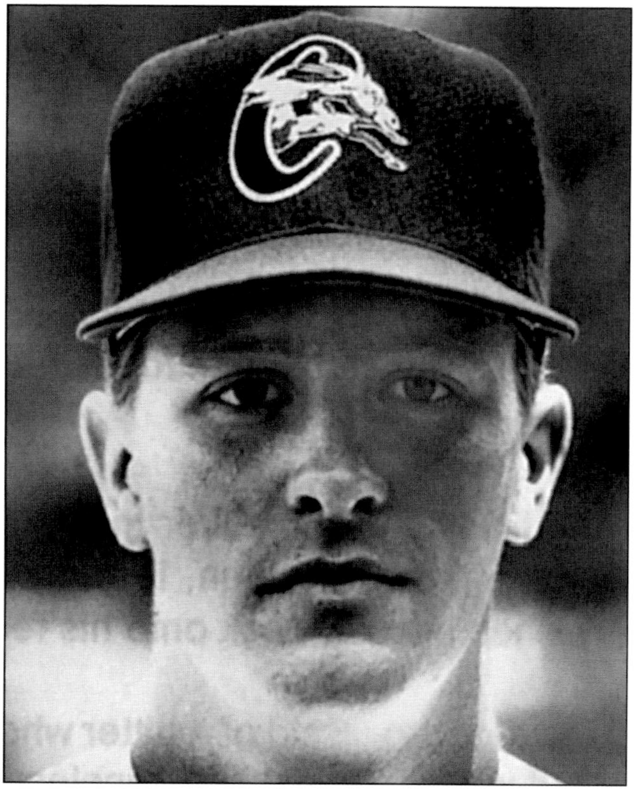

Outfielder Artie Schmitt, Jr., out of Monmouth (NY) College was the second player selected by the Paints in the first Frontier League draft. Artie scored the very first run in Paints' history and led the 1993 team in home runs with seven. He had a streak in the middle of the year when three consecutive hits of his over several games were all home runs. His father, Artie Schmitt, Sr., was so taken with Chillicothe that he rented an apartment and stayed in town all summer. In the second most at-bats on the team (144), Schmitt hit .257. He also tied for the lead in RBI (24) and doubles (7).

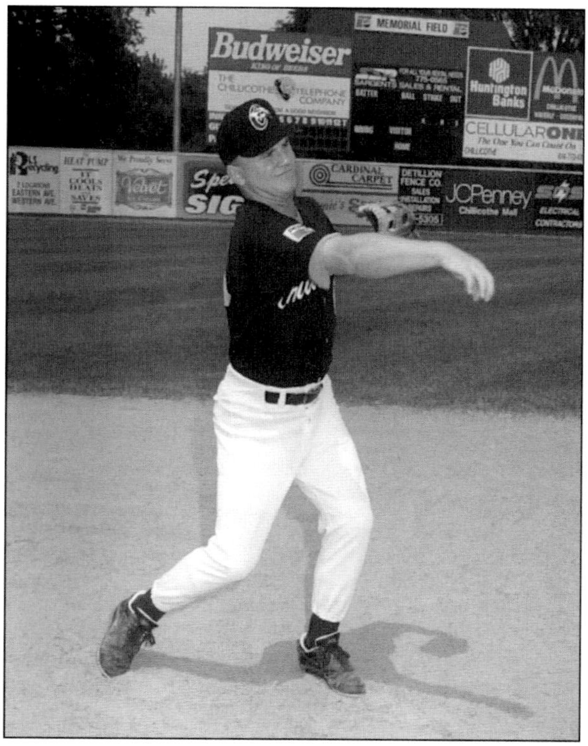

Greg Wittman of Bethlehem, Pennsylvania, was the regular shortstop for the 1993 Paints. He recorded the first out in Paints' history when, on Opening Day, he made a diving catch in foul ground behind third base of a pop up off the bat of the Portsmouth Explorers' leadoff batter. Greg batted a solid .278 in 1993 and was named to the West Division All-Star team. He returned to the Paints in 1994 and continued to hit the ball. He started the season as the regular shortstop but moved to third when Aaron Foley left the team in early August. He had a hitting streak of at least 14 games in 1994, and his three-run homer on August 25 helped the Paints defeat the Kentucky Rifles, 5-4.

Damon Treadway came to Chillicothe with Mark Jones, for whom Treadway had played college baseball at Howard Payne University in Brownwood, Texas. Treadway was signed primarily as a pitcher, but he began the season sharing second base with LaVonn Banks (out of Central State) and quickly solidified his hold on the position. He batted .297 on the year, got a hit in the All-Star Game, and was named the team's Most Valuable Player for 1993. On August 4 he relieved Jayson Smith (who left the game after throwing one pitch) and gave up two earned runs in 5 and 2/3 innings. On August 23 he started on the mound because a deep thigh bruise prevented him from playing second base. After his gutsy complete-game 7-6 victory over the Kentucky Rifles, Roger Hanners referred to him admiringly as "one Paint who plays with pride."

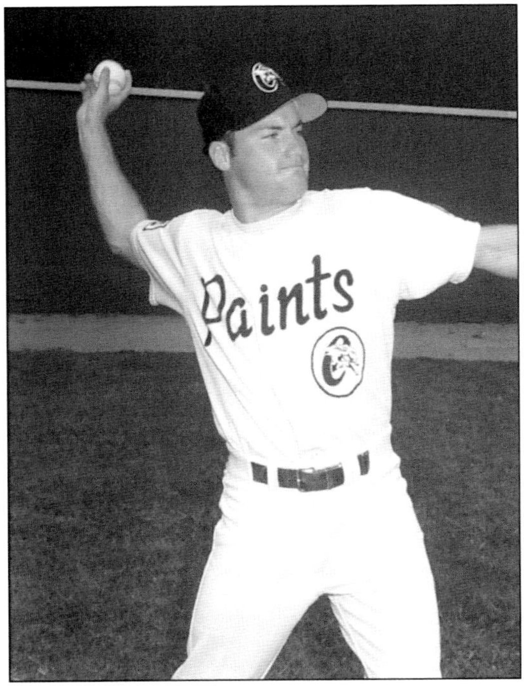

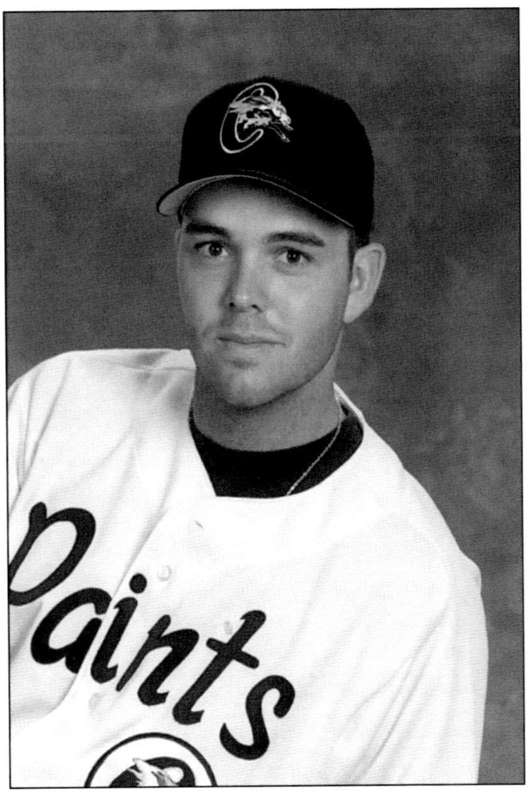

Starting pitcher Jayson Smith of Wright State University was another local boy, who hailed from nearby Washington Court House, Ohio. Smith possessed a wicked forkball but battled shoulder soreness all season. Jayson's best outing of the year came on August 17 when he picked up a victory by holding the Kentucky Rifles to a single earned run, scored in the first, over seven innings. After the game Roger Hanners said of him: "Jayson's a slow starter all the time. If he can get by those first couple of innings he's fine." Smith went 3-4 on the year with a 3.90 ERA and was invited back for 1994 but did not make the final cut. Nevertheless, on August 10 he re-joined the team (to replace pitcher Matt Cook who was released so that he could return to school) and pitched 7.2 innings over three games. Tragically, Jayson was killed in an auto accident in the summer of 2000.

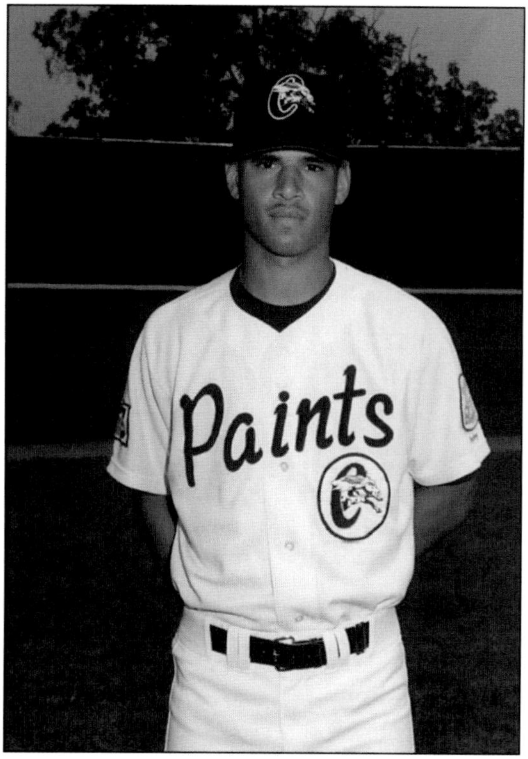

Players don't come any more "hometown" than Craig Brown, who not only had graduated from Chillicothe High School but had also played as a Cavalier for Paints' coach Marty Dunn. Prior to joining the Paints for their second season, the left-hander went 12-1 with a 2.10 ERA for Ohio Dominican, concluding his college career with a 37-8 record. Marty Dunn said of him, "He's shown that he's a competitor and he's a winner." Brown was given the honor of starting on Opening Day 1994, and he gave up four earned runs in 7 2/3 innings, earning a No Decision. He was a reliable workhorse the rest of the season, keeping the team in almost every game he started and deserving better than the 4-4 slate he finished with. He returned to the Paints the following year and started the 1995 Opener too. His record dropped to 2-7 in 1995, but again he deserved better. Paints' fans agreed and voted him as the left-handed starting pitcher to the All-Time Paints' 10th Anniversary Team.

Third baseman Aaron Foley of Boston, Massachusetts, played for the Kentucky Rifles in 1993, batting .294 with six home runs. Paints' fans remember him for two games. He won the 1994 Opener in dramatic fashion, bashing a walk-off grand slam to beat the Lancaster Scouts, 11-7, at V.A. Memorial. He was also at the center of the infamous composite bat controversy. After Aaron hit an RBI single with the Paints trailing Ohio Valley 5-3 in the bottom of the eighth On July 8, Redcoats' manager Greg Lemaster claimed Foley's bat was illegal. The umpires agreed with Lemaster, called Foley out, and sent Mark Tangen back to second base. The Paints lost the game but protested the umpires' decision. Commissioner Bill Lee ruled that the bat, while composite, was all-wood and thus legal. On July 13 the Paints won the "continued" game, 6-5, with Foley driving in the game winner on a 9th-inning sacrifice fly. Aaron made the 1994 All-Star roster but quit the team on August 5 for "personal reasons."

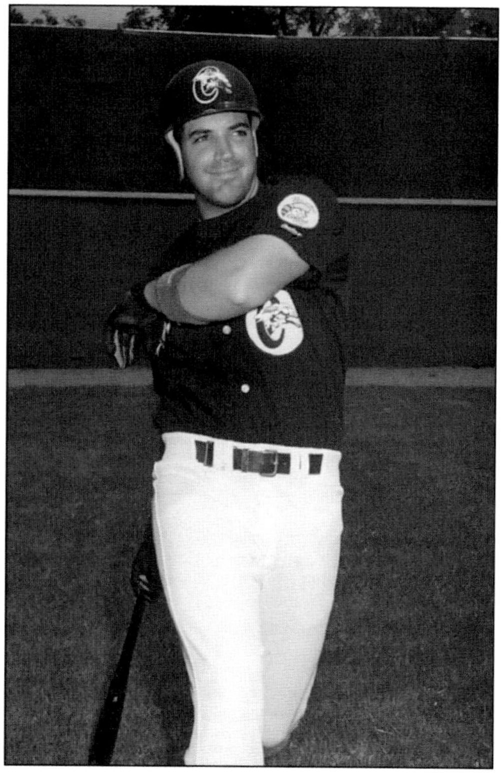

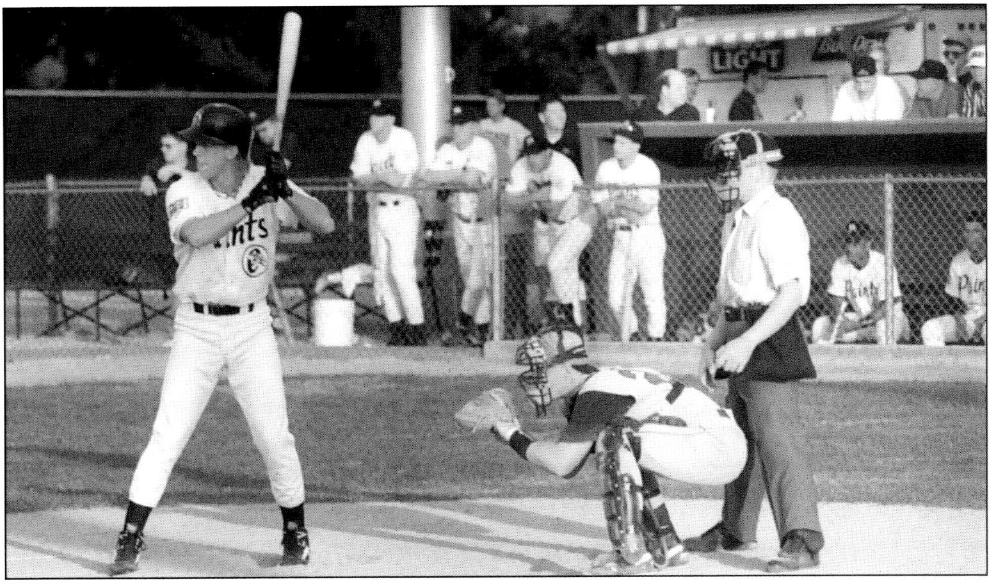

Long-haired Mark Tangen was a speedy outfielder with some pop in his bat. He and teammate Todd Smith appeared in the Division II World Series for the University of North Dakota in 1992. Tangen and Smith endured a circuitous 42-hour bus trip from Grand Forks, North Dakota, to get to Chillicothe and almost missed the team tryouts. Mark began the year leading off and playing center field but moved to left with the arrival of Steve Grandizio. A fan favorite, Tangen was often in the middle of Paints' rallies and batted .295 on the year. He returned to the Paints for the 1995 season and married a Chillicothe girl. He became more of a utility player than a regular in the outfield, but he hit for a high average and even started pitching relief to take some of the pressure off the beleaguered bullpen.

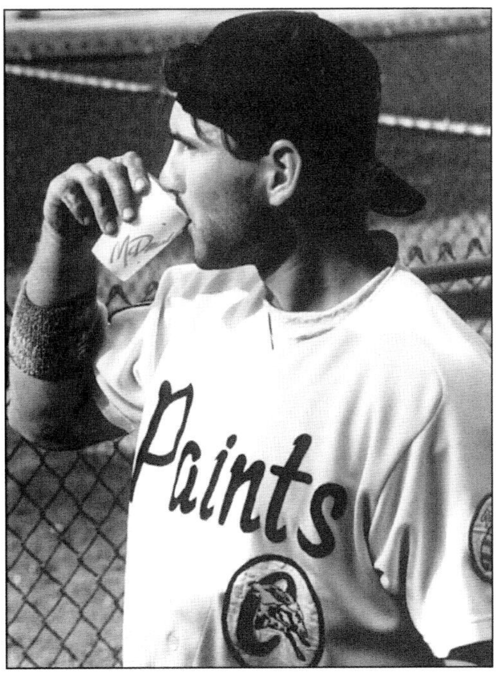

Catcher Jason Moore from Westerville, Ohio, played college ball at Florida International University and was voted Best Defensive Player there for 1994. He had a very good arm and was especially valuable to the Paints because he switch-hit. Early in the season he homered in three straight games, and half way through the season he was batting .344 (33-96). At the All-Star Game in Newark, Ohio, he put on a show, batting 3-3 with a double and two RBI and twice throwing out the league's top base stealer, Scott Pagano of the Ohio Valley Redcoats. When he was removed from the game after the sixth inning, the media voted him MVP of the game; however, they changed their votes and gave the award to Greg Slone when he got his fourth hit of the game. Although Moore tailed off at the plate in the second half of the season, he finished with a very good .285 average and six homers and was named to the Frontier League post-season All-Star Team.

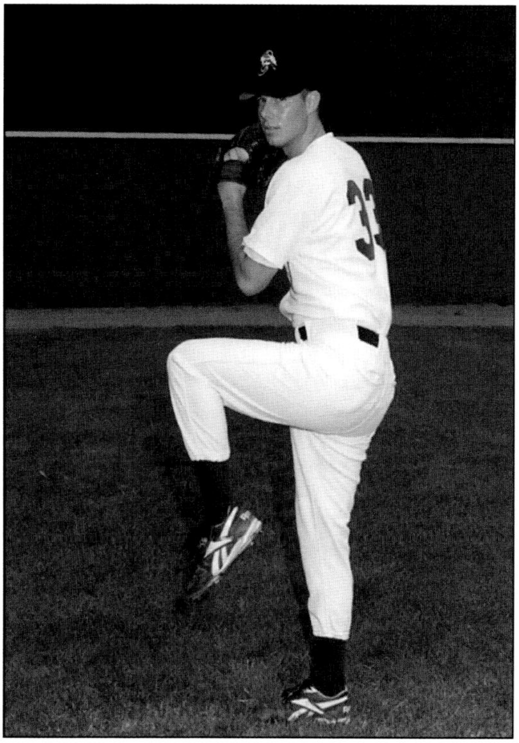

Lanky Tim Roth was a valuable member of the Paints' starting rotation in 1994. He'd played in the elite Cape Cod League in 1992, compiling an ERA of 0.00 in 15 innings. He played four years at Georgia Southern University for legendary college coach Jack Stallings. One of Tim's nine wins his senior year was the 1,000th victory of Stallings' career. Tim's father, Ron, had pitched for Stallings when Stallings began his career in 1960 at Wake Forest University (Ron Roth earned Stallings victory #6.) One of the highlights of Roth's year was his part (six innings, one hit) in a combined two-hitter (with Jayson Smith) against Kentucky on August 24. The nadir definitely came at Portsmouth on July 31. After pitching seven shutout innings, Tim developed a blister on one of his fingers and left the game after giving up a two-run single, with the Paints ahead 10-2. The Explorers bombed the Paints' bullpen and won the game 11-10 in nine innings.

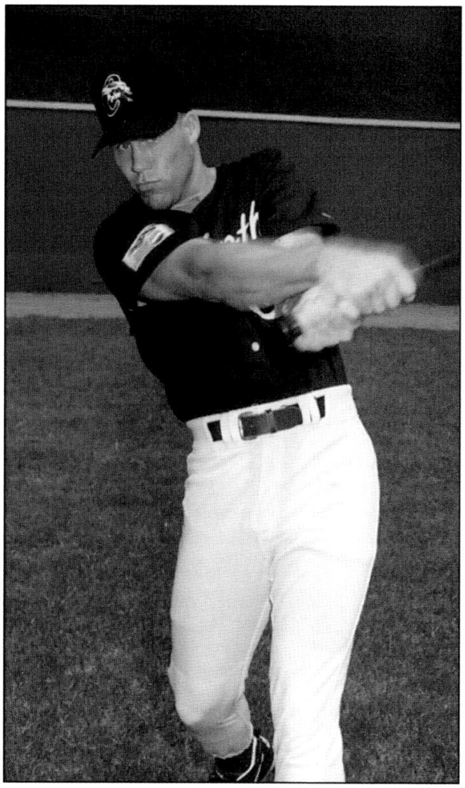

Called "The Bull" by Roger Hanners, outfielder Kurt Venneman was drafted by the Paints in the fifth round of the Frontier League draft. Venneman (St. Peters, Missouri) was an All-American at the University of South Carolina-Aiken, where he hit .329 with seven home runs and 71 RBI. On July 22 Kurt had a double and grand slam for six RBI, and a week later he went 4-5 with three RBI. The latter performance raised his average to .514 (first in the league) and caused Hanners to describe him as "the most dangerous hitter in the league." Venneman finished the year with four home runs, 42 RBI, and a batting average of .341, good for seventh in the league. Venneman returned to Chillicothe for 1995 and was one of the more reliable hitters in the lineup; nevertheless, he was traded to Zanesville in early August (for pitcher Mike Chrisman), hitting .282 with 20 RBI at the time.

Mark Avery was upset with the Detroit Tigers when they did not draft him out of Wayne State University, as a scout promised him they would, until the Tigers hired him to be their bullpen catcher for the 1993 season. After Avery hit some balls into the upper deck of Tiger Stadium during batting practice, Tigers' pitcher Bill Krueger called and recommended that the Paints sign him. Even though Jason Moore did most of the catching for the Paints in 1994, Avery added a potent bat to the everyday lineup as a first baseman and DH. Mark finished the year with a .333 batting average, good for eighth in the league, and he led the Paints in hits, doubles, and home runs with nine. His home run in the second game of the 1994 playoffs against Lancaster was also the first post-season homer in team history. Avery played in the Western League in 1995 and later became the baseball coach at Oakland University.

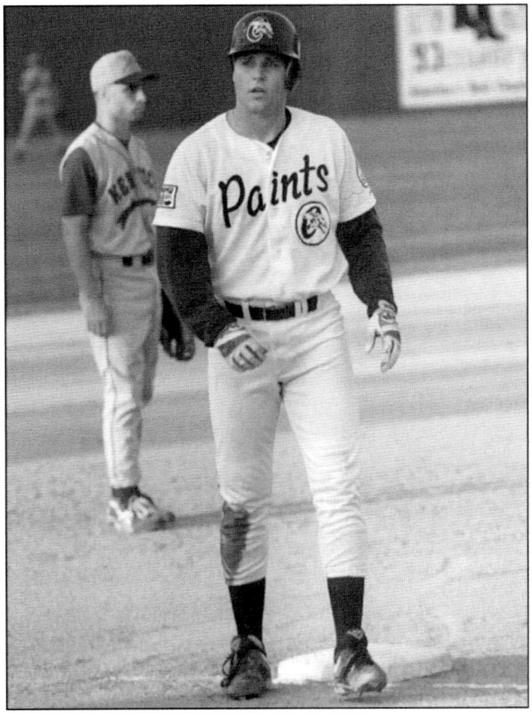

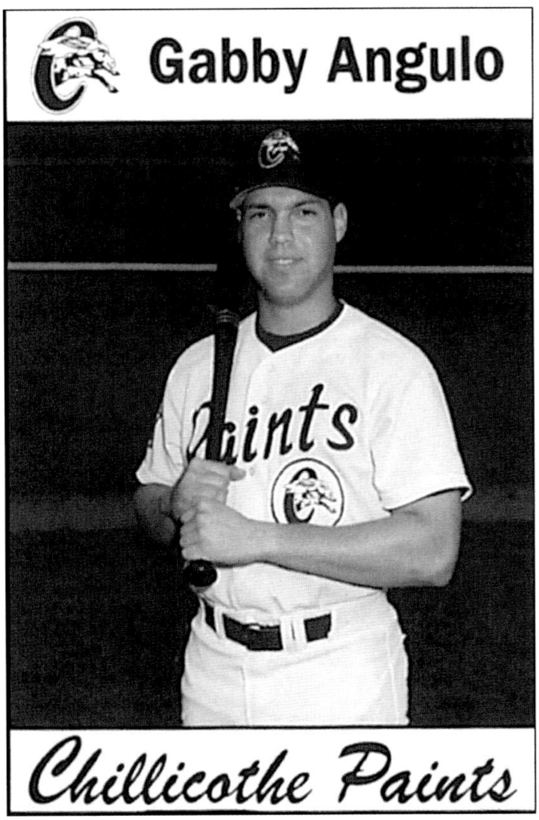

Even though Hurricane Andrew flattened his family home in Miami, nothing could dampen the spirits of first baseman-outfielder Gabby Angulo, who brought a sense of humor and an upbeat personality to the Paints' locker room. Angulo played against Alex Rodriguez in high school, and the Miami-Dade squad he played for was one of the top-ranked jucos in the country. Gabby had several multi-hit games in 1994, but he really hit his stride the following year when he led the team in batting, with a .317 average, tied for ninth in the league. Gabby also led the team in RBI (26) and doubles (12). For his efforts he was voted the team's MVP.

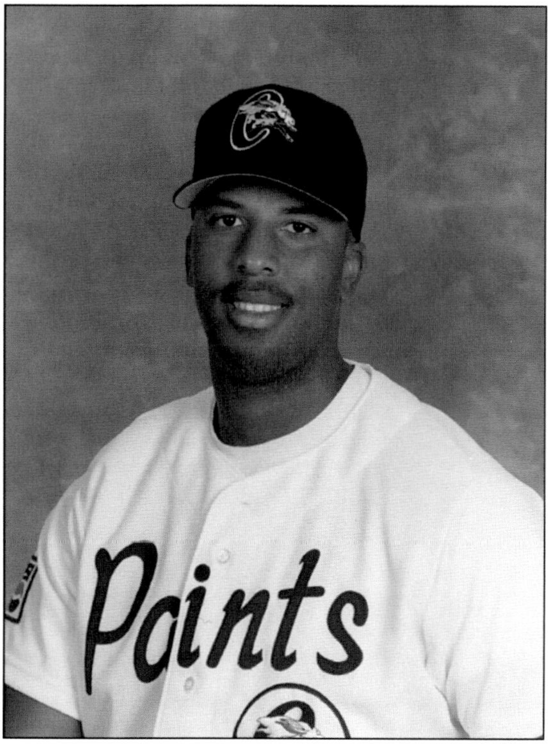

Brooklyn-born Ariel Martin joined the Paints two-thirds of the way through the 1994 season after being released by the Huntington (WV) Cubs of the Appalachian League. The brawny (6' 5", 230) first baseman-DH was inserted into the cleanup slot and immediately produced for the ballclub. He collected 22 hits and 9 RBI in only 19 games, and his slugging percentage of .417 was second highest on the team. He also got two hits in the first playoff game against Lancaster. In 1995 he played for the Grays Harbor Gulls of the Western League.

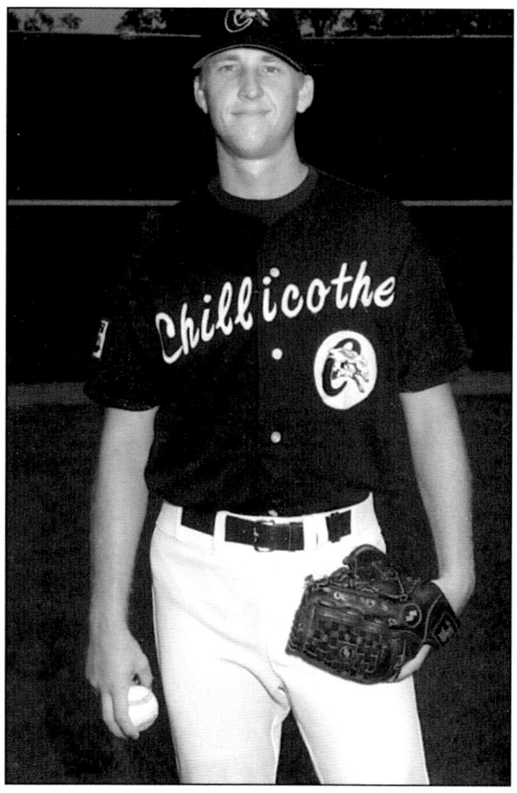

Brian Tollberg, out of the University of North Florida, began the 1994 season as the Paints' fourth starter and ended it as the team's ace. Possessing a good fastball and an even better curveball and control, Tollberg could be counted on to pitch deep into almost every game. He made the All-Star team and gave the Paints a chance to win the second playoff game against Lancaster by pitching 7 and 2/3 strong innings. He finished the year with a 7-4 record and a 2.85 ERA (tied for eighth in the league) and led the Frontier League in strikeouts with 69. He was voted the team's Most Valuable Pitcher for 1994. Tollberg was signed by the Milwaukee Brewers and eventually became, in 2000, the first Frontier League alumnus to make the majors.

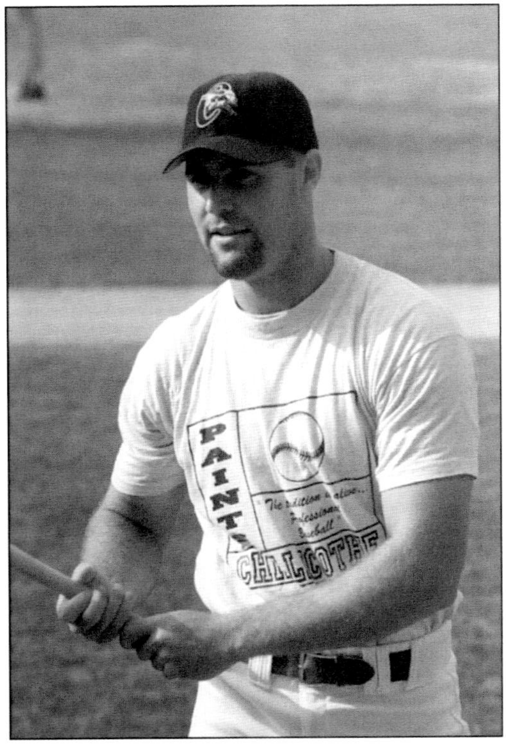

Although he was twice a second team NAIA All-American while playing at Wilmington (Delaware) College, speedy outfielder Steve Grandizio was not signed by a major league team upon his graduation. He went home to Philadelphia and starting working construction and sending faxes about himself to every team in the minor leagues. Fortunately for the Paints, the team beckoned Steve to Chillicothe after releasing first baseman-DH Marc DiCarlo on July 10. Grandizio was installed in center field and hit from the very start, going 2-5 and 2-3 in a double header against Newark. He kept hitting the rest of the summer, stringing together a 29-game hitting streak that still stands as the team record. For the year he batted .342 with 54 hits in 38 games and was named MVP of the team. The following winter he was signed by the St. Louis Cardinals and played for Peoria, Illinois, in the Midwest League.

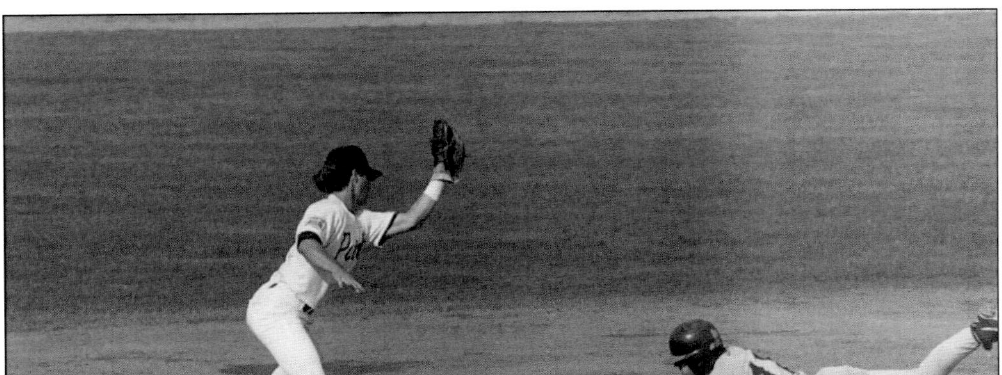

For most of the 1995 season the leadoff spot in the Paints' order was held down by second baseman R.J. Palma of San Jose, California. Palma was a good fielder and a legitimate stolen base threat, having swiped 59 bases during his career at San Mateo JC and 69 while at San Jose State. Short to begin with, Palma reduced his strike zone even further by batting out of a crouch and was more than happy to get on base via a base on balls. "I want to set the table for the bigger hitters in our batting order," he said, after the second game of the season during which he went 0-2 but reached base three times (twice by walks, once by error), stole four bases, and scored two runs. Hitting .333 after the first three weeks of the season, he finished at .207 with a team-leading 27 stolen bases. He was nominated for the Paints' All-Time 10th Anniversary Team.

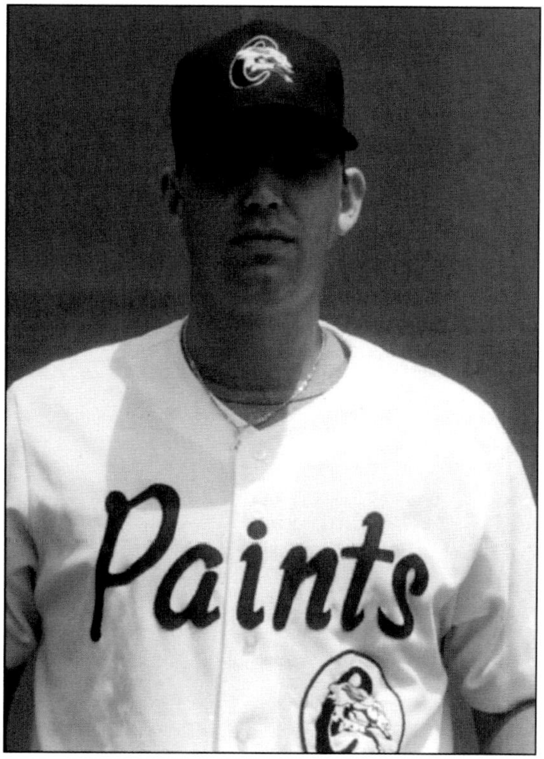

Chris Bristow was a 6-foot-6 left-handed hitting first baseman from the University of North Florida. He had tremendous power but didn't connect often enough. He did get the 1995 Paints off to a good start in the season opener, at V.A. Memorial; blasting a long home run with two runners on base to give Chillicothe a 3-0 lead over Portsmouth in the bottom of the first. In 47 games Bristow hit .197 with 16 RBI and three home runs.

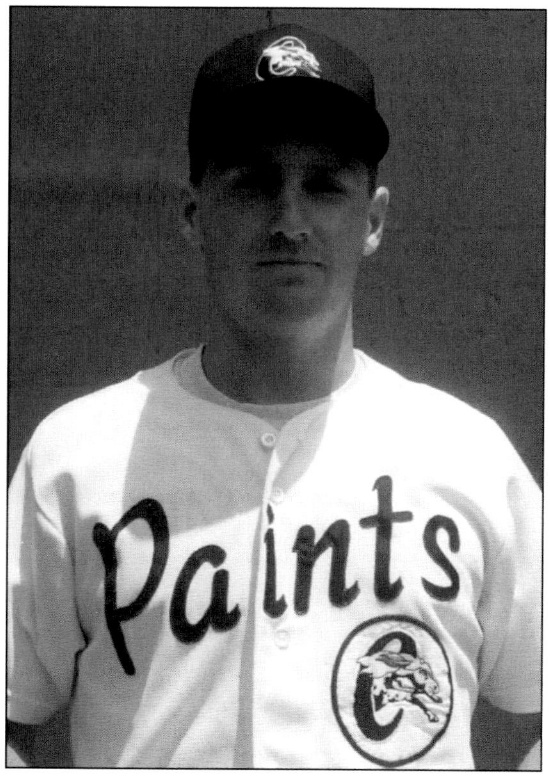

Outfielder-third baseman Troy Muckerheide was from Cincinnati and played his college ball at Dayton (OH) University. He started the season 0-8 but recovered enough to be named to the All-Star team, at which time he was batting .262 and leading the team in RBI (13) and triples (4). Troy singled in the All-Star Game won by the West Division, 4-2. On August 17 he went 3-5 against the Ohio Valley Redcoats, and on August 24 his single knocked in the game-winning run against the Richmond Roosters. Troy hit .242 for the season with 24 RBI, five doubles, and a team-high four triples.

Left-hander Keith Bozyk from Canton, Michigan, played for Adrian (MI) College and set the school record for wins and strikeouts. He struck out 21 in 30 innings for the Paints in 1994, and the team was counting on him to anchor the bullpen in 1995. Unfortunately, Bozyk's best two performances came at the very start of the year. In the Paints' second game of the season he pitched three and a third innings of hitless relief to pick up the win against Portsmouth. Two days later he pitched two more scoreless innings during a 10-0 Paints' win over the Evansville Otters. For the season he went 2-1 with an ERA of 4.63 in 23.1 innings.

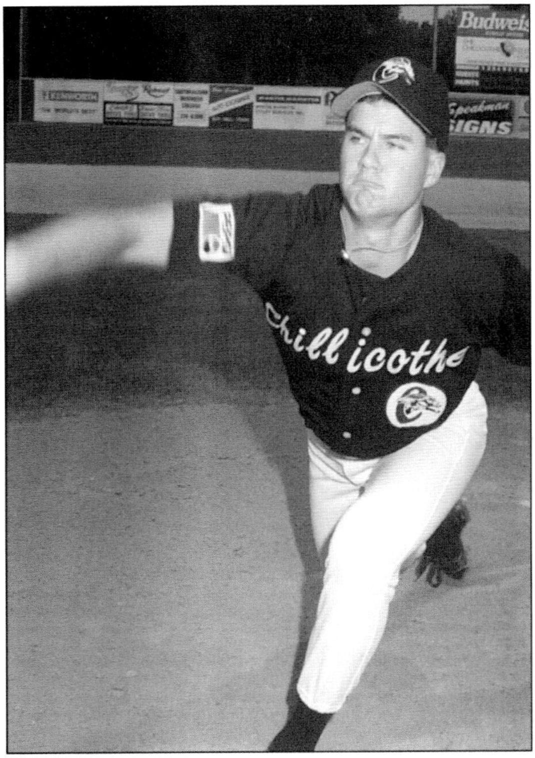

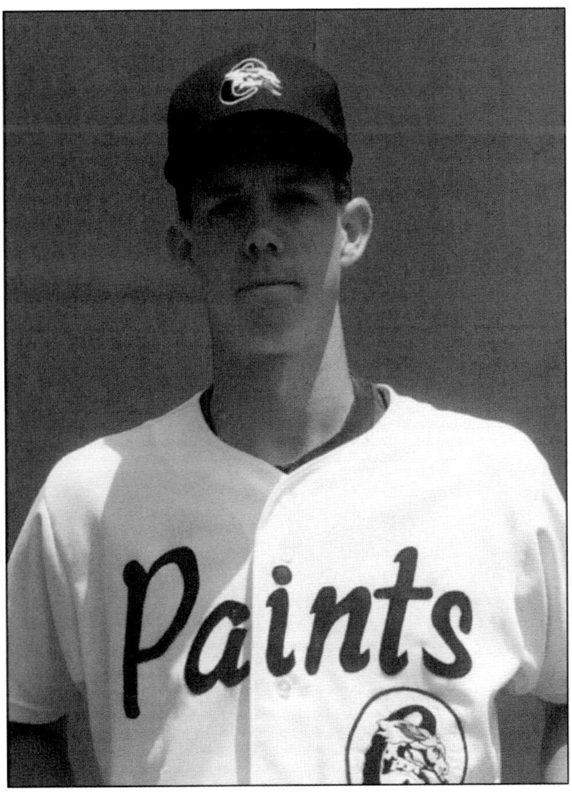

In his pre-season assessment of his players for 1995 Roger Hanners put the old "good field-no hit" label on Jon Geist of the University of North Florida: "As smooth looking a shortstop as you'll ever see. Can cover a lot of ground. Needs work with hitting." The 6-foot-3 Geist, who tried to pattern himself after another tall shortstop, Cal Ripken, Jr., performed better than expected. He accumulated at least ten multi-hit games and batted a respectable .271 for the season, his 54 hits tying him for fourth-best on the team. He also socked a solo home run on August 23 against the Richmond Roosters.

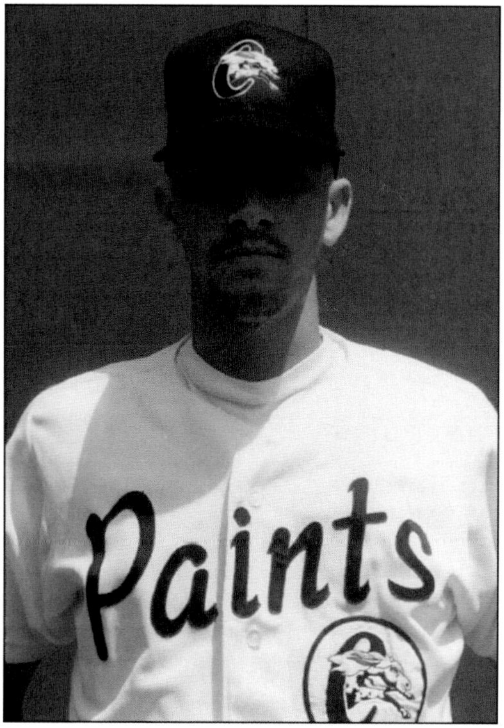

Skinny submarining reliever John Lynn from Brea, California, was the biggest character to ever don a Paints' uniform. Nicknamed "The Weasel," Lynn did bird calls from the bullpen, carried around a Pez candy dispenser, and did a dance on the mound to "Pop Goes the Weasel" before warming up. *Chillicothe Gazette* reporter Mark Sonka said of him: "He's as nutty as a Snickers bar." When he wasn't clowning around, Lynn did a pretty good job as the Paints' closer (3.56 ERA). Often victimized by shoddy fielding, Lynn saved four games and notched his two wins at the very end of the season. He got his first win on August 24, giving up one hit in two and a third innings against Richmond, and his second win in the last game of the year, on August 28, working two and a third hitless innings against the Newark Buffaloes.

Greg Reinhart out of Allegheny (PA) College DH-ed on Opening Day, but it didn't take him long to earn the #1 catcher's job on the 1995 Paints. Although Reinhart wasn't big for his position (5'10", 185 lbs), Roger Hanners loved him for his quick feet and his quick release on throws. The other managers in the division must have appreciated his work behind the plate too, as Greg was selected for the All-Star team despite his batting record of .223 with two home runs. His best day at the plate came on July 17 when he went 4-4 with two RBI to help the Paints beat the Ohio Valley Redcoats, 11-5. He finished the year with four home runs, 20 RBI, and a .275 batting average. Reinhart had another fine year for the Paints in 1996 and was nominated for the All-Time Paints' Dream Team.

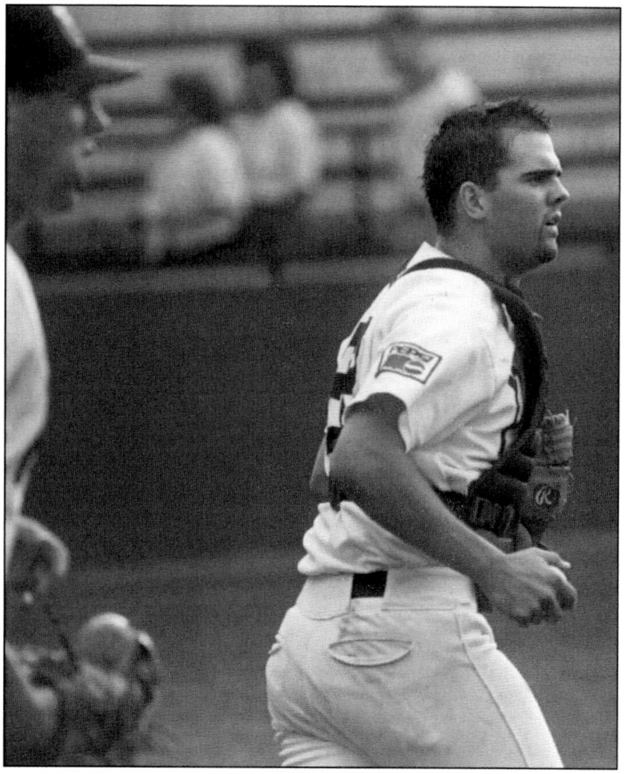

Brett Roehm was a left-handed curveballer who came to the Paints after having set the NCAA Division III career record for strikeouts (392). In his senior year at Ohio Northern he also established season records for wins (14), strikeouts (134), complete games, and innings pitched. Although Roehm preferred starting and did so at the beginning and end of the year, he worked out of the bullpen for most of the year and provided some of the best relief pitching the Paints got. His best starting appearance came on August 15 when he gave up no earned runs in 7 2/3 innings to help the Paints to an 8-5 victory over the Zanesville Greys. Brett struck out 59 in 24 games and finished with a 3-6 record in 1995. Back for another go in 1996, he pitched sparingly out of the bullpen.

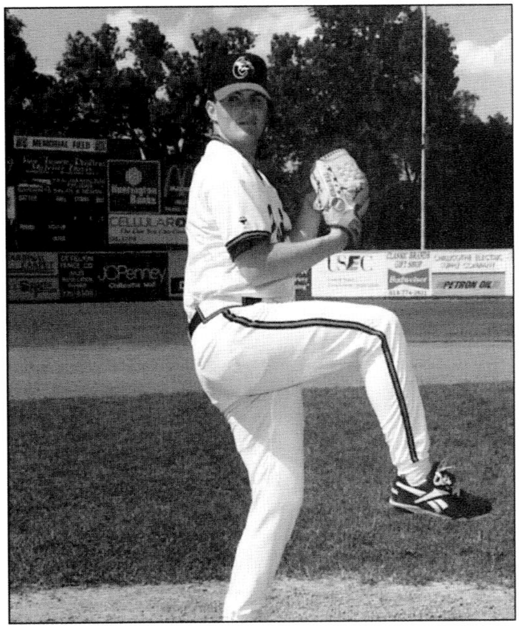

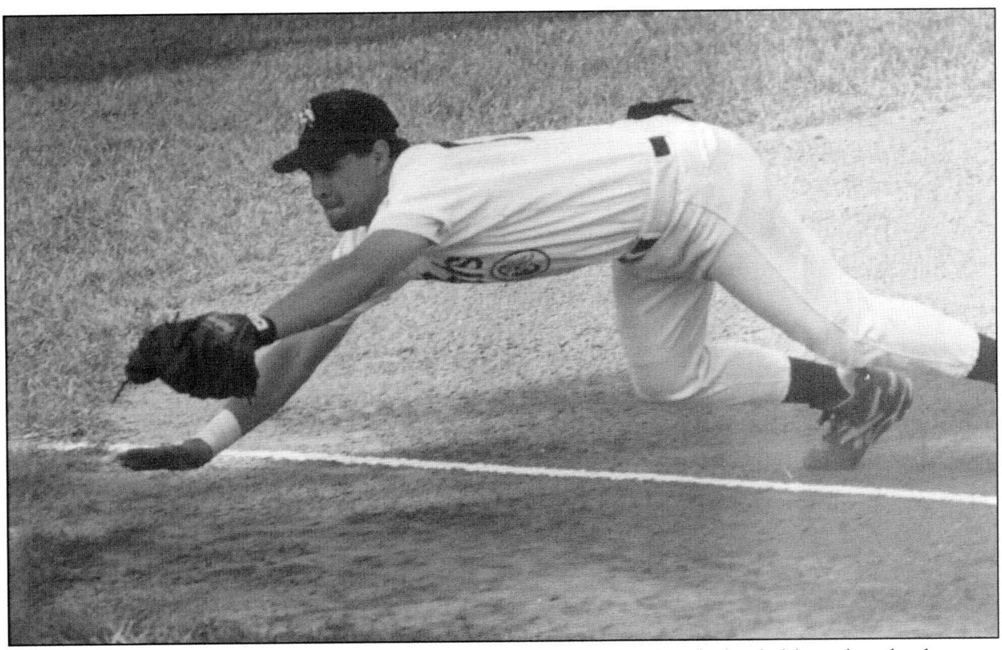

Regular third baseman Curtis Knight was in the lineup more for his flashy fielding than his hitting, but he wound up with the fourth-best batting average (.280) on the team. He went 3-4 at least twice. His 8th-inning home run on July 9 helped the Paints beat Portsmouth, 7-5, and on August 25 he knocked in the only run of the game as the Paints edged Portsmouth, 1-0. Knight was from Albuquerque, New Mexico, and played college baseball at NW Oklahoma State.

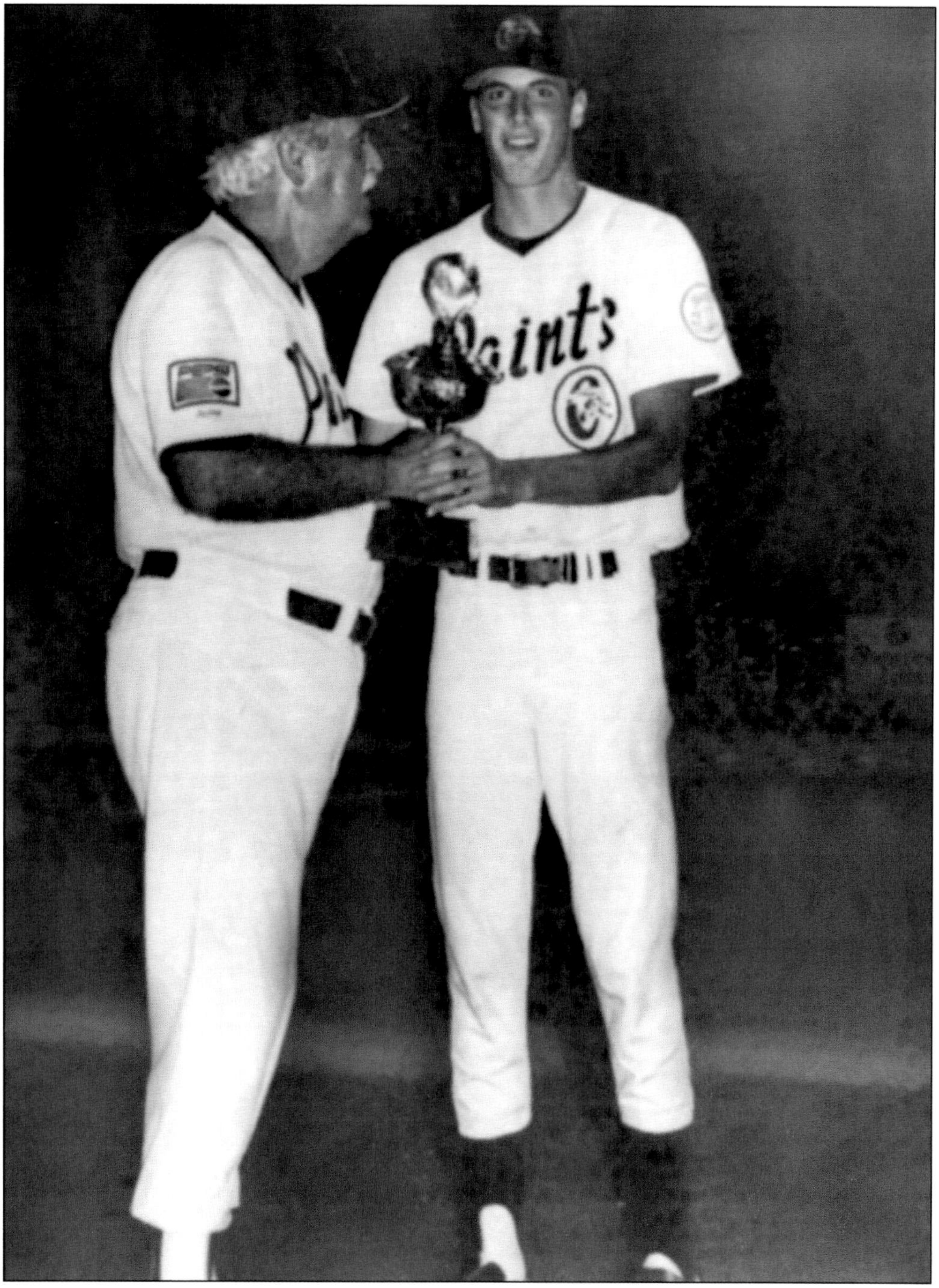

Matt Copp was a tall right-hander from Lakewood, Colorado, who enjoyed fly fishing as much as baseball. Armed with a good fastball and a good curve, Copp started the 1995 campaign 1-3 but rebounded to lead the team in wins with a 6-6 record and an ERA of 2.88, good for sixth best in the league. His best game was probably an eight-hit shutout of the Evansville Otters on July 29. He is pictured here accepting the team's Most Valuable Pitcher Award for 1995 from manager Roger Hanners.

THREE

'The Best Damn Baseball Team Chillicothe Will Ever See' 1996–1998

With an almost completely revamped roster, the Paints dominated the Frontier League in 1996 with a 48-26 record and a seven game edge over second-place Zanesville. The "Worst-to-First" Paints enjoyed an .811 winning percentage in home games (30-7) and pulled off five series sweeps. The pitching staff shut out the opposition ten times, and all five starters (Reenn Edmondson, Jon Hinkle, Kevin Loewe, Rob Cancel, and Tim Sheridan) posted winning records. The offense led the league in runs scored, was second in batting average (.297), and boasted three of the top four home runs hitters (Mitch House, Jackie Jempson, and Scott Pinoni). Chillicothe sent seven players to the mid-season All-Star Game (Edmondson, Sheridan, House, Jempson, Pinoni, shortstop Matt Reimer, and reliever Thad Chrismon), and four Paints were named to the post-season Frontier League All-Star Team: House, Jempson, Pinoni, and Reimer. Topping it all off, Roger Hanners was named Frontier League Manager of the Year. It was Hanners who gave the team the ultimate compliment a week before the start of the playoffs. "Regardless of what happens," he said, "this is the best damn baseball team Chillicothe will ever see."

The Paints clearly were the class of the league in 1996, but unfortunately they were not able to extend their season-long dominance through the playoffs. After dispatching the Johnstown Steal in three games in the first round, the Paints fell to the Springfield Capitals in two straight. What made the defeat an even more bitter pill to swallow was the fact that the Capitals' record against Chillicothe in the regular season was 1-7.

The Paints went through a strange, disappointing season in 1997. The team won its first five games of the season and ran off another streak of seven straight wins to start the second half but saw those bursts of excellence offset by losing streaks of four and five games. Similarly, the Paints' respectable batting and pitching efforts (ranked third in the league) were undercut by the team's leaky defense and their league-leading 148 errors. The team was bolstered by contributions from players signed after the season was underway (such as catcher Patrick Anderson, outfielder Josh Itzoe, and first baseman Brian Mannino) but hurt by the mid-season retirements of regulars Danny Collins, Bobby Jones, and Jesse Fluck. The final result of this mixture of good and bad was a mediocre sixth-place finish and a 41-38 record that left the team a game and a half out of the playoffs.

Once again, in 1998, the Chillicothe Paints pulled off a complete turn-around and put a team on the field that combined the best pitching staff in the league with a "Murderer's Row" batting lineup. The pitching staff was led by Bob Spears (10-5) and Brian Scarcello (13-1); while the trio of Mitch House, Scott Pinoni (who returned from a year in the Northern League), and the .403-hitting Gator McBride terrorized opposing hurlers. The team was so impressive that by July GM Bryan Wickline was quoted as saying: "This is the best team we've ever had in Chillicothe."

The 48-31 Paints downed the Canton Crocodiles in the first round of the playoffs, and then challenged the Springfield Capitals again in the Finals. After Chillicothe rode Bob Spears complete-game six-hitter and Pinoni's three-run ninth-inning home run to a Game One 4-2 win in Springfield, the Paints returned home, needing only one win in two games to claim their first Frontier League Championship. Springfield rebounded to take Game Two, 11-5; and then, despite the heroics of Gator McBride who went 4-5 with a home run in his final at bat in the game, the Capitals took the rubber game, 7-4. The gutsy Spears neatly summed up Chillicothe's disappointment and frustration by saying, "We are the best team in this league, but you've got to prove it."

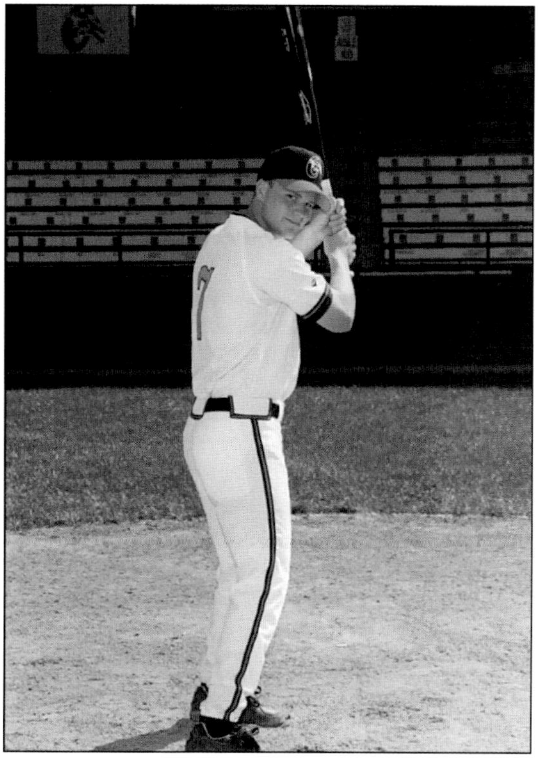

Despite hitting .528 and not striking out once his senior year in high school, Jesse Fluck (pronounced "fluke") received no interest from either the pros or Division I colleges, so he attended Franklin and Marshall College, where he set school records in four hitting categories. He played third and the outfield for the Paints and did an excellent job as the team's regular leadoff hitter in 1996, batting .298 with six triples and 20 stolen bases and putting together a 14-game hitting streak. He returned to Chillicothe in 1997 and was having another good year for the team as a leadoff hitter (.303, 17 steals) and a valuable utility player when a case of mononucleosis knocked him out of the lineup in early August.

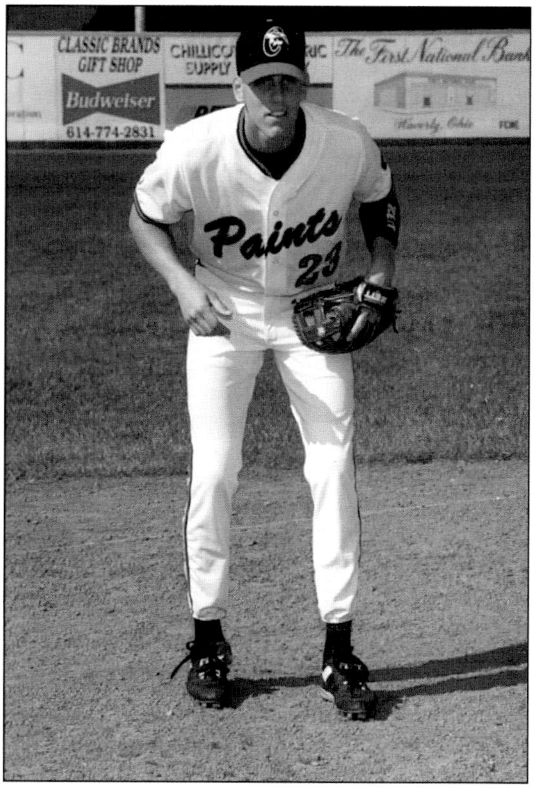

One of the best fielding shortstops to ever don a Chillicothe uniform, Matt Reimer came to the Paints in 1996 after having played a couple of seasons in the Baltimore Orioles' organization. Reimer set the team record for stolen bases in a season (42), and he got some big hits from the bottom of the batting order, such as his game-winning RBI triple against Zanesville on Opening Day and his grand slam against Ohio Valley on August 1. Reimer was named to the East All-Star team and was the only East Division player to get two hits in the game. In August *Baseball America* named him the Best Base Runner and the Best Defensive Shortstop in the Frontier League. Matt played the part of the Chicago White Sox shortstop in the Charlie Sheen movie Major League II, which was filmed in his hometown of Baltimore, Maryland. He hit .272 on the year with 17 doubles (third best on the team) and 37 RBI (fourth best).

Mostly used as a reliever at the University of North Florida, Reenn Edmondson was converted into a starting pitcher by the Paints and became the staff ace in 1996. The big right-hander gave up 55 hits and struck out 63 in 83 innings while fashioning an ERA of 2.82 (fourth best in the league) and a record of 9-3, which tied him for most wins among league pitchers. He pitched a scoreless inning in the 1996 All-Star Game and was named the Paints' Most Valuable Pitcher for 1996.

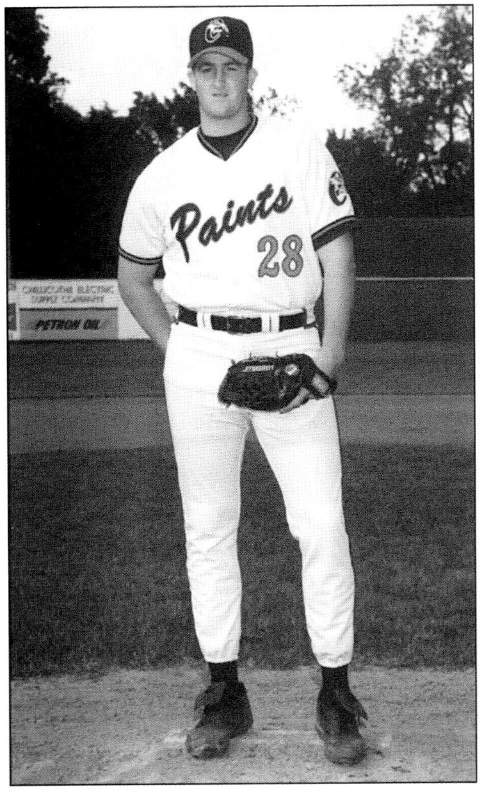

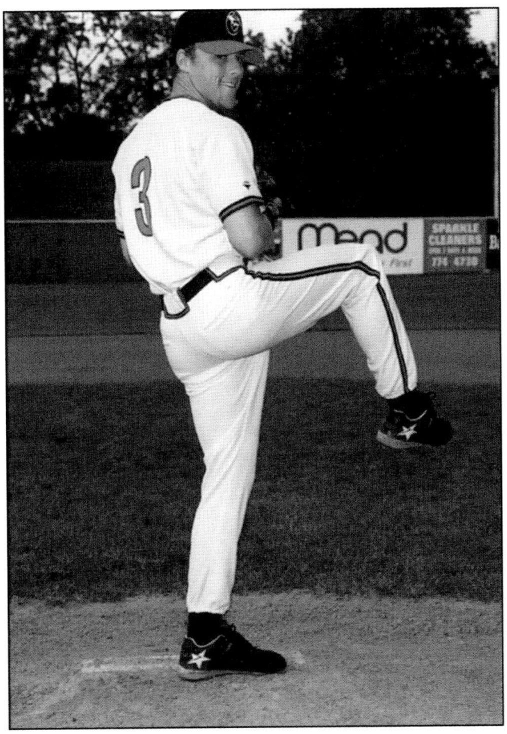

As a junior at The Citadel, left-hander Jon Hinkle had one of the best strikeout to walk ratios in the nation (65-4). The following year, in 1995, he had an 8-2 record and an ERA of 2.50. A workhorse for the 1996 Paints, Hinkle led the staff in games started (16), complete games (5), and innings pitched (106). He compiled an 8-2 record and an ERA of 3.93. His best game was a three-hit shutout of Richmond on July 12; but his most important start came in the second game of the first round of the playoffs, when he helped the Paints avoid elimination by holding Johnstown to two runs over seven and a third innings.

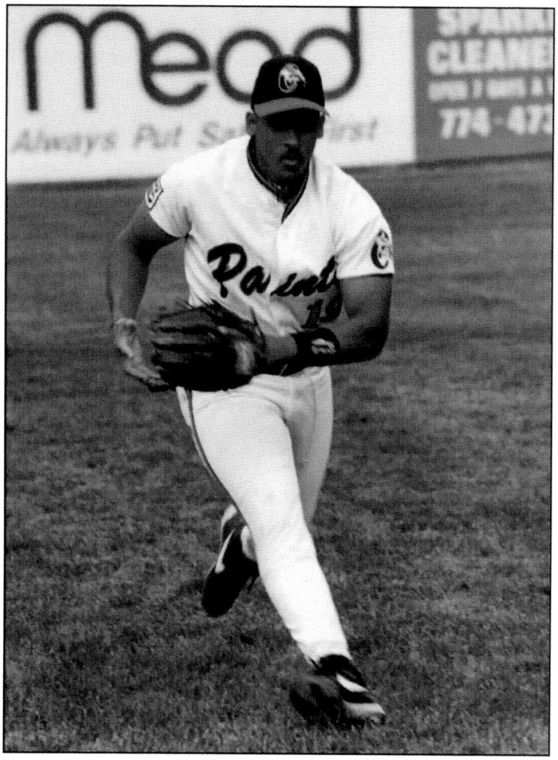

The regular left fielder on the 1996 Paints was Jackie Jempson, a slugger with power to all fields, who had played college ball at Colorado State and Cal. State-Bernadino. Jempson teamed with Scott Pinoni and Mitch House to give the Paints a fearsome heart of the batting order. Jackie hit .340 on the year, fifth best in the league, and clubbed a league third-best 13 home runs. After hitting a moon shot over the CF wall at V.A. Memorial on August 12, he said, "It felt like a golf ball off my bat. I knew it was gone." Jempson almost single-handedly keep the Paints from losing the first round of the 1996 playoffs. His bases-loaded single in the bottom of the ninth of Game Two evened the series, and his three-run home run in the bottom of the first led Chillicothe to a 5-2 win in the clincher.

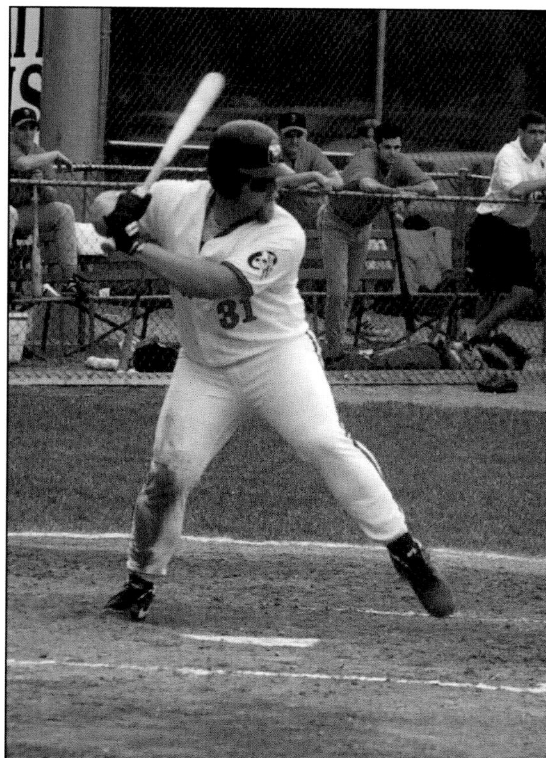

Scott Pinoni came to Chillicothe in 1996 with most impressive credentials. A two-time All-ACC 1st team selection at Duke University, he had made the California League All-Star team the previous year while playing for the Visalia Oaks of the Kansas City Royals' organization. Pinoni simply terrorized Frontier League pitching, winning the batting (.384) and RBI (65) titles, and setting a new record for hits (108). A native of Columbus, Ohio, Pinoni had the build, strength, and disposition of a "Gentle Ben"; which made his nickname, "Bear," almost a given. He was also a surprisingly good fielder as a first baseman. His 11 home runs in 1996 were good for fourth best in the Frontier League.

Like Pinoni, muscular(6'3", 225) third baseman Mitch House was already a veteran of professional baseball when he joined the Paints in 1996, having spent the previous five seasons in the Pittsburgh Pirates' minor league system. House led the league in home runs in 1996, and many of his homers were tape-measure jobs. He hit his final and 18th dinger on the last day of the regular season to break a tie with Richmond's Morgan Burkhart. (The 18 home runs were also a Frontier League season record.) For the season House batted .305 with 53 RBI, 139 total bases, and 63 runs (2nd in the league).

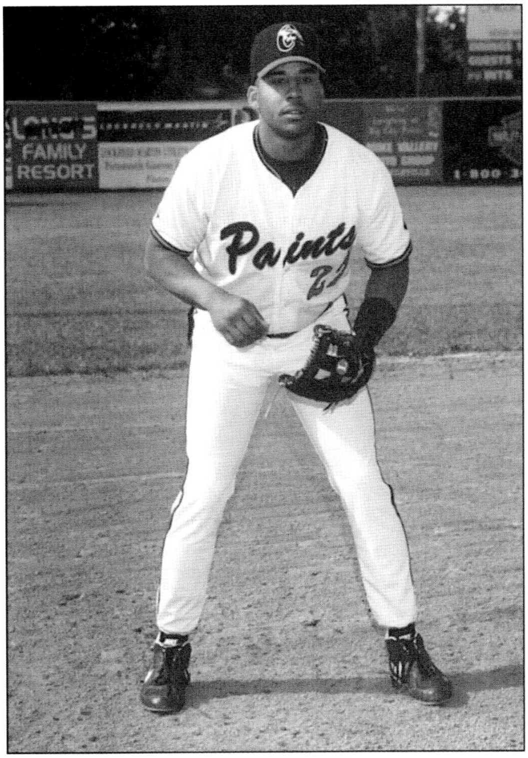

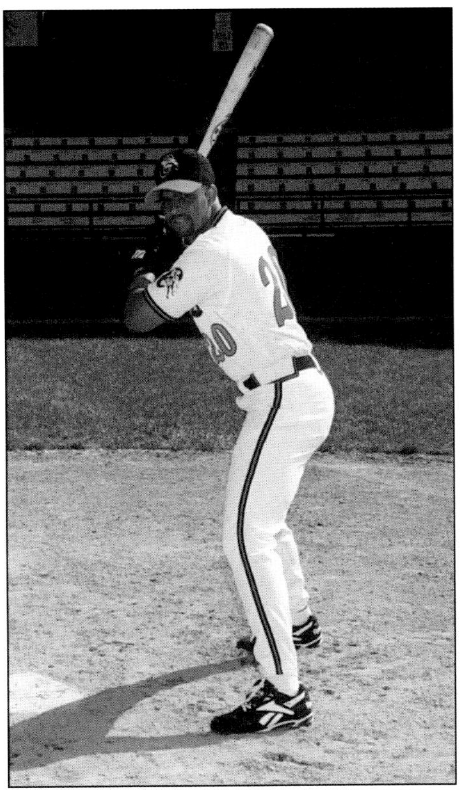

A graduate of the University of San Francisco, Danny Collins was a talented player whose playing time in 1996 was limited due to a crowded Paints' outfield and a groin injury he suffered during the first week of the second half of the season. Still, he made his contribution to the team, batting .274 in 53 games with 17 RBI and 16 runs. His best days came on July 13 when his two-run triple in the bottom of the 11th beat Ohio Valley, 6-5, and on August 4 when he went 3-3 to help Chillicothe beat the Zanesville Greys, 7-3. Although he hit no home runs in 1996, he blasted what observers described as the longest homer ever hit at V.A. Memorial Stadium on Opening Day the following year and hit a total of three long balls in the season's first five games. He abruptly retired July 11, ending the year batting .270 with 3 homers and 18 RBI.

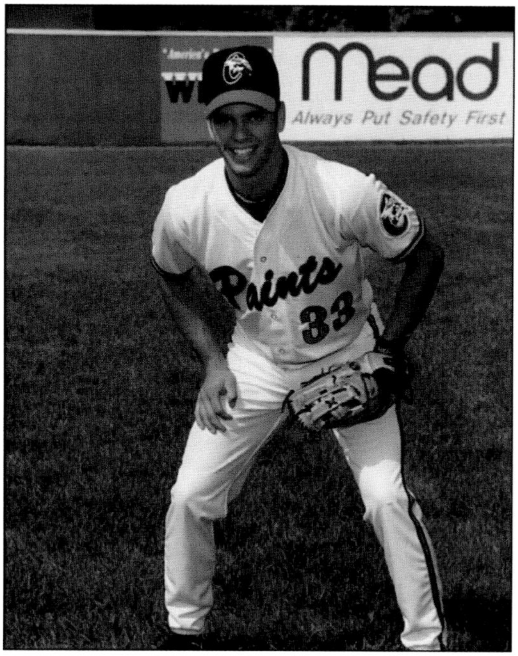

A native of Hubbard, Ohio, Jamie Palumbo joined the Paints after a stellar career at Youngstown (OH) State University. He platooned in center field and had several days at the plate worth remembering. His bases-loaded single over the center fielder's head produced the GWRBI in the bottom of the 11th inning against the Kalamazoo Kodiaks on July 24; and on August 19 he went 4-5 to help the Paints knock off the Johnstown Steal, 10-4, in Johnstown, Pennsylvania. Palumbo batted .268 in 57 games.

Starting pitcher Tim Sheridan from Downington, Pennsylvania, was a teammate of Jesse Fluck in college and a two-time Pitcher of the Year for Franklin and Marshall. The highly competitive Sheridan, who liked to pitch inside, psyched himself up before games and took a football player's mentality to the mound; not surprising since he played outside linebacker on the Franklin and Marshall football team. He threw a one-hit shutout on Opening Day at Zanesville and was sporting one of the best ERAs in the league when he was named to the All-Star team; however, the Paints announced his retirement on August 5. "He just wore his arm out," said GM Bryan Wickline. Tim finished the 1996 season with a 4-3 record, a 3.69 ERA, and 40 Ks in 63 1/3 innings. He returned to Franklin and Marshall for his senior season in football.

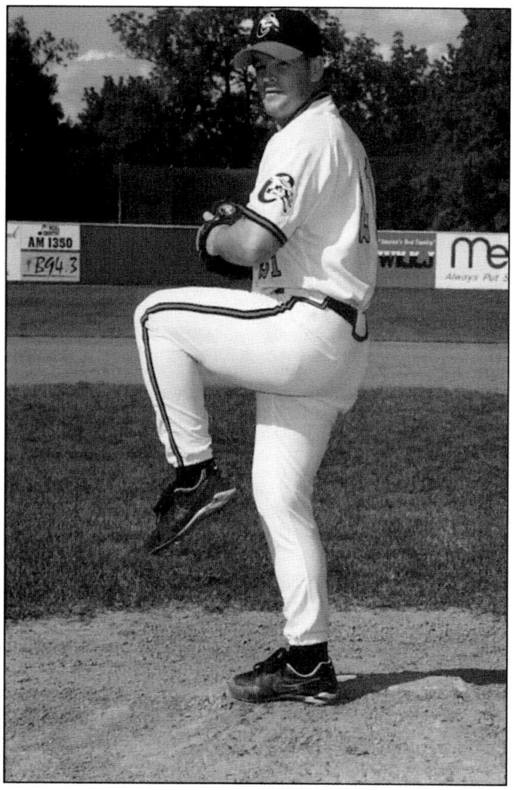

Hard throwing Keith Mayhew was a three-time All-American at Ferrum (VA) College, where he set nine school records, finishing his career with a 35-5 record and a 2.15 ERA. Before signing with Chillicothe he added a spectacular 1995 season in the Northwest League to his impressive resume, compiling a 15-1 record with a 1.96 ERA and 145 strikeouts. He began the 1996 season as a starter but quickly moved to the bullpen where he was most effective. He finished the 1996 season with a 5-3 record and nine saves, which tied him for fourth in the Frontier League.

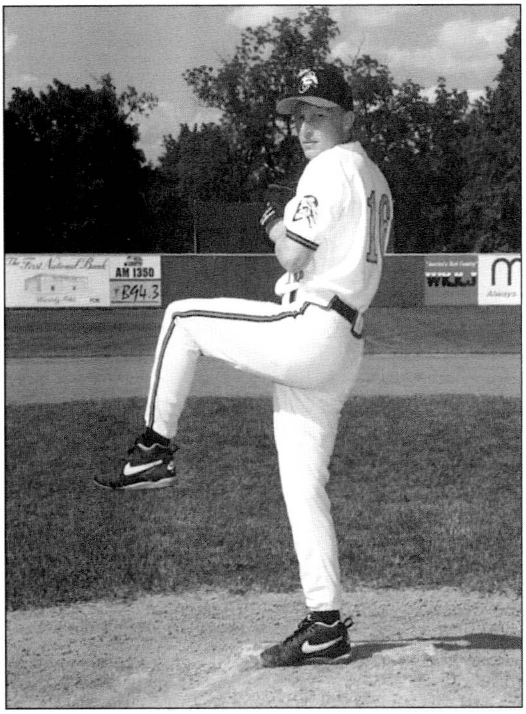

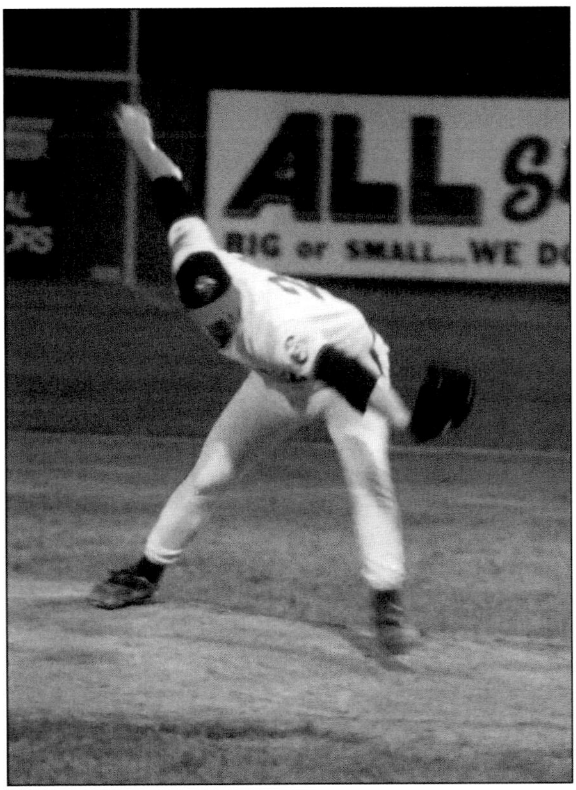

While pitching for the University of North Carolina, submarining reliever Thad Chrismon set the ACC record for saves in a season (18) and for career saves (41). He got plenty of work with the Paints in 1996, making 24 appearances which tied him for fourth in the league. He wound up with eight saves and three wins on the year to go with a sparkling ERA of 1.96. On two different occasions he put on the team mascot's costume and entertained the crowd without anybody finding out about it until the end of the season.

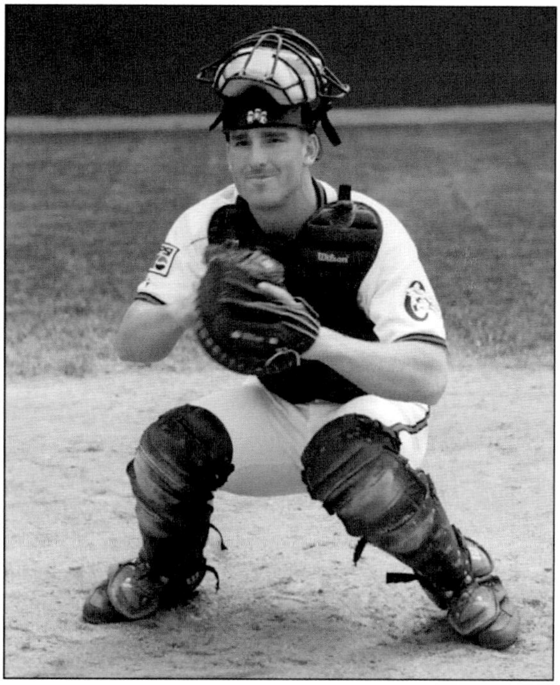

Slated to be a backup in 1996, Brad Plackemeier filled in admirably when first string catcher Greg Reinhart suffered a hamstring injury in the middle of the season. The tall (6'5") receiver with a strong arm batted .270 and did not commit an error in 29 games in 1996. Brad returned to Chillicothe for the 1997 and 1998 seasons as the first string catcher, and he performed so steadily at the plate that through the 2000 season he was listed among the Paints' Top Ten in four batting categories (home runs, RBI, doubles, and at-bats). In 1997 he set a Frontier League record for hit-by-pitch (20). At the end of the 2002 season, Paints' fans voted Plackemeier as the catcher to the 10th Anniversary Dream Team.

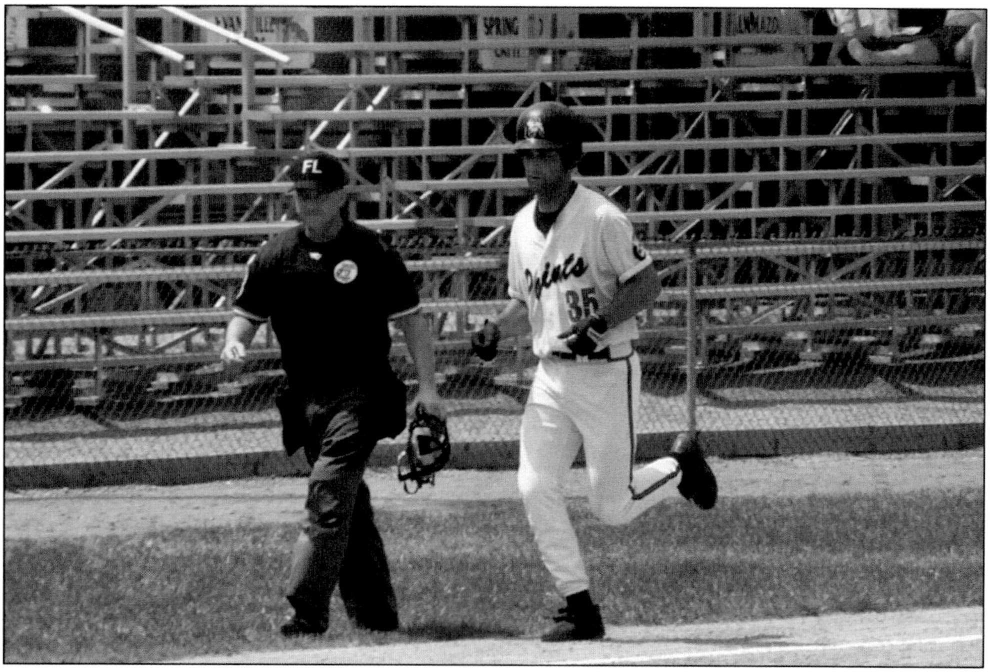

Mike Roche, who'd played in the Milwaukee Brewers' organization, started the season as the Paints' regular second baseman, but Jason Benyo, who joined the ballclub two weeks into the season, gradually beat him out for the job. A product of the University of Rio Grande (OH), Benyo played in 55 games, batted .288, stole 16 bases, and compiled 182 assists. The following year Benyo had numerous multi-hit games and batted .283 with 16 doubles and 32 RBI. He was nominated for the Paints' 10th Anniversary Dream Team.

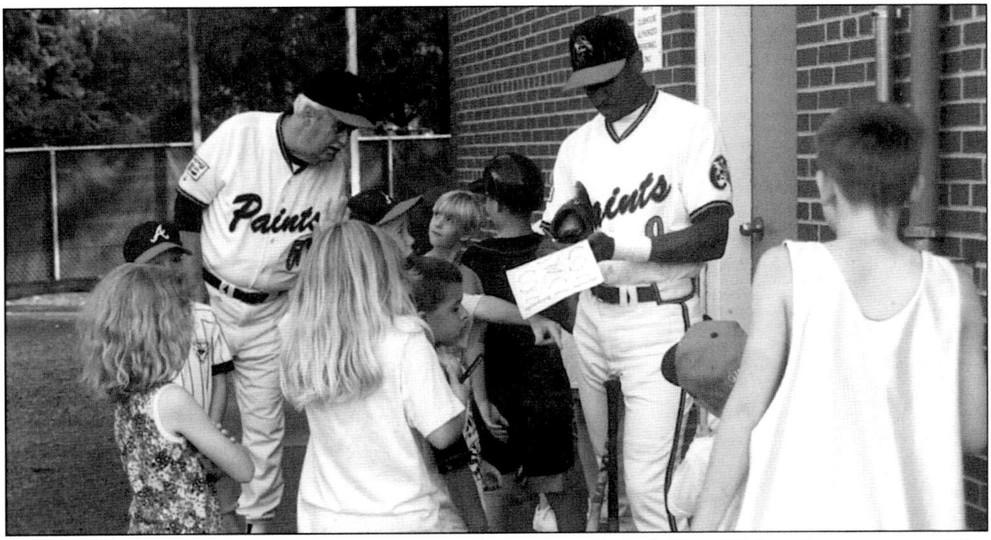

After batting only .232 for the Paints in his rookie season of 1995, Troy Wilcox became one of the outfield regulars in 1996 and upped his performance considerably. In 64 games he batted .314 with six doubles, four triples, and 35 RBI. His 23 stolen bases (in 27 attempts) were also second on the team. A fan favorite in Chillicothe, the Michigan (Clinton Township) native had been the MVP of his Aquinas College team his senior year. Wilcox is pictured here (with Paints' manager Roger Hanners) signing autographs outside the Paints' clubhouse at V.A. Memorial Stadium. Troy was a candidate for the Right Field position on the Paints' 10th Anniversary Dream Team.

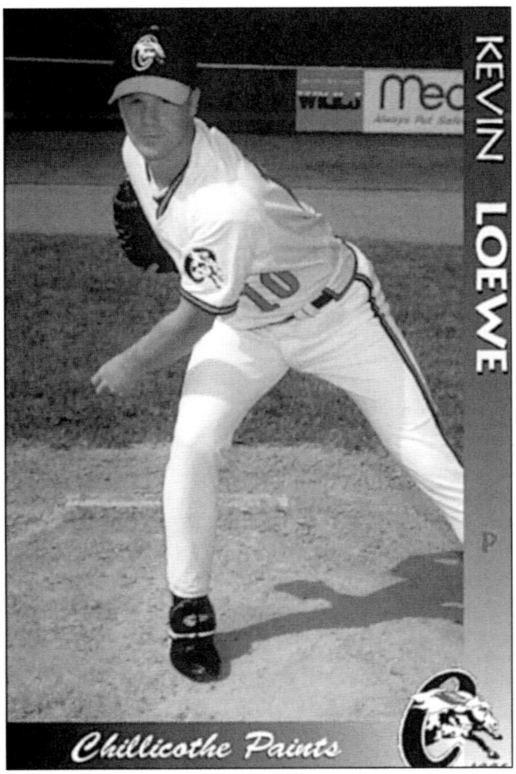

Kevin Loewe from Baltimore, Maryland, was one of the stalwarts of the Paints' starting rotation in 1996. He was second on the team in starts (14) and innings pitched (87.2), and his seven wins (against three losses) were third-best. He threw a five-hit shutout against Ohio Valley on August 15, but his most important victory in a Paints' uniform came when he pitched Chillicothe to a 5-2 win to clinch the first round of the playoffs against Johnstown. In that game Loewe scattered five singles, and both runs he allowed were unearned. At the University of Maryland-Baltimore County, Kevin set the school record for career wins with 27. He was a starting left-handed pitcher nomination to the Paints' 10th Anniversary Dream Team.

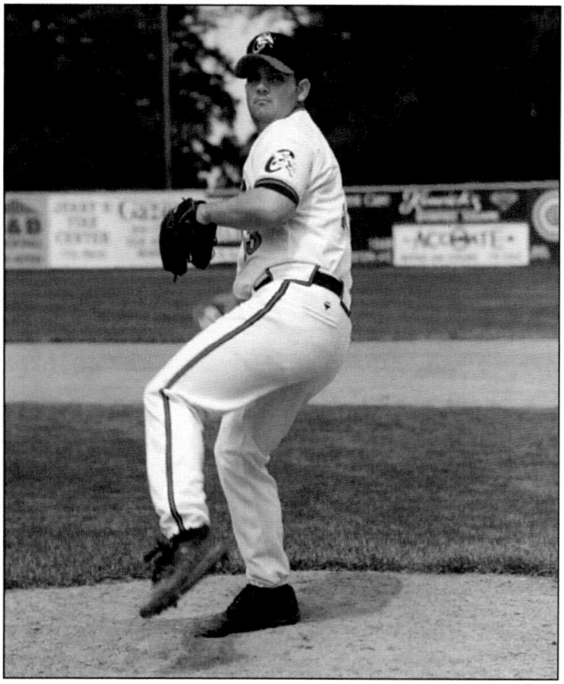

Andy Mycheck posted a 17-5 record with a 2.80 ERA and 190 strikeouts in 150 innings during his four-year career at Saginaw Valley State University. The Rochester, Michigan native was cut from the Paints during spring training, but Chillicothe signed him shortly after the 1997 Frontier League All-Star Game. He was a good addition to the roster, chalking up a 4-0 record with a sparkling 1.90 ERA. Working mainly as a middle reliever, Mycheck also had a nine to one strikeout-to-walk ratio.

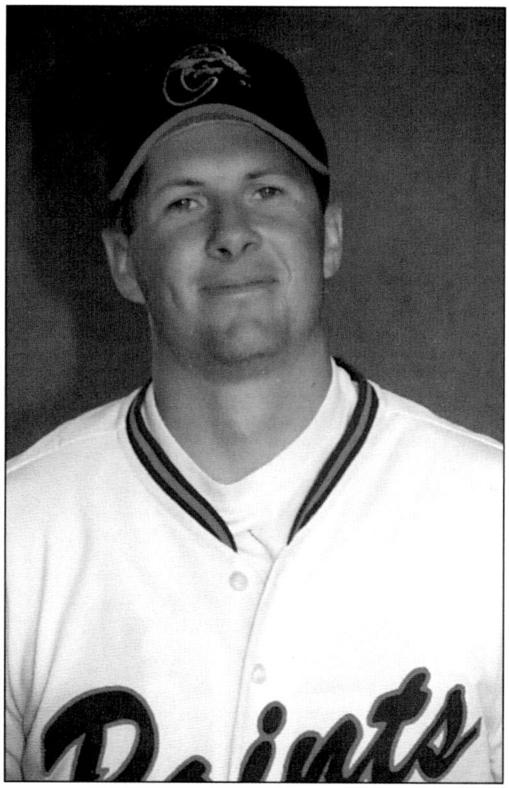

The ace of the Paints' pitching staff in 1997 was right-hander Bob Spears, a Zanesville Grey in 1996 and a former captain of the Ohio State baseball team which won four straight Big Ten titles while he was a member of the team. In 1997 Spears led the Frontier League in complete games (7) and innings pitched (112), and he was third in ERA (3.05). His 8-6 record tied him for second in wins, and his 92 strikeouts placed him second. He started the All-Star Game for the East Division and was voted the Paints' Most Valuable Pitcher for 1997.

Rick Heineman was another dependable arm in the Paints' rotation in 1997, but he suffered from a lack of run support and deserved better than his 5-4 record. His ERA of 3.73 was 13th best in the league, and he was named to the East Division All-Star team. A Culver City, California native, Heineman went 7-4 in his senior year at UCLA, won All-Pac 10 honors, and received the Tommy John Award. He was drafted by the Chicago White Sox but played only one year (1996) at Bristol, Virginia, before he was released by the organization.

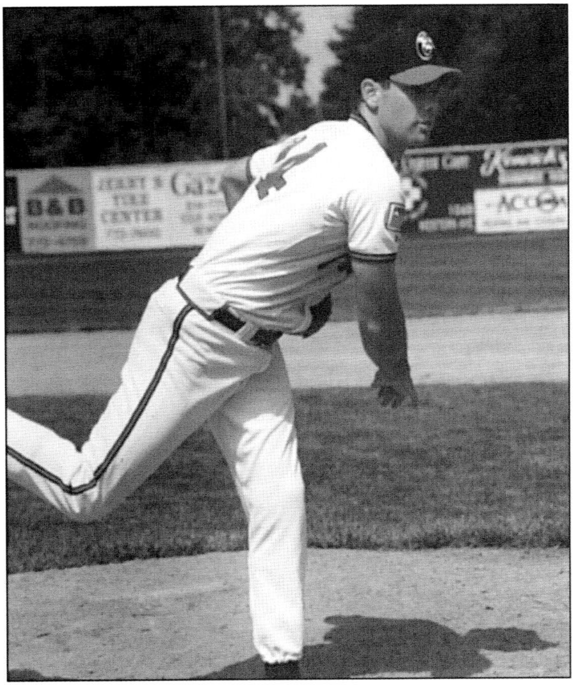

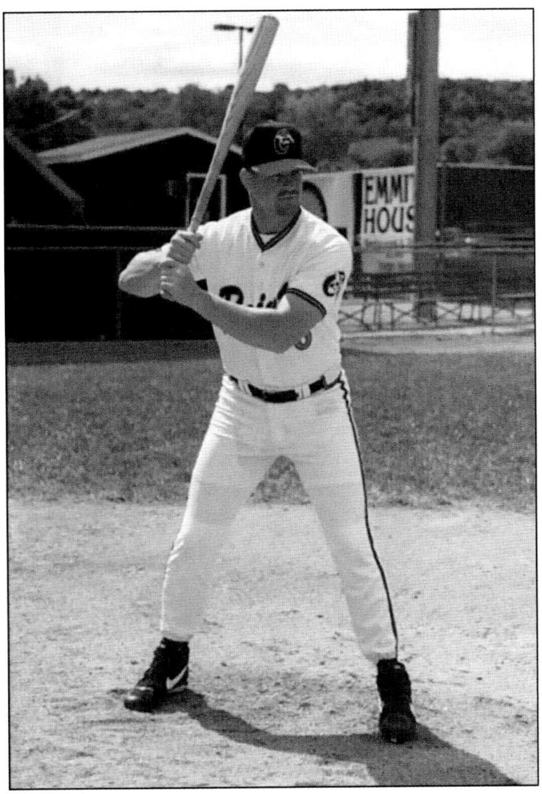

A nephew of former Cincinnati Reds' second baseman Tommy Helms, Telly Helms was from Charlotte, North Carolina, and played at Coker College (Hartsville, SC). The Paints signed him as an infielder-backup catcher, but he got most of his at-bats in 1997 as a designated hitter. He batted .289 with 14 doubles, one home run, and 28 RBI in 1997. His best games came on July 20 when he went 4-5 with four RBI against Johnstown, and on July 24 when his single in the bottom of the tenth inning drove in the game-winning run against Ohio Valley. Back with the Paints in 1998, he rode the pine for most of the first month of the season but got red-hot when given his chance. In three games between July 7 and July 9, Telly cracked out eight hits and had back-to-back games of two two-run home runs. He made the East Division All-Star team and went 1-4 in the game. He batted .288 for the year.

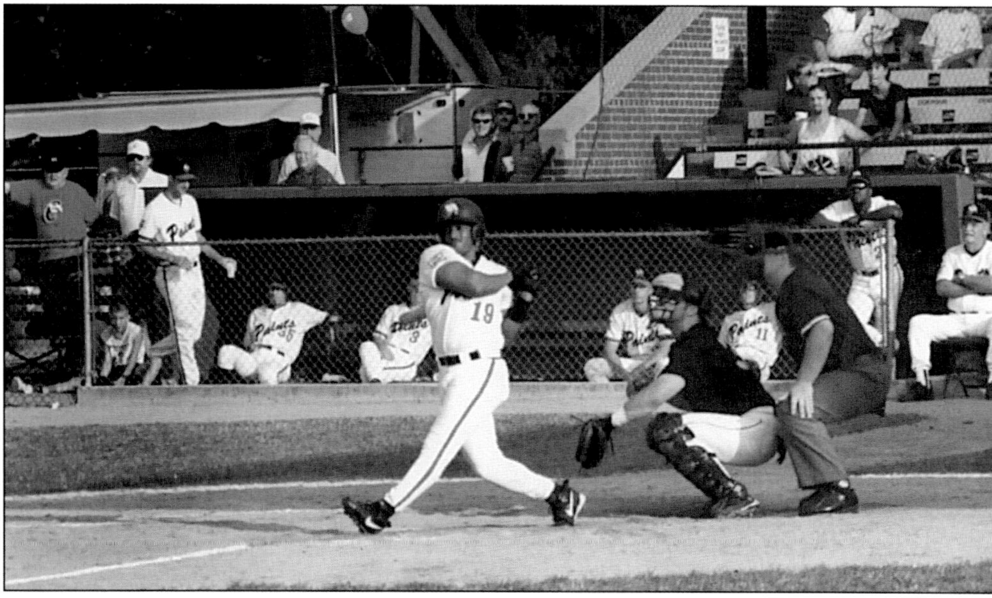

In his second tour of duty with the Paints Jackie Jempson again put up some of the best power numbers in the Frontier League for 1997. He tied for second in the league with 17 home runs, placed fifth with 64 RBI, and led the Paints in both categories. He hit a two-run home run in the 1997 All-Star Game and for the second year in a row was one of the three outfielders named to the post-season Frontier League All-Star Team.

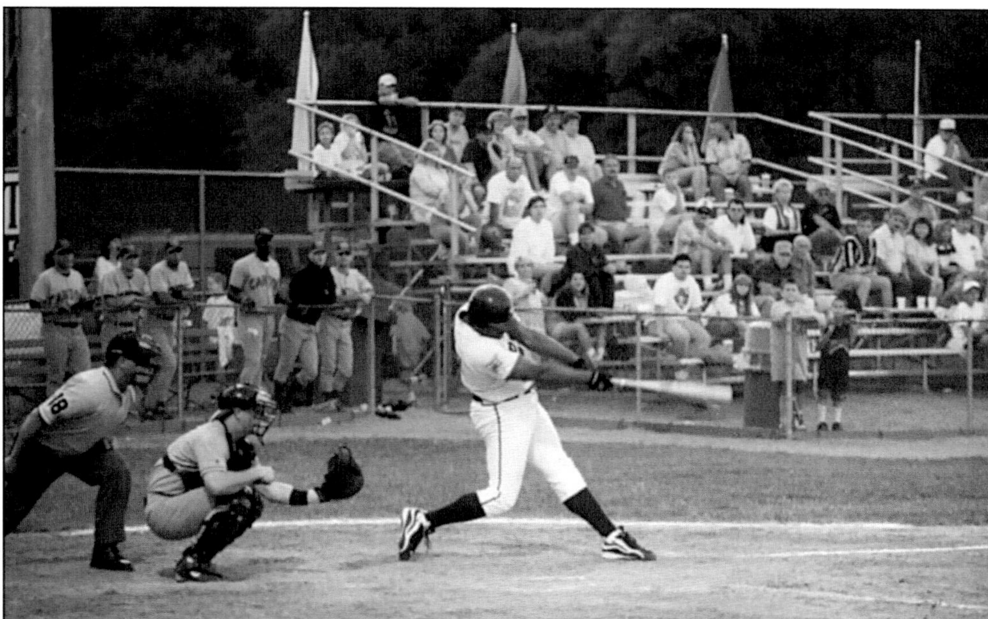

After the 1996 season, big Mitch House retired from professional baseball. He decided to "un-retire" by the following spring, and Paints' fans were ecstatic that he did. In 1997 House batted .319 (15th in the league), with 15 home runs (4th), and 62 RBI (6th). He also led the league in walks (74) and on-base percentage (.471). He was voted the team's Most Valuable Player and named again to the post-season Frontier League All-Star Team, this time as the first baseman.

Bobby Jones didn't play in the 1997 Opener, but he won the center field job by hitting three home runs between the third and seventh games of the season. A former first-team Junior College All-American at Riverside (CA) Community College, Jones had been a 15th round draft choice of the Detroit Tigers in 1993. He continued to play well but retired on July 7 because of injuries. He batted .299 on the year.

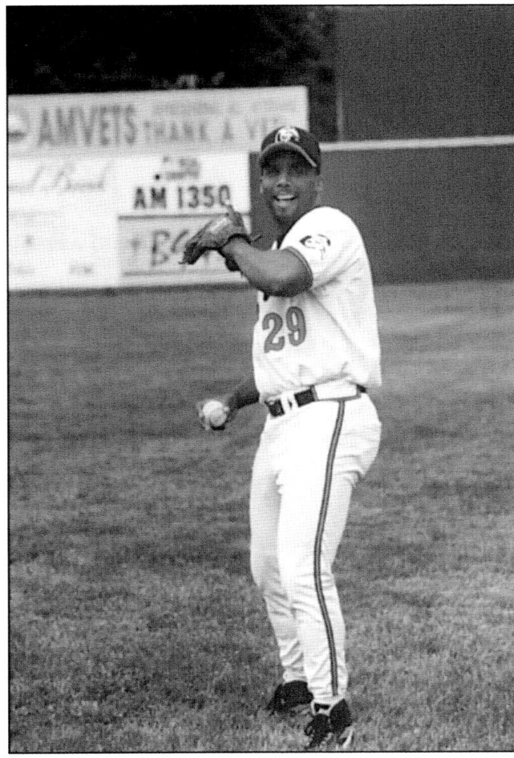

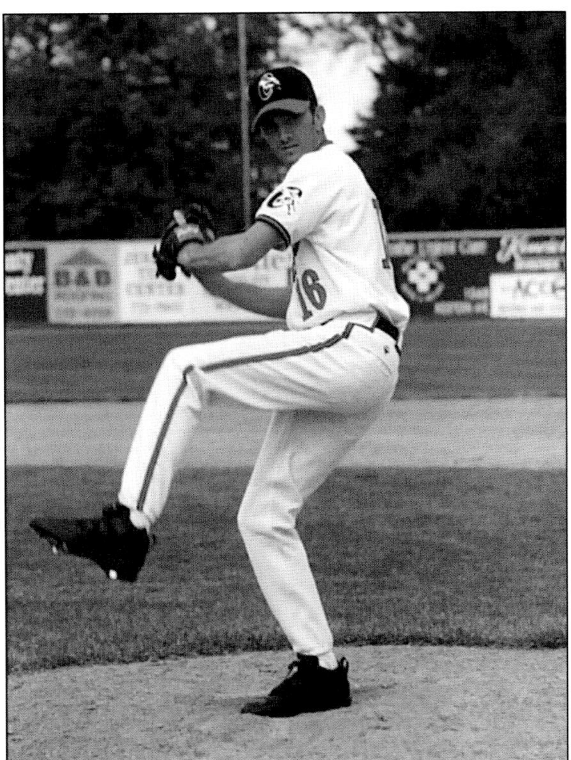

Nicknamed "Smoke" for his blazing fastball, Joe Montgomery worked as the Paints' closer for most of the season but moved into the starting rotation towards the end of the year. He picked up his fifth win of the season (against seven losses) on August 25 by scattering nine hits in a complete-game 11-3 victory against Ohio Valley. Before coming to the Paints he had pitched at Eastern Kentucky University and in the farm system of the Cincinnati Reds for two seasons. His ERA for 1997 was 2.84, and he was nominated for the Paints' 10th Anniversary Dream Team.

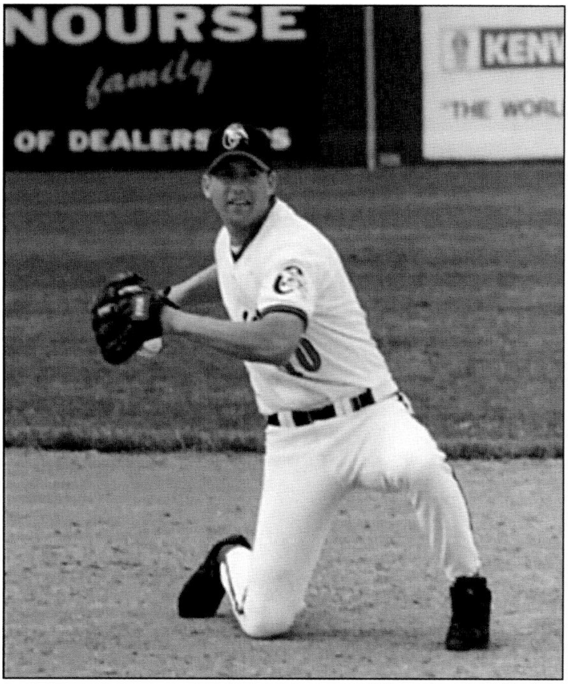

The Paints planned to play Eddie Acosta, a four-year veteran of the Montreal Expos' and Milwaukee Brewers' farm systems, at shortstop in 1997. They released him after he started the season 0-9 at the plate in six games and replaced him with Delaware, Ohio, native Jon Clinger, who'd just finished his career at Otterbein College. Clinger batted .246 for the season, with three home runs and 22 RBI in 68 games, and he was nominated for the Paints' 10th Anniversary Dream Team.

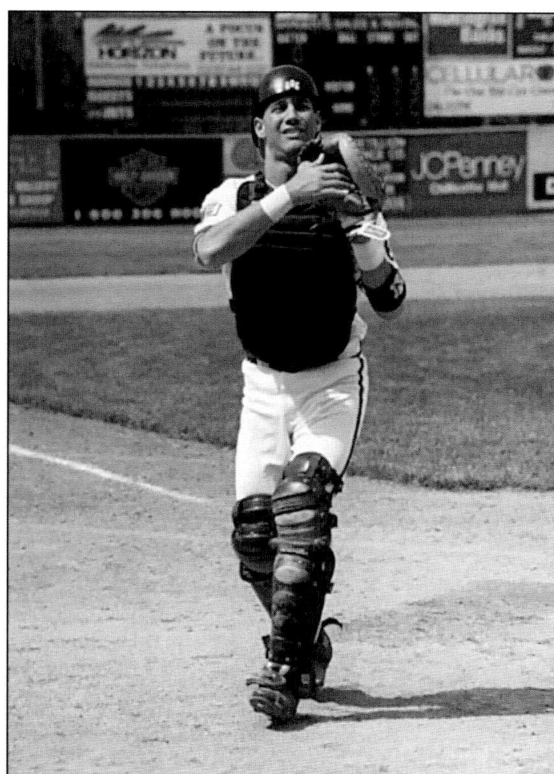

Before signing with the Paints for 1997, catcher Patrick Anderson (Asheville, NC) had been a two-year starter for the Zanesville Greys and a Frontier League All-Star in 1996. Expected to be a reserve, he was forced into action when Brad Plackmeier went down with injury. Anderson hit so well that when Plackmeier return to his duties, the Paints continued to give him at-bats as a first baseman and as a DH. He produced several game-winning hits, made the 1997 East Division All-Star team, and finished the year with a .307 batting average (second-best on the team), with three home runs and 29 RBI.

Nathan Gardner was a rookie in pro baseball in 1997, coming to the Paints from the University of North Carolina at Asheville, where he averaged better than a strikeout per inning his senior year and set the school record for consecutive scoreless innings (16). Gardner appeared in 29 games in 1997 and led the Paints in saves with eight. He pitched one and a third scoreless innings in the All-Star Game and struck out three West Division All-Stars. After the season he was signed by the Cincinnati Reds and spent the next two seasons in their minor league system, recording a 9-6 composite ledger for Charleston (WV) and Rockford (IL). After his release by the Reds, Gardner returned to Chillicothe in 2000 and again worked out of the Paints' bullpen.

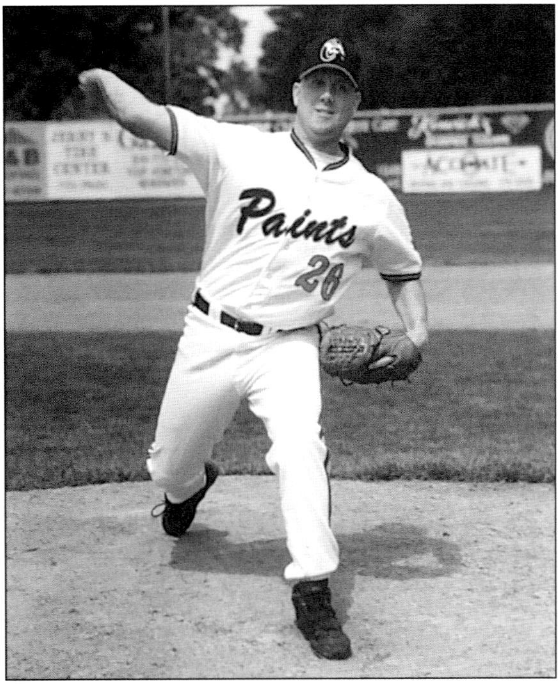

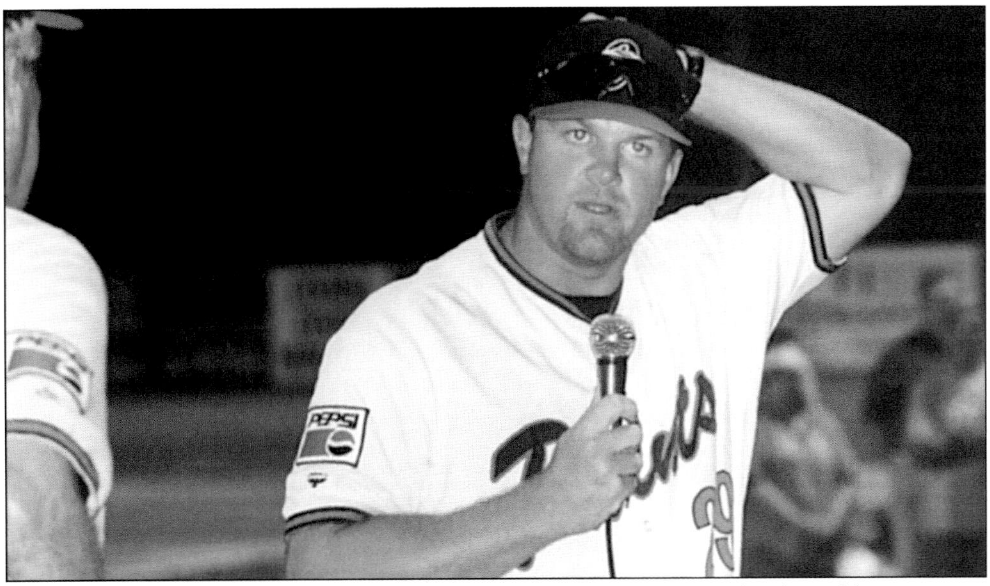

Brian Mannino only played half a season for the Paints, but he made such a favorable impression that he was one of the five players nominated to the first base position for the 10th Anniversary Dream Team. A teammate of pitcher Bob Spears at Ohio State, Mannino was a four-year starter for the Buckeyes and a two-time First-team All-Big Ten player and All-American. After having played for the Rhode Island Tigersharks of the independent Northeast League in 1996, Mannino joined the Paints on July 16, 1997. He had at least nine multi-hit games in his half season, and his best day came on August 25 when he hit two home runs and knocked in six runs against the Ohio Valley Redcoats. Brian hit .295 with four home runs and 28 RBI on the season, and he returned to Chillicothe in 1998 as a coach.

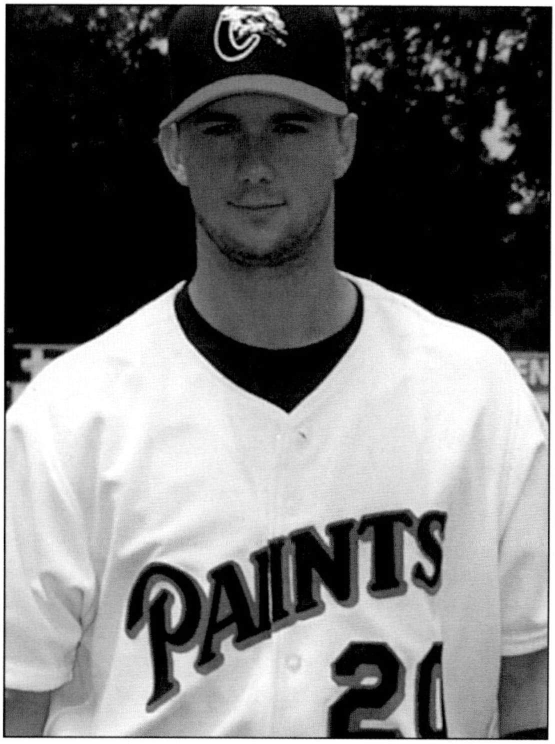

Outfielder Charles "Gator" McBride played in the farm system of the Atlanta Braves for five years before his leg injuries caused the Braves to give up on him. The Atlanta scout who recommended him to Roger Hanners said, "The Braves will never send you a better hitter than this guy." McBride simply tore up the Frontier League in 1998, and he combined with Mitch House and Scott Pinoni to form the most devastating trio of sluggers ever to play on one Frontier League team. Voted the Paints' MVP for 1998, McBride hit .403 for the year and lost the batting title by a single point. He added 12 home runs and 63 RBI. He doubled and homered in the mid-season All-Star Game, hit .385 with two homers in the Playoffs, and was voted to the end-of-the-season 1998 Frontier League All-Star team.

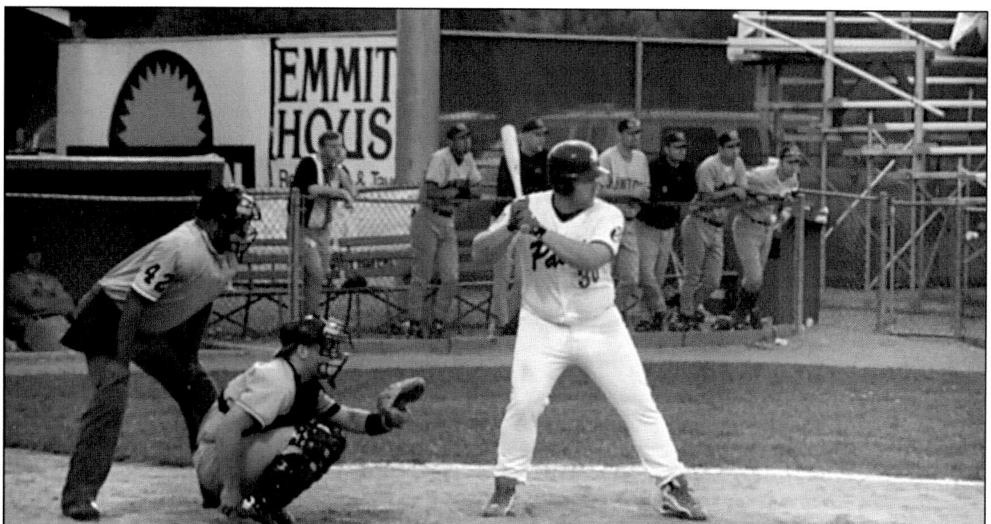

After an excellent year (.315, 23 HR, 92 RBI) with the Sioux City Explorers of the Northern League in 1997, Scott Pinoni returned to Chillicothe for 1998 and picked up where he'd left off. His average dropped to .309, but his 25 home runs tied him for second in the league while his 98 RBI tied him for first. Scott also hit two of the most notable home runs in Paints' history in 1998. His three-run blast in the ninth inning led Chillicothe to a dramatic 4-2 victory over Springfield in the opening game of the Frontier League finals, and his moon shot over the trees beyond the left field wall at V.A. Memorial on July 2 traveled 506 feet, according to the "walked-off" measurement by pitcher Stephen Byrd.

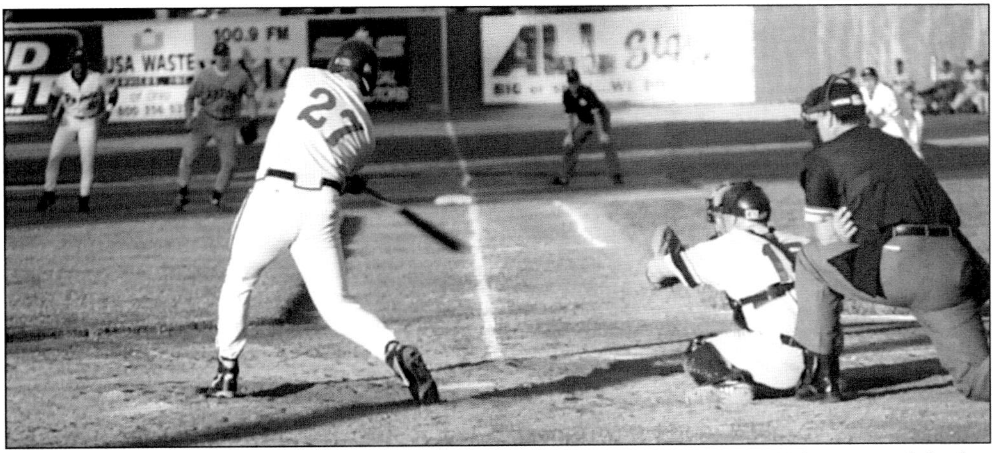

Mitch House, who would be too old to play in the Frontier League in 1999, returned for his final season with the Paints in 1998. His stats (.277, 17 HR, 66 RBI) were below par for him but still good enough to land him on the league All-Star team for the third straight year. His 41st career home run on July 16 made him the Frontier League all-time leader, and on the last day of the season the Paints gave him the honor of being the first player in team history to have his uniform number retired. House celebrated by hitting his 50th career home run (a game winning-three run shot) and an infield single which gave him a .300 lifetime average with the Paints. Mitch's solo home run was the game-winning hit in the first playoff game against Canton, and his solo homer two days later accounted for Chillicothe's lone run in Game Two.

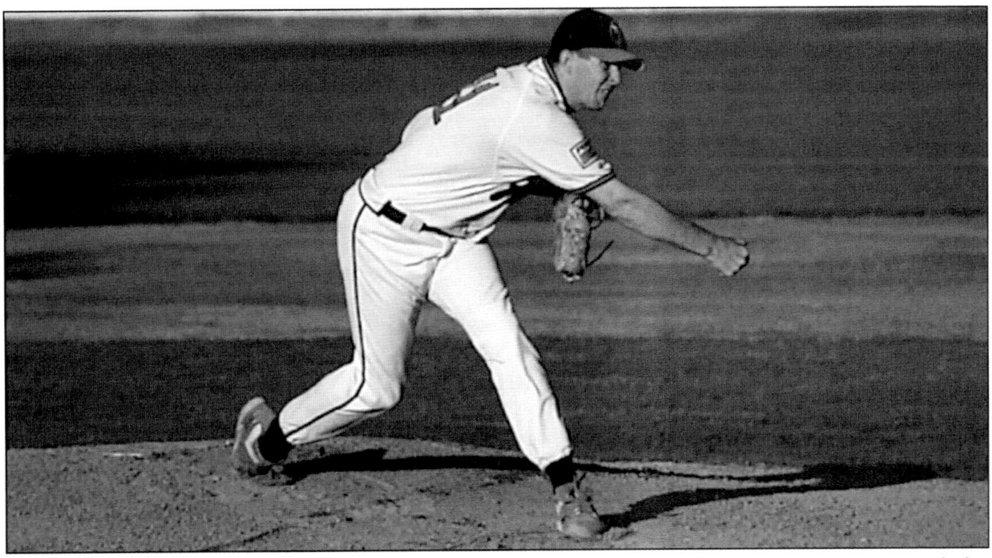

For his outstanding performance in 1998 Bob Spears became the first player to be voted the Paints' Most Valuable Pitcher in consecutive seasons. Spears posted a 10-5 record with an ERA of 3.38 (fifth best in the league), and his 124 strikeouts established a new league record for a season. He pitched a three-hitter and a four-hitter, and his one-hitter in a scheduled seven-inning contest on August 13 was almost the first no-hitter in league history. After playing in the Taiwanese professional league, Spears returned to Chillicothe in 1999 a month into the Frontier League season, but his results were not up to his usual high standard. Still, after the 2000 season, he was the Paints' all-time leader in starts, innings, complete games, wins (tied at 20 with Stephen Byrd), strikeouts, and shutouts.

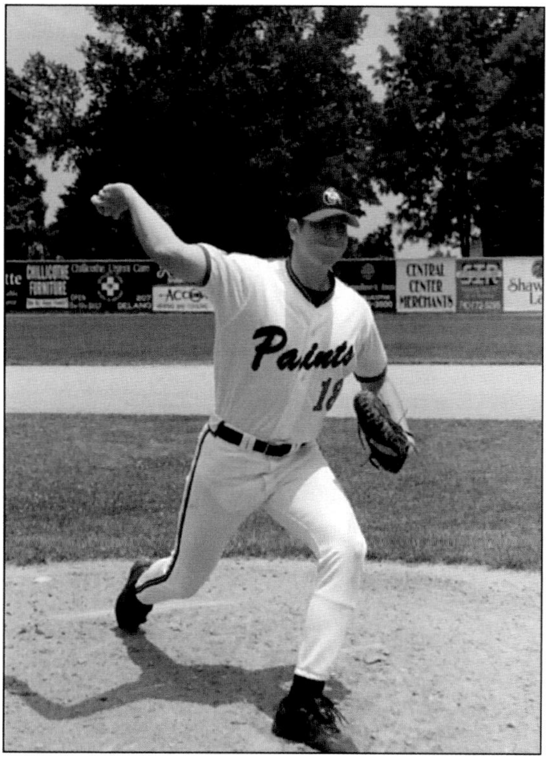

Kansas City native Brian Scarcello was an amateur magician who amused his teammates with tricks like disappearing napkins and pouring water into his left hand and then dumping it out of his right. He also cast a spell over the Paints' potent bats, reserving their most lethal attacks for days he pitched. Scarcello set a league record by starting the 1998 season 8-0, and in those games the Paints outscored the opposition, 65-32. He was named Frontier League Pitcher of the Month for June, made the All-Star team, and set a new league record for wins with a 13-1 slate to go along with a 4.57 ERA and 65 strikeouts in 102 innings. Scarcello, who played baseball for three different colleges, went 12-1 in his senior year at Benedictine College. He began his pro career in 1997 with Amarillo of the independent Texas-Louisiana League.

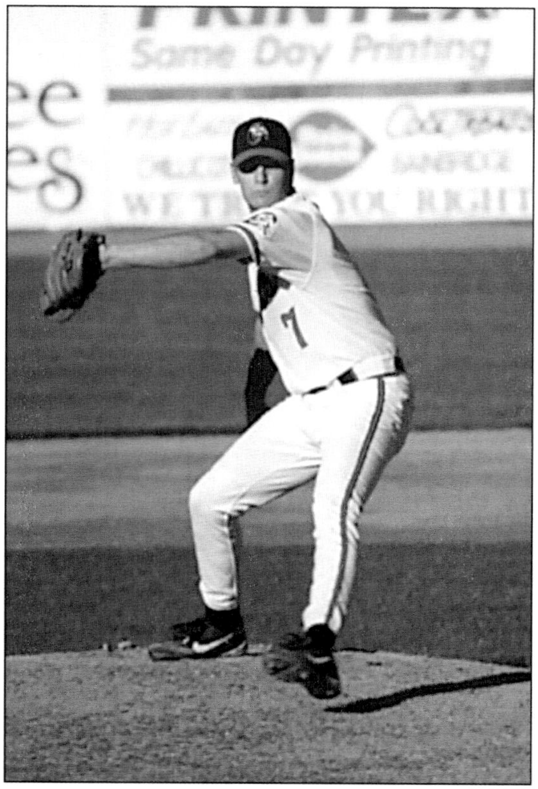

Although he stood just 5-foot-11, rookie pitcher Stephen Byrd was a hard thrower and a feisty competitor. A good old Southern boy out of West Alabama University, Byrd loved the rodeo and actually brought a mechanical bull with him to Chillicothe so that he could practice bull riding. He started 14 games for the 1998 Paints and posted a mediocre 5-5 record, but his excellent strikeout total (82 Ks in 82.2 innings) was more indicative of his performance. Byrd, who liked to be called by his last name, would go on to have one of the best careers by a starting pitcher in a Chillicothe uniform.

Bobby Chandler, who would eventually become the Frontier League All-Time saves leader, began his pro baseball career with the Paints in 1998. A native of Salinas, California, Chandler had posted a 7-2 record and a 3.50 ERA at California State University in the spring. Bobby made the East Division All-Star team and finished the season with a 1-2 record and seven saves, which tied him for the team lead with Rick Blanc. He posted an ERA of 3.90 in 32.1 innings and allowed 27 hits and 19 walks while fanning 22. Chandler, who always seemed to have a smile on his face, was a talented pantomine as well as one of the originators of the Chicken Dance routine which the Paints' bullpen made famous.

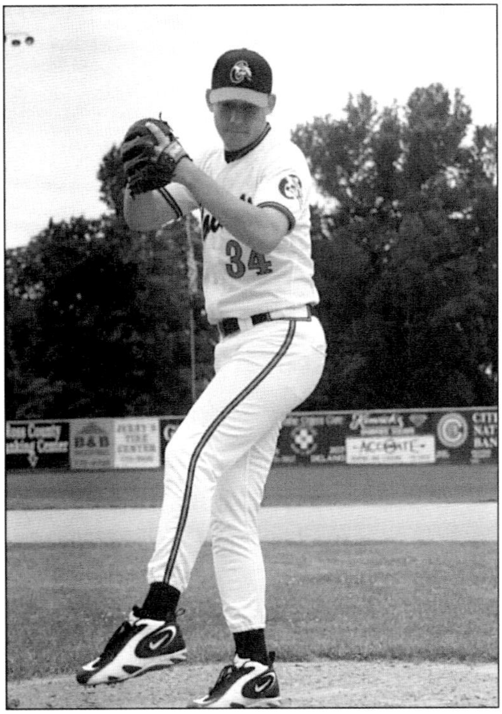

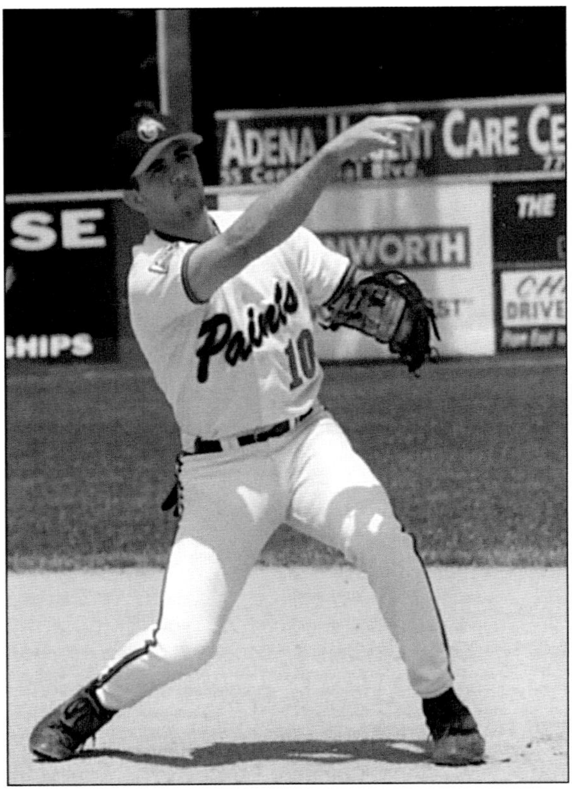

Rookie shortstop David Daulton teamed with second baseman Mike Horning, yet another rookie for 1998, to give the Paints one of their best double play combos ever. Daulton hailed from Greenville, South Carolina, and had sold Kirby vacuum cleaners to help pay his way though college. He played college ball at Liberty University (Lynchburg, VA) where he hit .410 his senior year and was named the MVP of the Big South Conference Tournament. Freddy Flores started the year at short, but Daulton's bat was too good to keep on the bench. Daulton's .330 season average turned out to be the second best on the Paints and the 14th best in the league. He added seven home runs and 39 RBI.

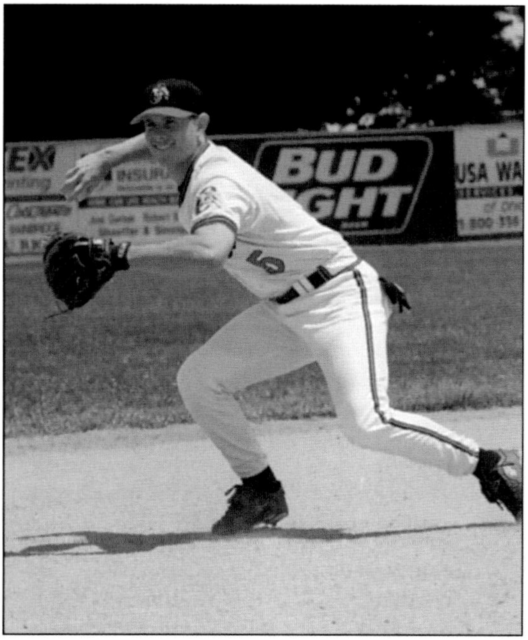

On the heels of an excellent senior year (.330, 9 HR, 44 RBI) at Le Moyne College (Syracuse, NY), second baseman Mike Horning immediately won over Paints' fans with his gritty play and constant hustle. He suffered several nagging injuries but still put together a solid season, batting .273 from the leadoff spot, with a pair of home runs and a pair of triples. Horning was the regular second baseman for the next two years too, and when he retired after the 2000 season he ranked in the Paints' All-Time Top 10 for most batting categories. The highly superstitious Horning practiced a number of different rituals involving the number 3 throughout every game, and he took pride in getting his uniform dirty every night. Chillicothe fans rewarded his spirit by voting him onto the Paints' 10th Anniversary Dream Team.

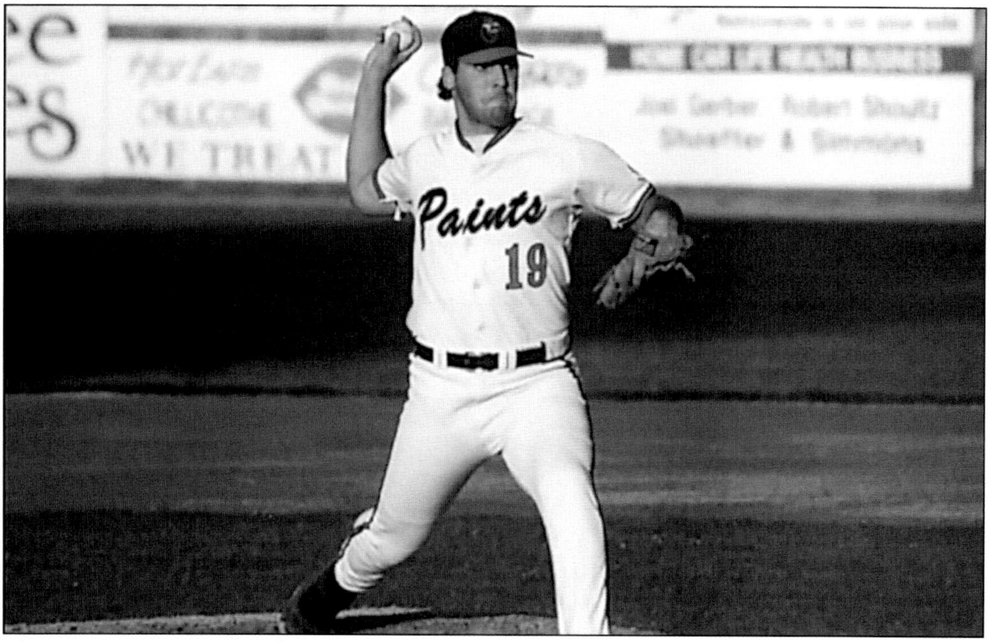

The 1998 Paints received a huge boost in the arm when they added Mike Roberts, a Massachusetts boy who loved country music, to the team on July 3. Roberts, who'd been released by the Atlanta Braves, started out working in relief, but on July 13 he moved into the starting rotation as the fifth starter. He went 7-1 on the year with a 4.22 ERA, which was seventh best in the league. Mike's best game was a complete-game, five-hit 11-1 victory over the Richmond Roosters on August 6. Roberts was also a key factor in the playoffs. He picked up the Game Three win that clinched Chillicothe's first round defeat of Canton, but he also absorbed the loss to Springfield in the deciding game of the championship round.

Big (6'4", 230lbs) John Peck was another important starting pitcher for the 1998 Paints. He went 7-4 with an ERA of 4.75 and struck out 35 batters in 72 innings. His best effort came on August 15 when he held the Springfield Capitals to one earned run over eight innings during the Paints' 7-3 win. Peck started his professional career in 1997 with the Bend (CA) Bandits of the independent Western League. At Sonoma (CA) State College he'd posted an 11-4 record his senior year and set school records for career wins and innings pitched.

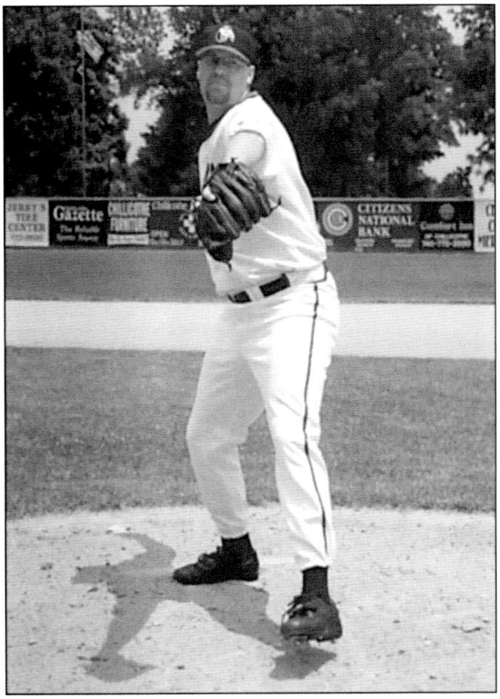

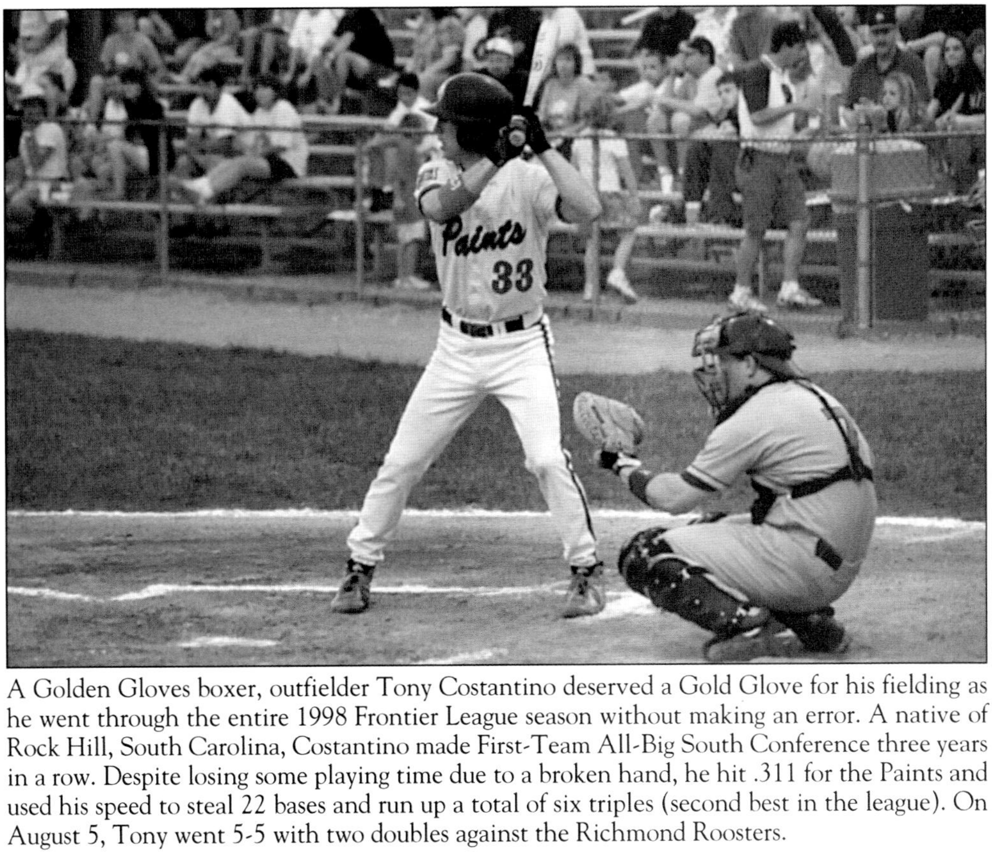

A Golden Gloves boxer, outfielder Tony Costantino deserved a Gold Glove for his fielding as he went through the entire 1998 Frontier League season without making an error. A native of Rock Hill, South Carolina, Costantino made First-Team All-Big South Conference three years in a row. Despite losing some playing time due to a broken hand, he hit .311 for the Paints and used his speed to steal 22 bases and run up a total of six triples (second best in the league). On August 5, Tony went 5-5 with two doubles against the Richmond Roosters.

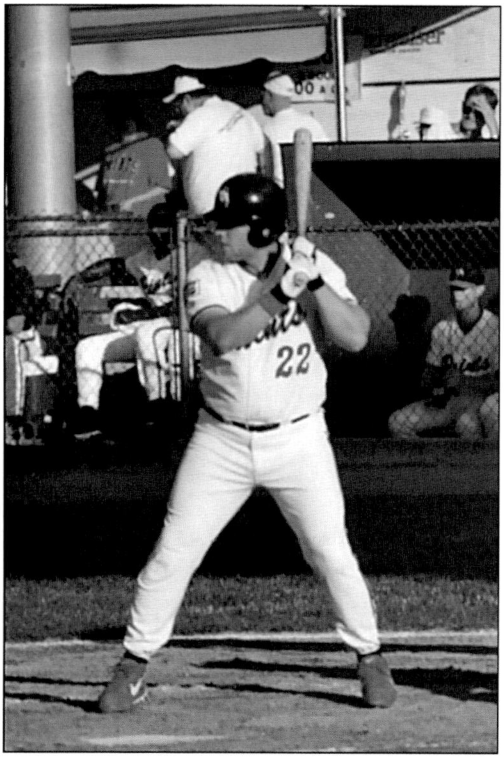

Dan Seimetz came to the Paints with some pretty big credentials, having established the records at Ohio State University for career home runs (52) and RBI (236). Since no one was going to take Scott Pinoni's position away from him, Seimetz filled in at first base and spent most of 1998 as a DH for the Paints. He batted .260 on the year with five home runs and 41 RBI.

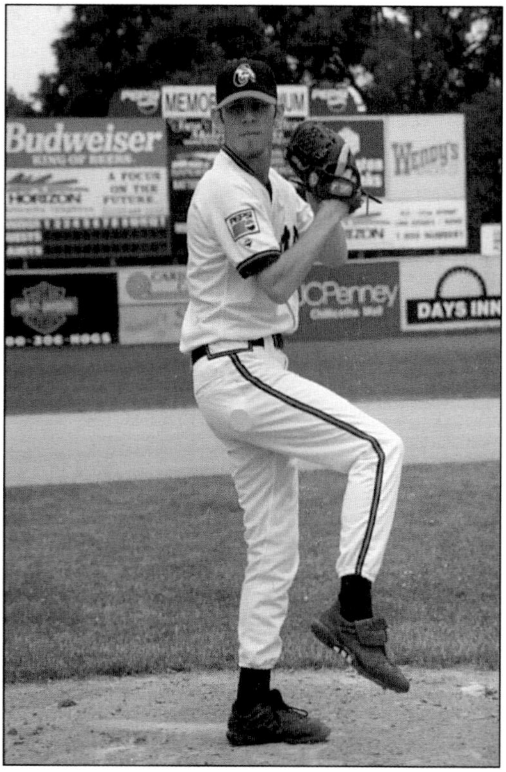

Skinny Donnie Collins, a rookie out of Coker (NC) College, was an important member of the Paints' bullpen in 1998, as he was the only left-hander on the staff at the beginning of the season. He pitched well but got homesick and left the team on August 6, at the time sporting a 2-1 record with two saves, an ERA of 2.70, and 29 strikeouts in 30 games. Management talked him into returning to Chillicothe from Stafford, Virginia, and he rejoined the team on August 11. He was one of five pitchers nominated for the left-handed reliever position on the Paints' 10th Anniversary Dream Team.

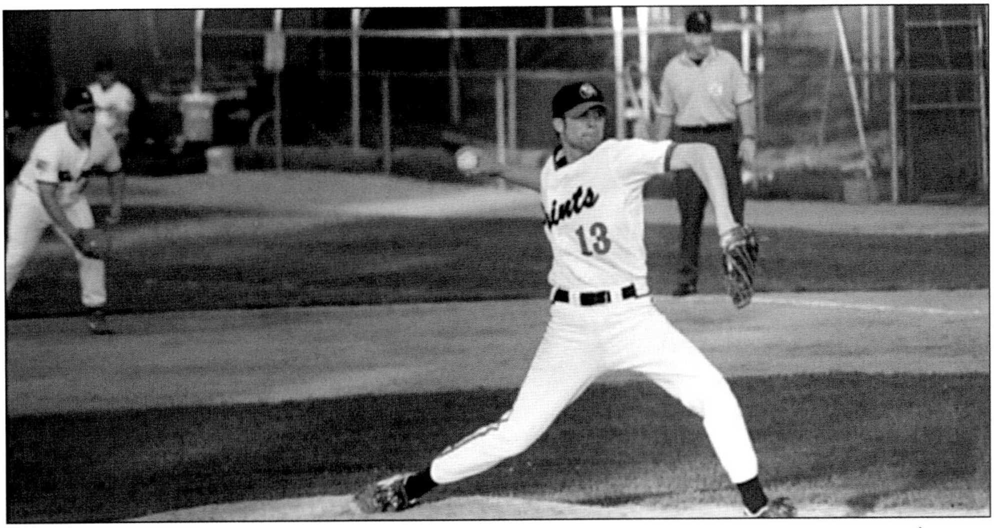

Standing at 6 feet, 165 pounds, Rick Blanc did not physically intimidate Frontier League hitters, but he did know how to get them out. A product of Bowling Green State University, he worked out of the Paints' bullpen in 1998, tying Bobby Chandler for the team lead in saves with seven and posting a 1-1 record with an ERA of 2.97. He earned his first win in a Chillicothe uniform on July 2 with three scoreless innings (one hit) against the Canton Crocodiles, and his first save on July 7 with 3.1 hitless and scoreless innings against Ohio Valley. Blanc later became a starting pitcher for the Paints and had such success that Chillicothe fans voted him the right-handed starter on the 10th Anniversary Dream Team.

The third outfielder on the 1998 Paints, Michael Fletcher was a Duke University graduate who had been named Second-Team ACC in 1998 for batting .342 with 11 home runs and 59 RBI. Fletcher was the Paints' hottest hitter at the start of the season, going 3-5, 2-4, and 3-4 in three of the first four games. On the year he batted .285 with 2 homers and 39 RBI. The Greenville, South Carolina native's biggest hit came in the eighth inning of the opening game of the first round of the playoffs against the Canton Crocodiles. His solo home run tied the game, eventually won by the Paints, 8-6.

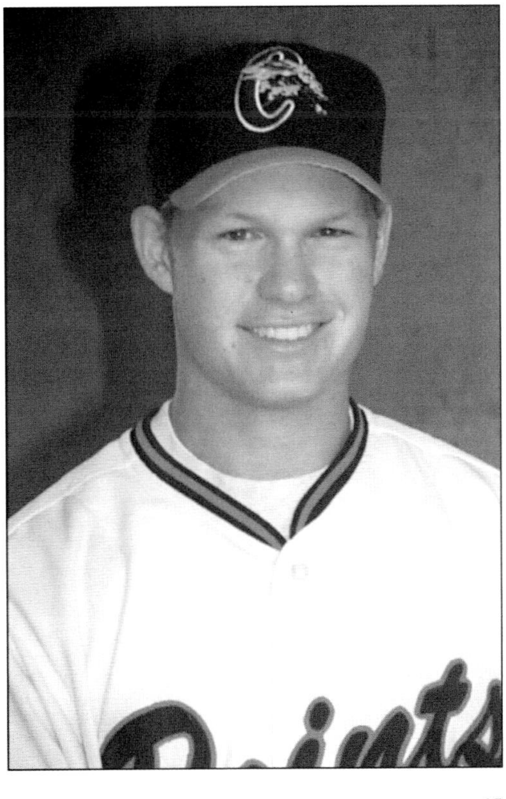

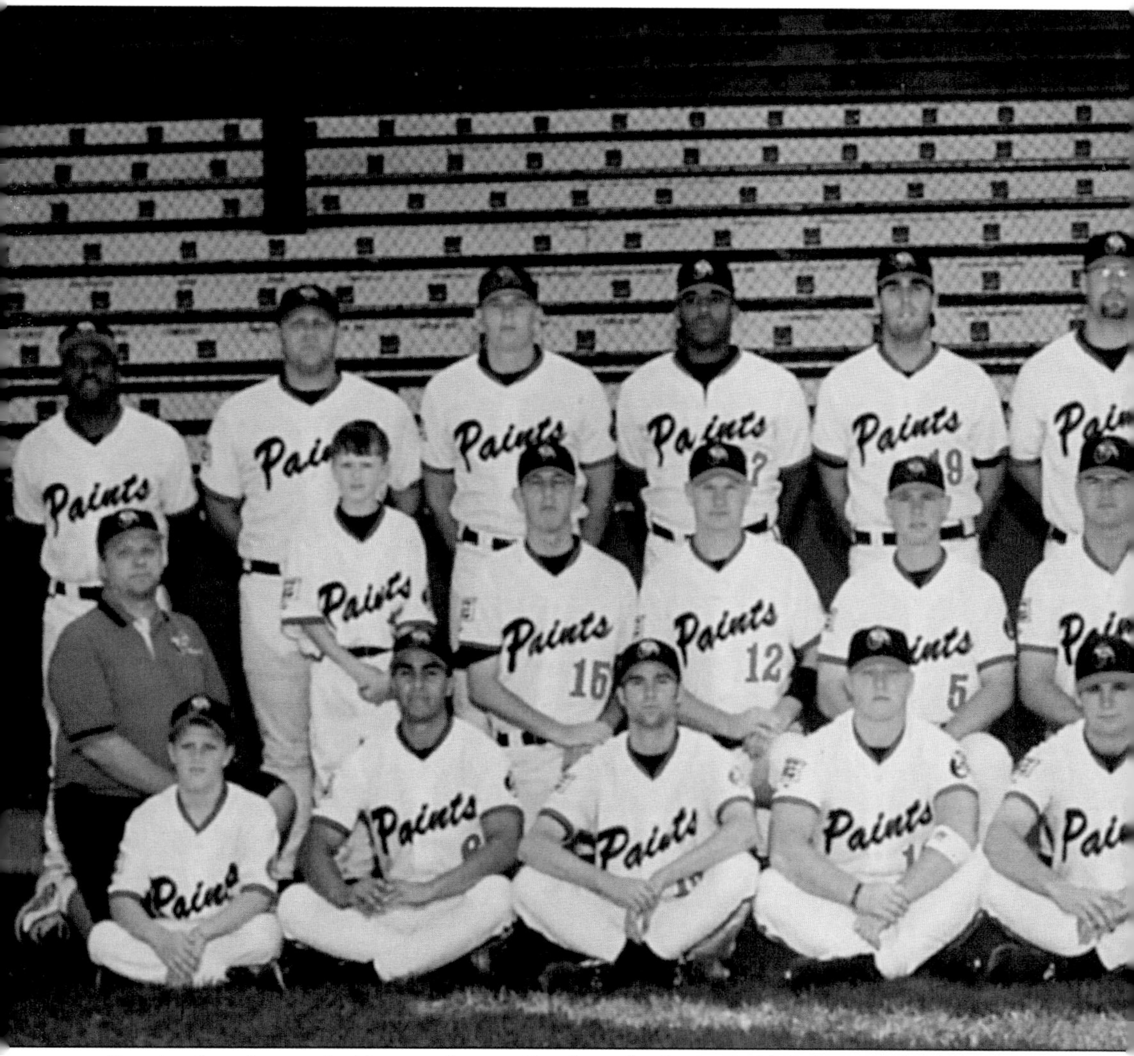

Despite their losing the Frontier League Finals to the Springfield (IL) Capitals, the 1998 Paints are considered to be the greatest squad in team history. Pictured from left to right are: (front row): Christopher Pinoni (bat bay), Freddy Flores, Rick Blanc, Pat Daly, Stephen Byrd, Gator McBride, Tony Costantino, Sam McAninch, David Dalton, and Cary Sayers (bat boy); (middle row) Scott Kaser (trainer), Cody Chenault (bat boy), Donnie Collins, Michael Fletcher, Mike

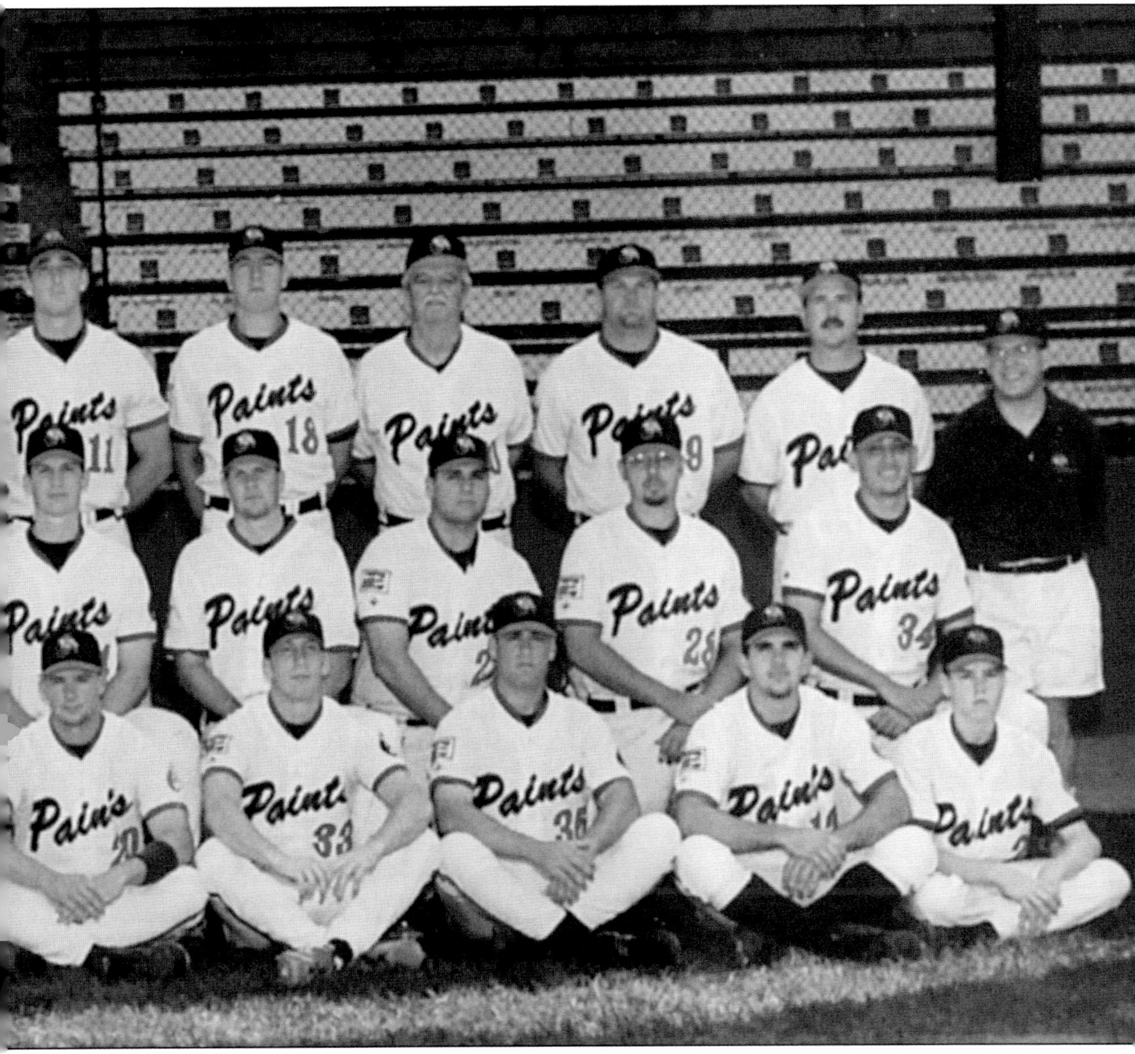

Horning, Telly Helms, Eric Tryon, Bob Spears, Dan Seimetz, Hank Soto, and Bobby Chandler; (back row) Marty Dunn (coach), Scott Pinoni, Ronnie Boggs, Mitch House, Mike Roberts, John Peck, Brad Plackemeier, Brian Scarcello, Roger Hanners (manager), Brian Mannino (coach), Eric Welch (coach), and Butch Atteberry (equipment manager). (Courtesy of Maleine Davis.)

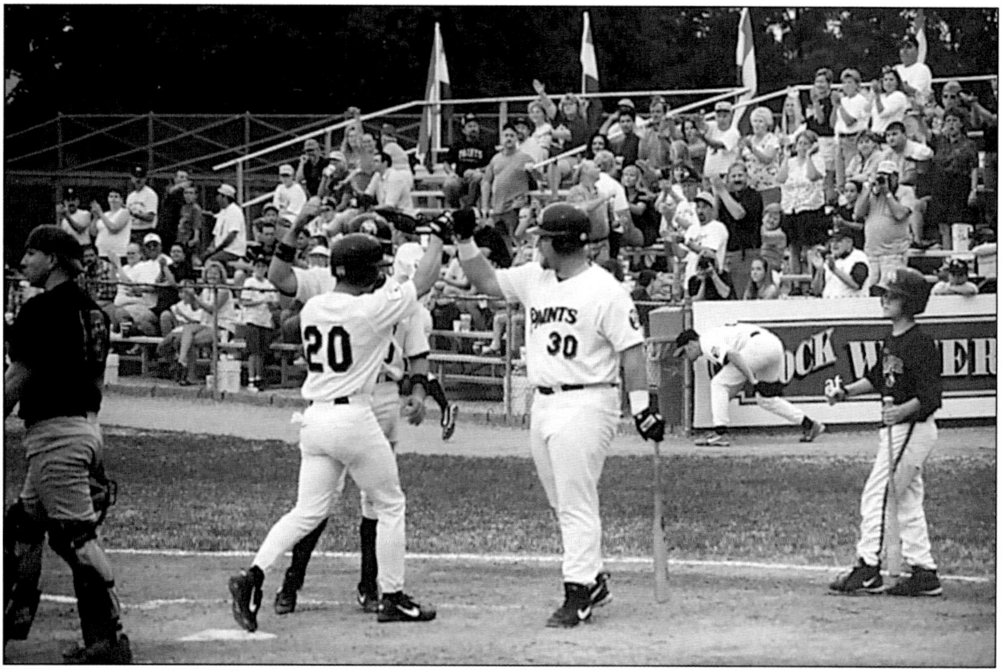

Scott Pinoni and an obscured player congratulate Gator McBride, who has just finished his trot around the bases after hitting a home run. Paints' fan saw the home team hit a lot of dingers in 1998; in fact, the 89 long balls hit by Chillicothe players that year is still the team record.

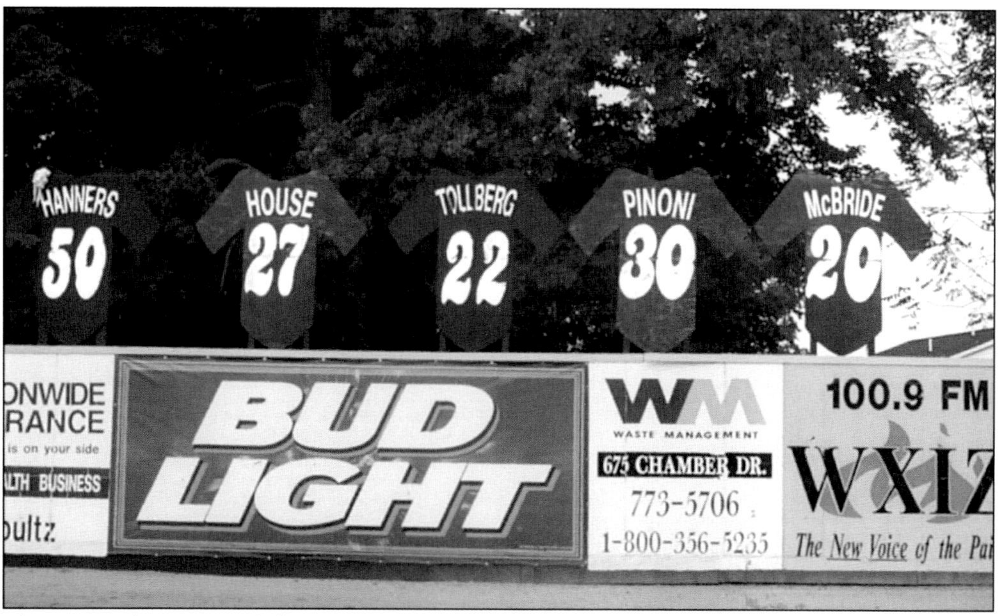

The Paints have retired the numbers of four players, plus that of manager Roger Hanners. Wooden jersey-signs symbolizing the honor stand atop the right field wall at V.A. Memorial Stadium. All four of the players were retired by the end of 1999, and all four returned for ceremonies celebrating the Paints' 10th Anniversary in 2002.

Four

Major League Fun & Big Time Commitment

It is no accident that as the Frontier League enters its 13th season in 2005, the only original franchise still in existence is the Chillicothe Paints, who play in one of the smallest markets in professional baseball. Since 1993, when the Frontier League got off to its rocky start, the Paints have been an example for the rest of the teams in the league to emulate. From the beginning the Paints got it right in making each and every game a joyous experience for the baseball fan who loves the game with a pure heart, and they have striven to improve on near-perfection every season since.

What is the big appeal? Oh, nothing much more than a venerable classic red-brick ballpark with wooden fences, real grass, huge trees inside (yes, inside!) the walls of the stadium, and a grandstand right on top of the action. Plus, the cheapest tickets in pro sports of any kind, free parking, great food (don't miss the chili dogs), promotions between every inning, give-aways of souvenirs you'd really love to have, a live organist who knows exactly when and how to get the crowd more into the game (thank you, Bryan Fields), a netted playground for the kids too antsy to sit in their seats all game long, and the funniest dance routine you've ever seen performed by a group of uninhibited bullpen pitchers. This is not to mention the baseball itself (a pretty good brand of ball, indeed), the players who (we can tell) are thrilled to be following their dreams, and the fans themselves, who are knowledgeable, friendly, and passionate about their team.

Go to a Chillicothe Paints' game and experience "The Hottest Game on Dirt," as they say in Southern Ohio. It really is baseball as it was meant to be played. It will all seem as natural and as effortless and as fun as having a backyard catch with a wide-eyed youngster in the summertime. The truth is that all this fun only comes about through a tremendous amount of hard work, preparation, and dedication by Paints' employees and because of the loyal support of the businesses and citizens of Chillicothe and Ross County. You don't have to think about this when you are enjoying a Paints' game, but here in the following pages are some of the features and the behind-the-scenes folks who make Chillicothe Paints baseball the most fun you can have in public with your clothes on.

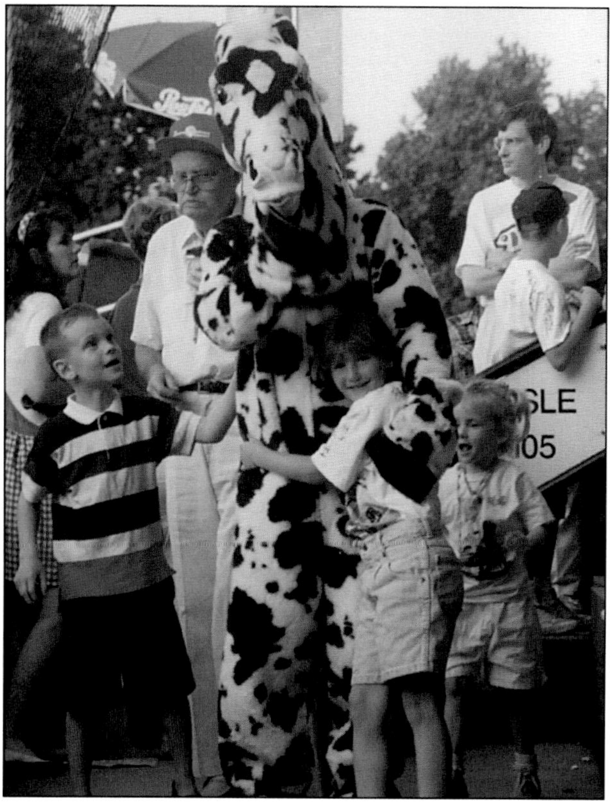

The Paints are named after the spirited, spotted horses that were favored by the native Indian tribes indigenous to the Chillicothe area ("Chillicothe" itself is an Indian word meaning "principal town"). The nickname gave rise to the team's mascot, an enthusiastic, fun-loving, mischievous stallion named Chief Krazy Horse. Sporting the patches and spots that are characteristic of his breed, Chief Krazy Horse made his debut in 1994 as a black and white pinto. He was an immediate sensation with kids of all ages and quickly established himself as the best mascot in the Frontier League. The team's annually published program, *The Stable Report*, is named in his honor.

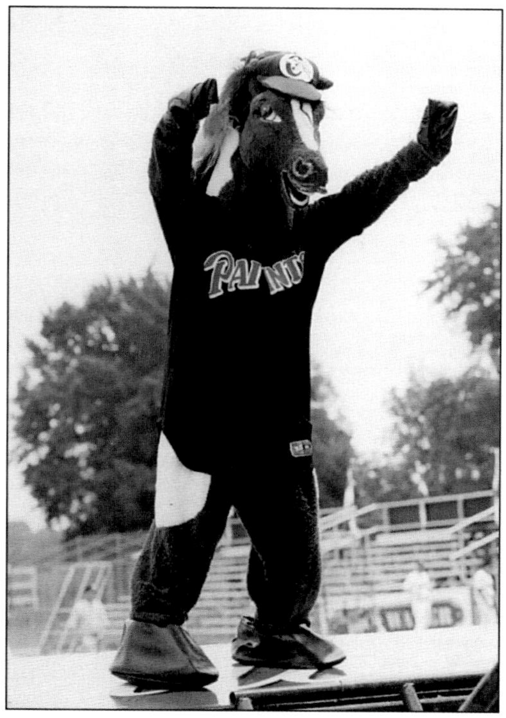

Like any celebrity in the public eye, Chief Krazy Horse has changed his look to keep up with the times. By 2000 he was primarily brown-colored and had grown a red and yellow mane in keeping with the officially designated accents in the Paints' uniform. Every inch of V.A. Memorial Stadium is natural habitat for Chief Krazy Horse, but his favorite stage is probably the top of the Paints' dugout, from where he likes to lead the crowd in singing and dancing to The Village People's hit "YMCA." Of the several performers who have brought Chief Krazy Horse to life, the most accomplished is Marty Parker (the "Bobcat" mascot at Ohio University for four years) who became the mascot of the San Francisco Giants after leaving Chillicothe.

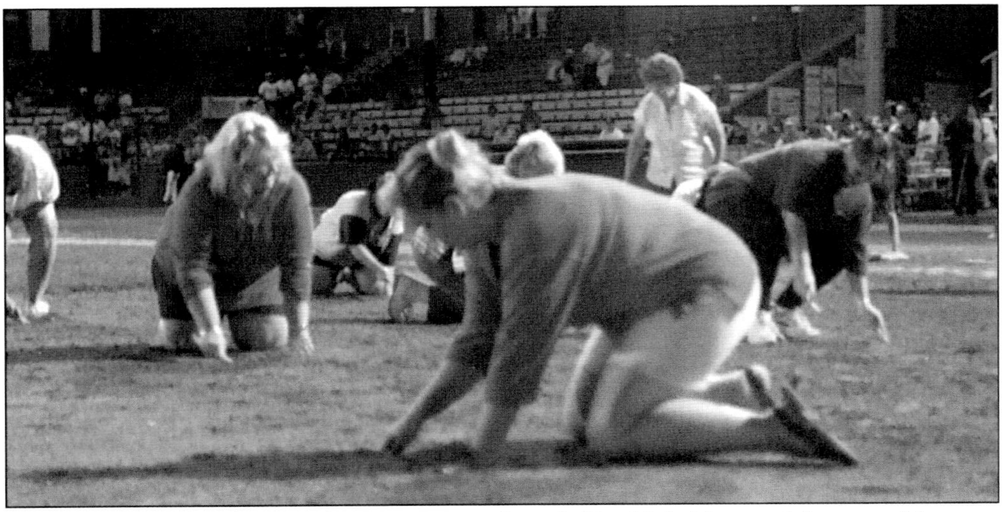

This is not an all-female grounds crew restoring the infield at V.A. Memorial, but one of the most popular promotions run anywhere in professional baseball: the Diamond Dig. In this promotion a local jeweler (Kenrick's or E.M. Smith) donates a piece of jewelry which the Paints secretly bury in the clay somewhere between first and second base. At the end of the game all ladies in attendance are allowed on the field to dig for the diamond. If the participants have trouble locating the buried box of jewelry, John Wend gives them directional hints from the press box. As popular as the Diamond Dig promotion is with female Paints' fans, it is not the favorite of GM Bryan Wickline, who has to employ the wisdom of Solomon when two participants divine the location of the prize at the same time.

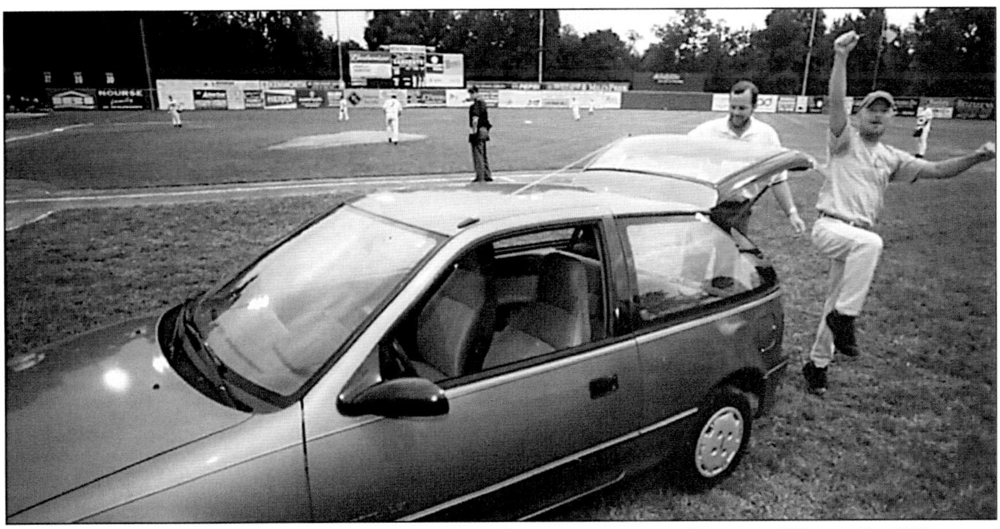

The only Paints' promotion more popular than the once-a-season Diamond Dig is the "Winning Wednesday" event, held every Wednesday the Paints play at home. Sponsored by the Nourse Auto Mall, "Winning Wednesdays" are opportunities for fans to win one of two used cars given away each night. For each car, five fans who have bought programs and entered the drawing are given keys. One by one, the contestants try their keys, and whoever has the key that opens the trunk wins the car. You might assume that the automobiles given away are clunkers, but you'd be wrong. Each car is definitely worth winning, as the excited winner in this photo demonstrates.

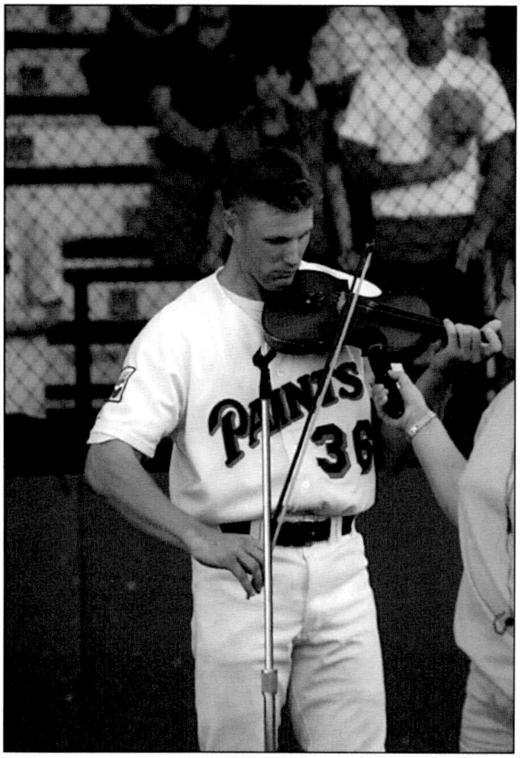

How many professional baseball teams can boast of having a violinist on the roster accomplished enough to play a flawless rendition of "The Star-Spangled Banner"? The Paints had one in Jason Baker, a graduate of Liberty University seen here performing before Opening Day 2000. Baker grew up in Rome, New York, and his musically inclined parents turned him and all five of his brothers into musicians. After playing for the Paints in 1999, Jason had a stint in the Dodgers' farm system as a flame throwing relief pitcher; but he missed playing everyday and returned to Chillicothe in 2000 as an outfielder, batting .315 with eight home runs.

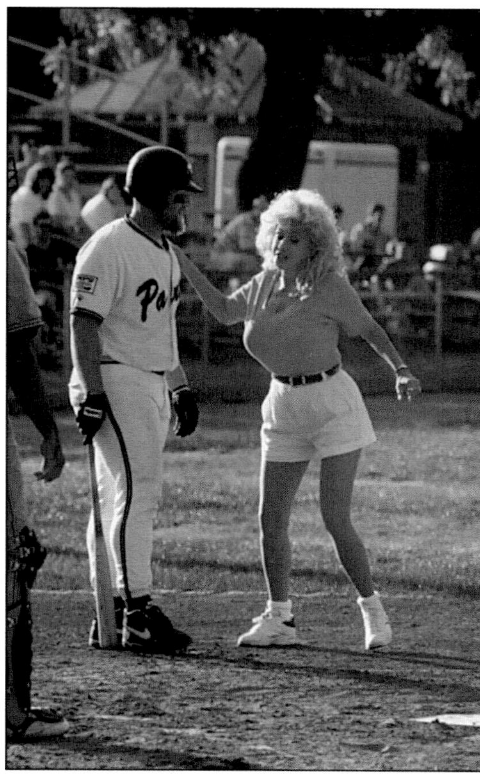

Morgana, the Kissing Bandit, who gained notoriety for interrupting major league baseball games to kiss startled players, made a scheduled appearance at V.A. Memorial Stadium on July 11, 1996. The buxom entertainer did her thing in the first inning with one out, Jason Benyo on first base, and Paints' star Scott Pinoni at bat. Pinoni flied to center after getting his smooch; but after Mitch House walked, Jackie Jempson hit a home run to give Chillicothe a 3-0 lead on the way to a 11-7 victory over the Richmond Roosters. Morgana posed for pictures with fans and other players throughout the evening.

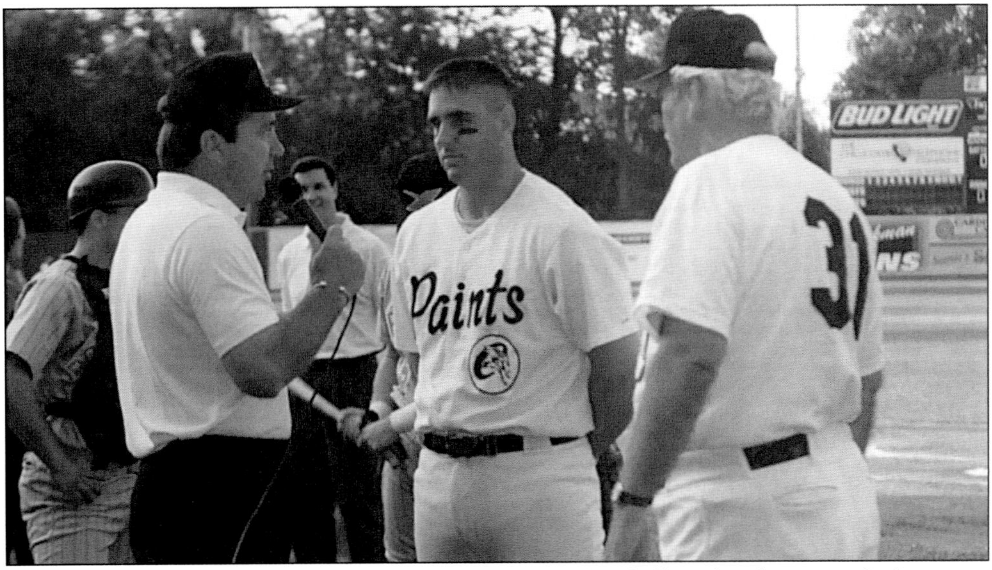

To commemorate Opening Day 1995 the Paints had the baseball used to throw out the honorary first pitch delivered by skydiver Steve Smith who parachuted out of an airplane 3,000 feet above V.A. Memorial Stadium. Former Cincinnati Reds Hall of Fame catcher Johnny Bench threw out that honorary first pitch, which was caught by the young man Johnny is facing, Paints' catcher Tim Tackett. Bench attracted a sellout crowd of 4,000, which created long lines for the bathrooms and concession stands all night long.

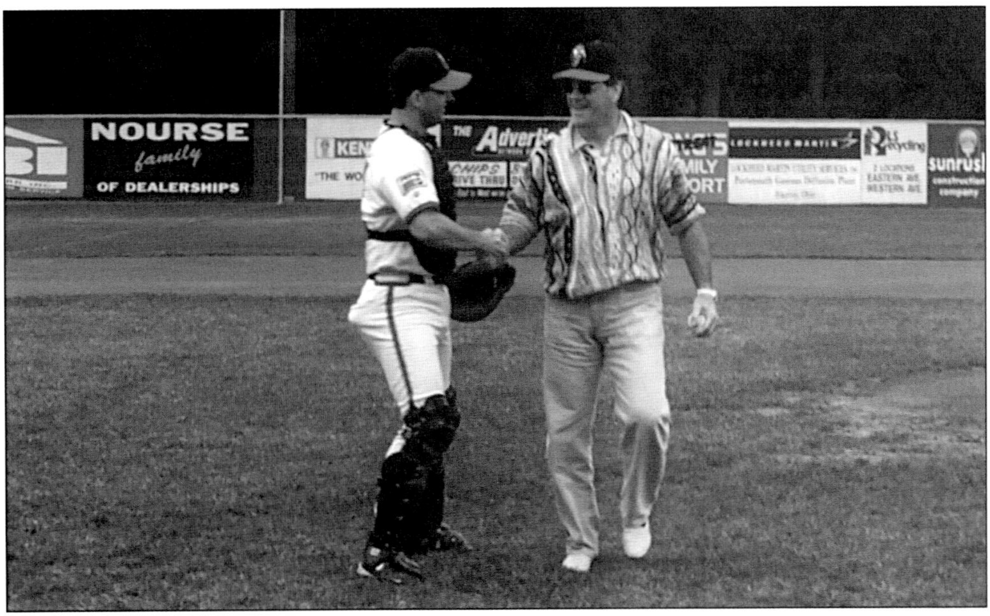

The following year (August 12) Pete Rose came to Chillicothe. Pete was feted at a luncheon and afterwards held court behind the cage while the Paints took pre-game batting practice. That evening an overflow crowd celebrated "Pete Rose Night" at V.A. Memorial Stadium. The first 2,000 fans through the gate received a free Pete Rose autograph, and 250 baseballs autographed by Rose were sold at $20 a piece in less than an hour. Pete is shown here, having just thrown the ceremonial first pitch, with Paints' catcher Greg Reinhart.

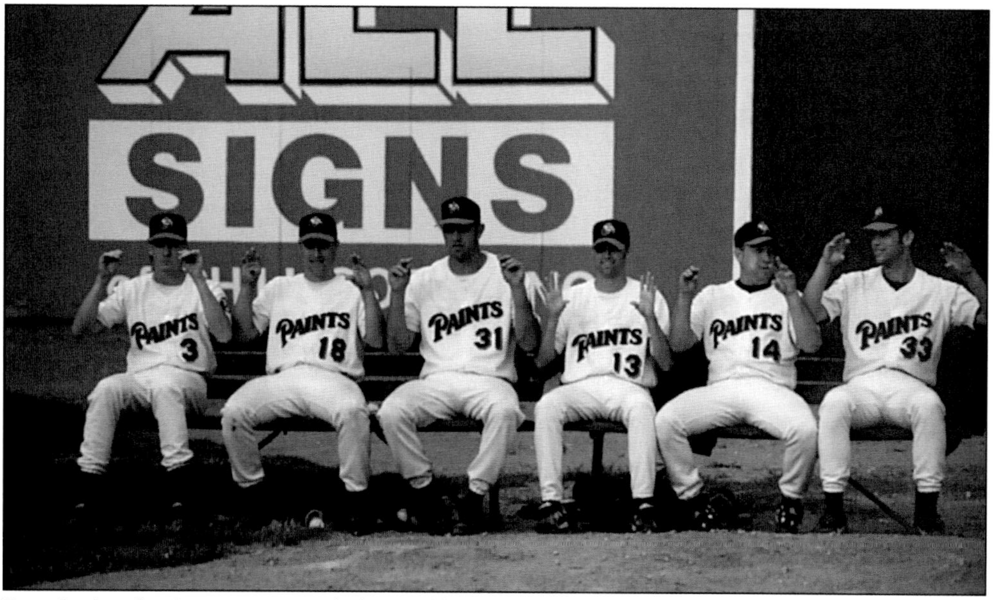

Everybody who has ever attended a wedding in America has seen the silly movements that accompany the tune popularly known as "The Chicken Dance" song. But only Paints' fans have seen ballplayers do these antics at the ballpark. Relief pitcher Bobby Chandler is credited with organizing the routine in the Paints' bullpen that has become a beloved tradition in Chillicothe. Here six members of the 2000 Paints' bullpen do the first part of the Chicken Dance routine. Pictured from left to right are Eric Frodsham, Ryan Sawyers, Josh Lamberg, Rick Blanc, Nathan Gardner, and Woody Fullenkamp. All but catcher-DH Lamberg were pitchers.

The Chicken Dance song is made up of two parts: a polka, when the silly choreographed movements are done, and a waltz, when wedding-goers join hands and rotate around the room in a big circle. The Paints, on the other hand, partner up and do some doe-se-doe square dancing during the waltz part of the song. Especially fearless Paints' dancers will also break off and perform some individual moves during the waltz. No Paint was ever more inventive and entertaining than reliever Woody Fullenkamp, who mimicked all sorts of activities unrelated to baseball, such as mowing the lawn and shooting basketballs. Here Woody is seen imitating a rotating lawn sprinkler.

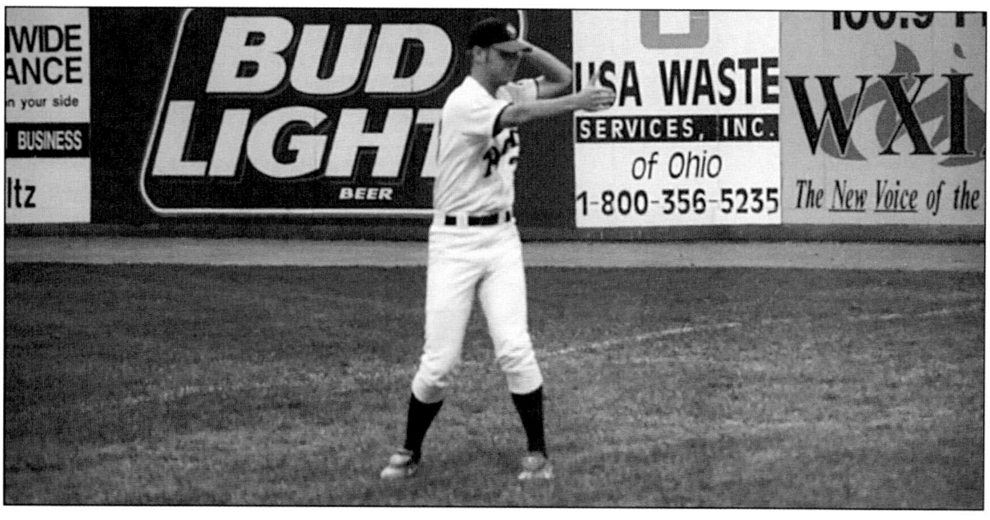

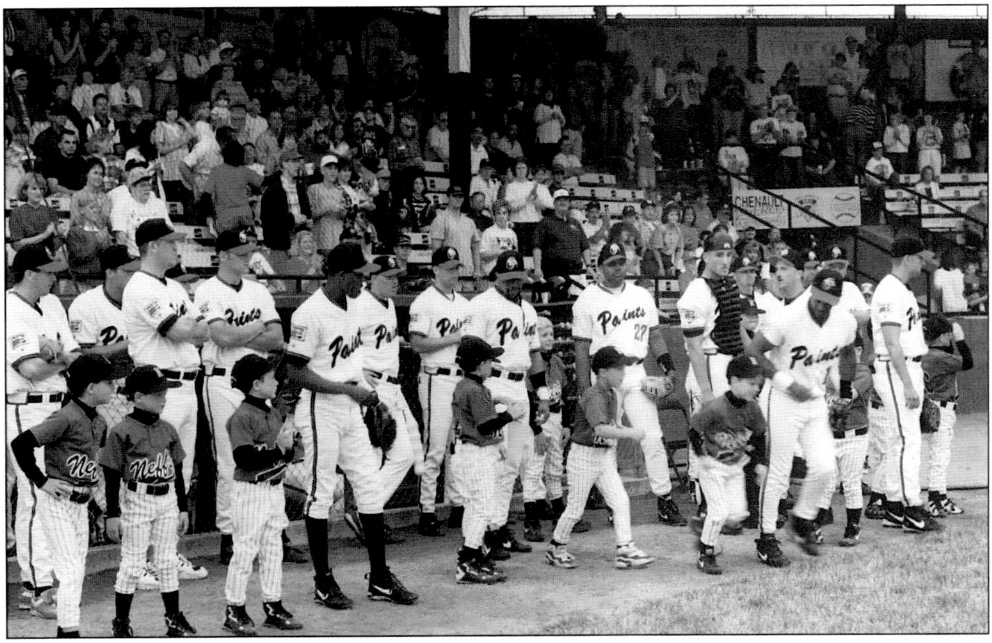

The Paints have always done a great job of reaching out to their youngest fans, the kids. Through the Field of Dreams program, the members of an area youth league team receive free tickets to the game, pair up with the Paints' players in the starting lineup, and run onto the field with the players for the playing/singing of "The Star-Spangled Banner." Here Jackie Jempson is beginning his trot out to left field with his thrilled youth leaguer at his side. The Paints also sponsor a player-run instructional clinic each summer.

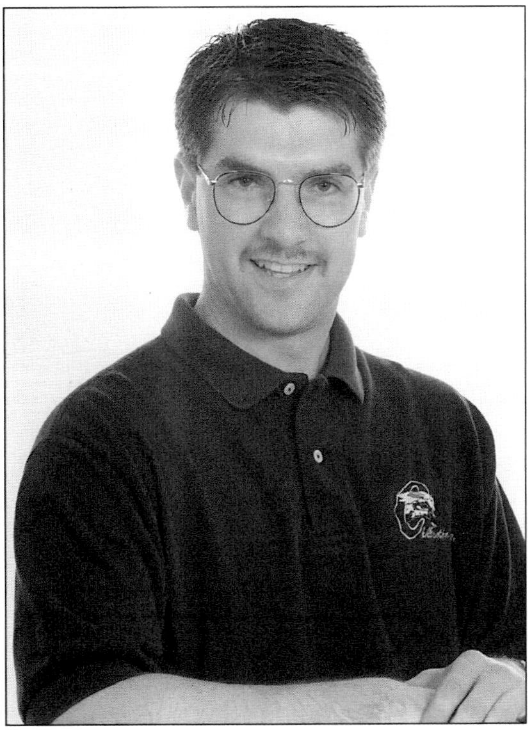

A native of Chillicothe and a graduate of Zane Trace High School, where he played baseball and basketball, Bryan Wickline began working for the Paints in 1994 as a college intern. He graduated from Ohio University with a degree in sports management in 1995, and a year later he was made General Manager of the Paints at the tender age of 23. It was one of the best decisions ever made by the organization, as the workaholic Wickline was named Frontier League Executive of the Year in 1996 and 1998. A closet romantic, Bryan ambushed his wife, Karen, with a surprise proposal on the field behind home plate during a game at V.A. Memorial Stadium in 2000.

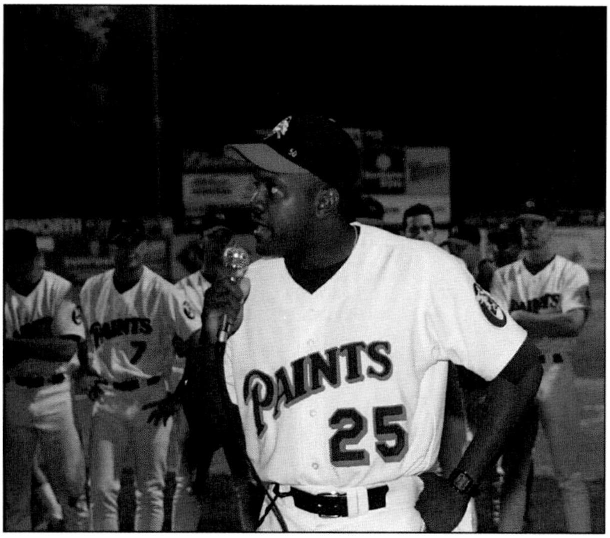

The varsity baseball coach at Chillicothe High School since 1988, Marty Dunn has been an assistant coach with the Paints since the team's inception in 1993. A graduate of Alabama State University, Dunn was a three-year starter there as an outfielder and captain of the team in 1980 and '81. He moved to Chillicothe in 1983 and became the chemistry teacher at CHS. Low-key but respected by players and fans alike, Dunn served as Interim Manager for part of the 2000 season after health problems forced Roger Hanners out of uniform. Shown here presiding over the presentation of the player awards at the end of the 2000 season, Dunn said, "I say it every year because it's true: 'There's no better place to spend your summer than Chillicothe, Ohio.' "

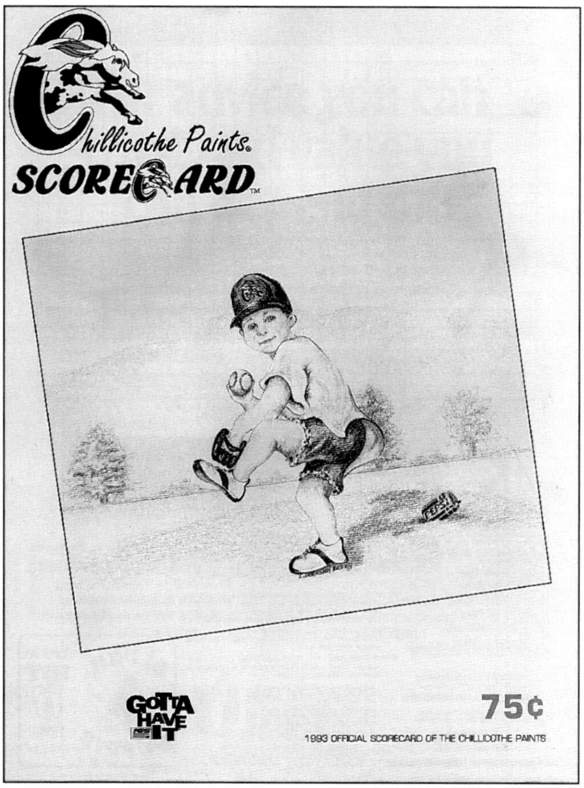

Scorecards have always been an important part of the Chillicothe Paints' game experience. Diehard Paints' fans keep scorecards not only to stay mentally involved in the game, but also to obtain the page of entry blanks for the contests run throughout the ballgame. This scorecard from the 1993 inaugural season cost 75¢. (Courtesy of Harry Chenault.)

By 2003 the scorecard had gone up to $1.00 but was still a bargain, and the somewhat amateurish illustration on the 1993 cover had been replaced by a spectacular photo of a night game at V.A. Memorial. Notice the new Paints' logo (top) that was trotted out for the team's 10th anniversary and the slogan (bottom), which fit like a glove.

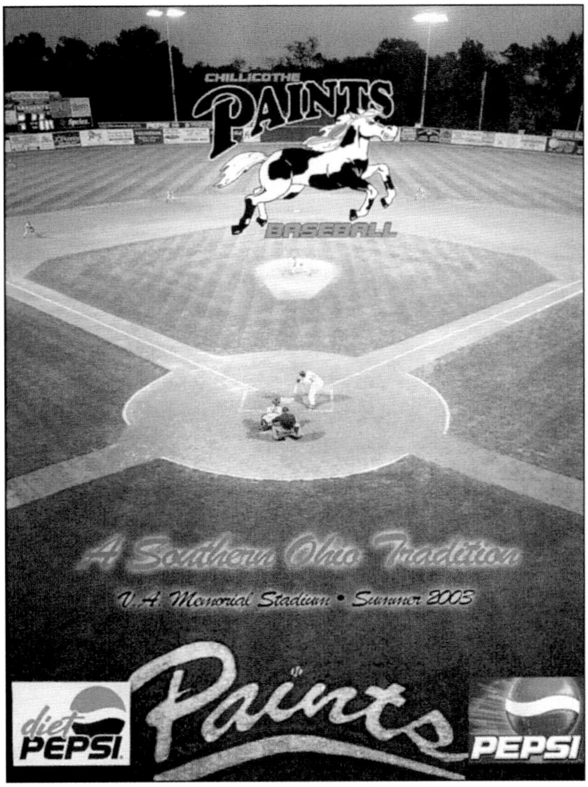

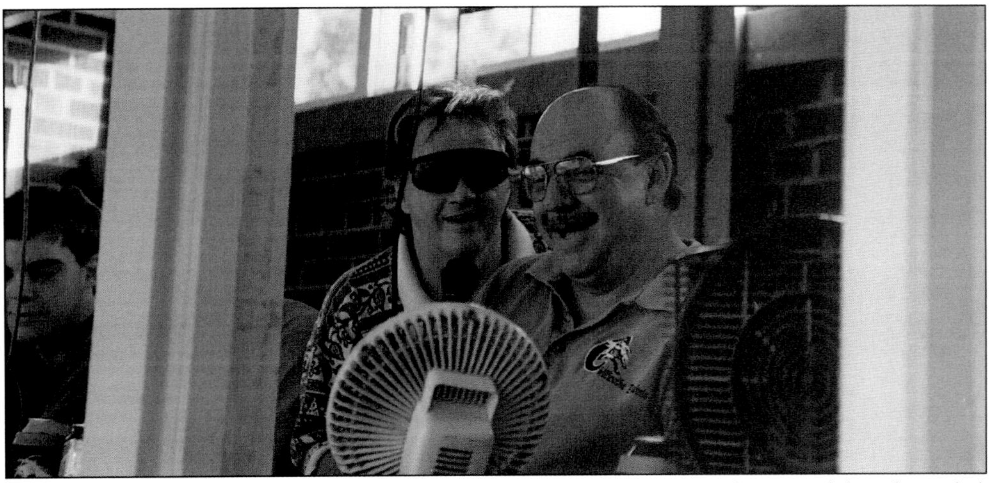

A native of Logan, Ohio, and a 1967 graduate of Ohio University, John Wend (on the right) is the only Public Address announcer in Paints' history. Although Wend has held a number of different jobs, he was born to sit behind a microphone. His rich baritone voice is a highly effective instrument which has become a commanding, reassuring, and essential part of every Paints' home game at V.A. Memorial Stadium. The genial and witty Wend is also a superb story teller and a fountain of baseball and Paints' knowledge. Wend became a full time Paints employee in 1998 when he assumed the position of Director of Sales & Marketing, in addition to his duties as P.A. announcer.

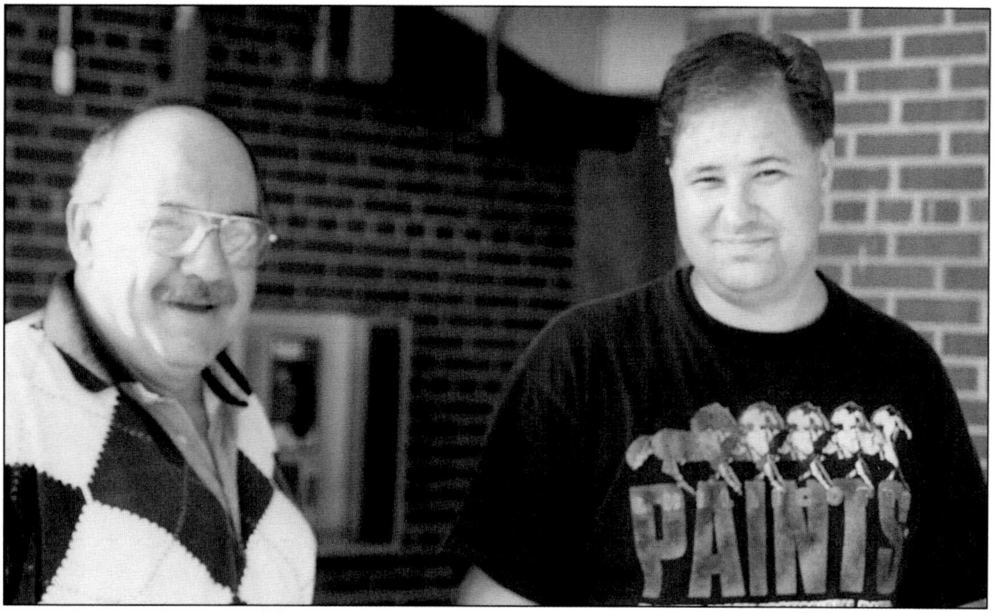

Aaron Lemaster, pictured here with P.A. announcer John Wend, is another key member of the Paints' press box crew at VA Memorial Stadium. A graduate of Zane Trace High School and Ohio University, Lemaster has been the Paints' official scorer and music director since 1995. A social studies teacher (grades 7-12) in the off-season, Aaron has also been an amateur umpire since 1992. The most memorable play Aaron ever scored was a rundown between home and third base when eight different Paints' players touched the ball. "Fortunately, it was one of the few times I thought to write down the players who touched the ball as they did it in a rundown," he says. "The crowd gave the players a standing ovation for the play."

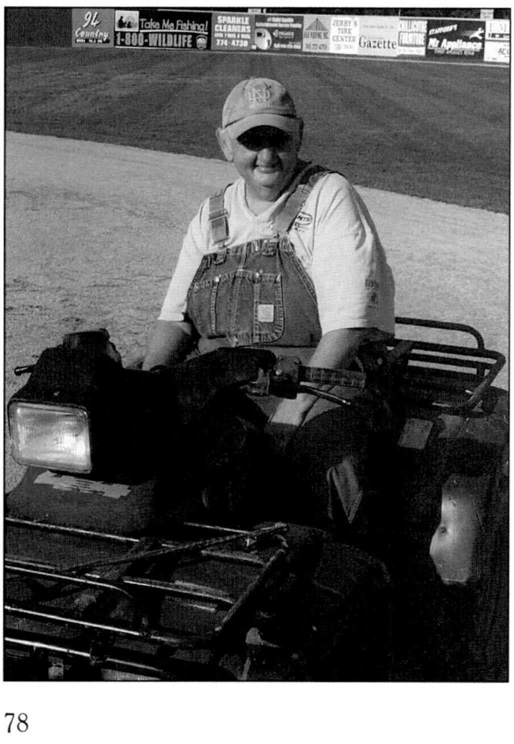

Jim Miner has worked for the Paints since the team's inception in 1993. At first a volunteer, he has been the team's head grounds keeper (or "Stadium Superintendent") since 2000. A self-proclaimed "diamond rat" who learned his trade by osmosis, Miner puts in 100 hours or more a week during the season. After the Paints installed an irrigation system over the winter of 2003–04, Miner re-seeded the entire field at V.A. Memorial Stadium. He also invented an ingenious piece of grounds keeping equipment: a rolling base cart specially designed to hold three Hollywood bases which can be easily pulled around the diamond by one person. (Courtesy of the author.)

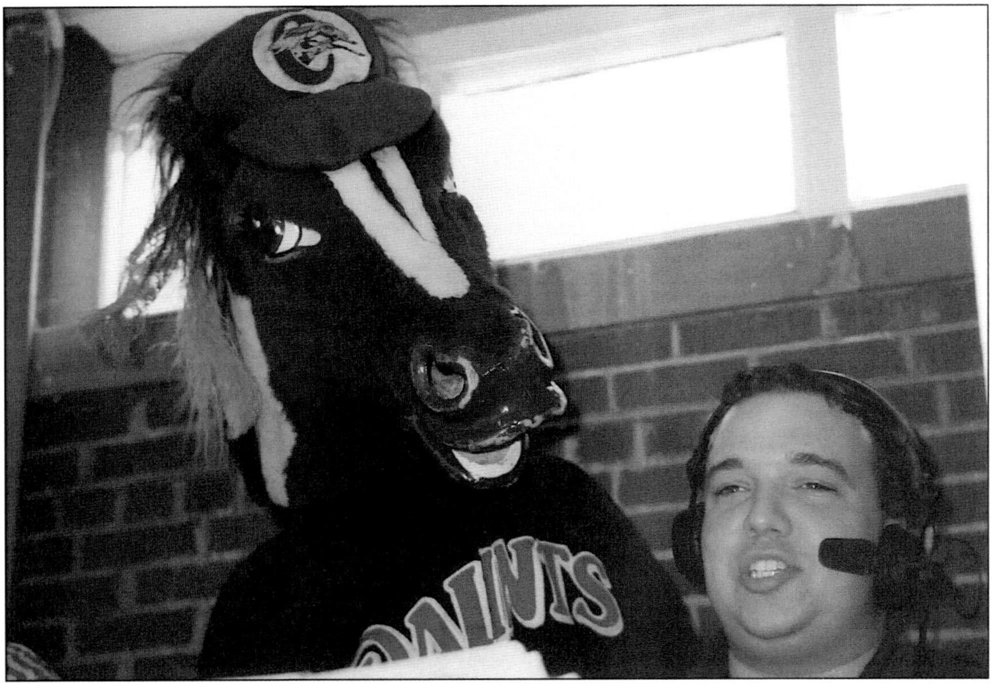

A native of Bloomingburg, Ohio (just south of Columbus), Matt Andrews came to the Paints right out of Ohio State University where he majored in journalism and communications, broadcast four sports for the OSU student radio station, and called the Buckeyes' National Championship victory over Miami (FL) University in the 2003 Fiesta Bowl (Tempe, AZ). Remarkably glib and polished for such a young broadcaster, Andrews (who could get an interesting interview out of anybody, even Chief Krazy Horse) stayed behind the mic for only two seasons in Chillicothe. He left after the 2002 season to take a position as the color man assisting play-by-play man Jim Kelch in the broadcast booth of the Louisville Bats of the Triple A International League, where he remains today, only a bad case of laryngitis away from the major leagues. (Courtesy of Matt Andrews.)

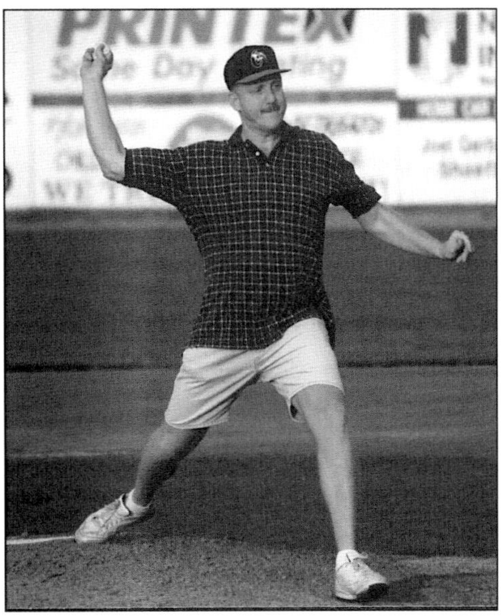

Doug Kimsey of Portsmouth, Ohio, covered the Paints for the *Chillicothe Gazette* (1994–1999) and for the Ross County Advertiser and *Circleville Herald* (2000–2001), and he is the only person to ever win the Frontier League Sportswriter of the Year Award twice (1998 and 1999). From 2000 to 2002 Kimsey wrote a very informative column on the Paints' website called "Kimsey's Korner," and he has broadcast the Adelphia Paints' Game of the Week (with partner Scott Graham) on cable television since its inception in 2000. Doug has also visited 21 foreign countries during his 18 1/2 years as a journalist in the U.S. Naval Reserve, and he spent six weeks aboard the aircraft carrier USS Kitty Hawk off the coast of Pakistan in the opening days of Operation Enduring Freedom.

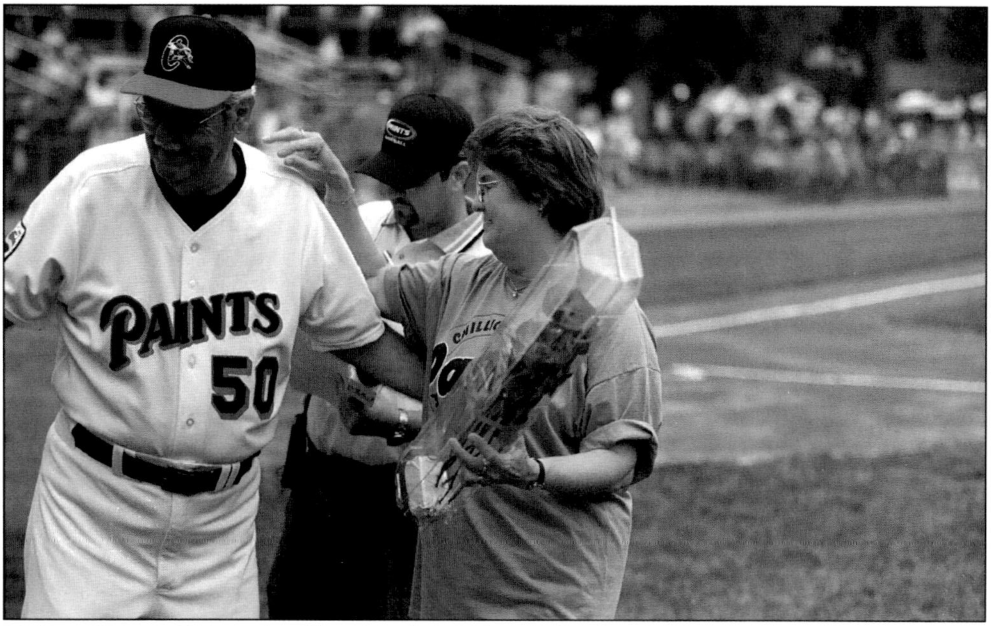

Maleine Davis of Waverly, Ohio, has donated countless hours of time to the Paints since the beginning of the organization. Formerly a grade school teacher for 30 years, she serves the Paints as the team's Director of Finance and as the manager of the beer booth; the latter a job Chris Hanners felt her experience in the classroom made her the perfect person for. Maleine also sponsors the team's magnetic schedule give-away promotion every year and throws out the honorary first pitch on that night. Asked if she has ever bounced the honorary first pitch, as so many grown men do, she replied: "I never bounce it! I was always the pitcher when my class played baseball in gym." Maleine, being hugged by Roger Hanners in this photo, was inducted into the Paints' Hall of Fame in 2000.

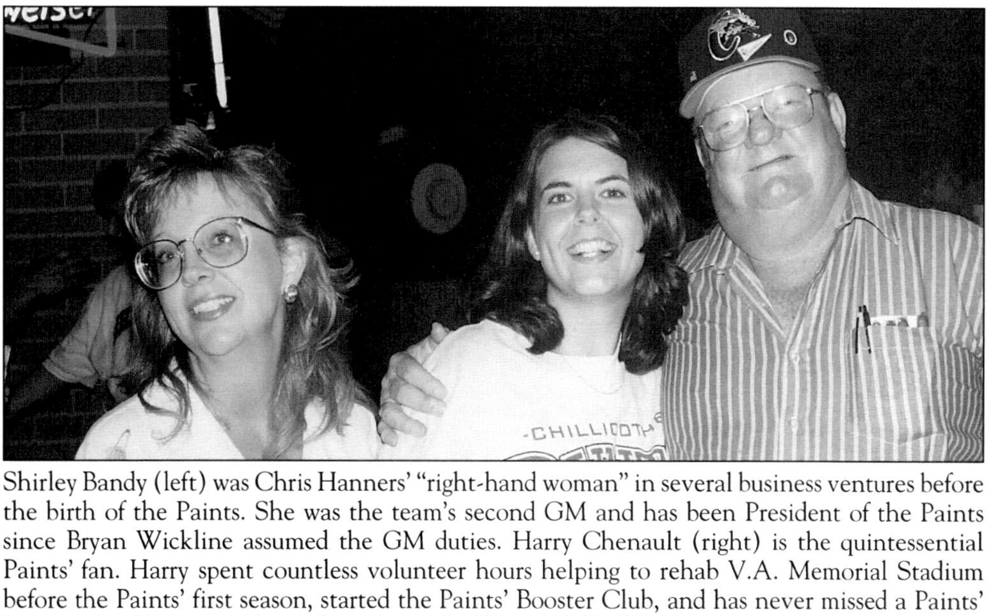

Shirley Bandy (left) was Chris Hanners' "right-hand woman" in several business ventures before the birth of the Paints. She was the team's second GM and has been President of the Paints since Bryan Wickline assumed the GM duties. Harry Chenault (right) is the quintessential Paints' fan. Harry spent countless volunteer hours helping to rehab V.A. Memorial Stadium before the Paints' first season, started the Paints' Booster Club, and has never missed a Paints' home game. Harry was also inducted into the Paints' Hall of Fame.

FIVE

'Our Day is Coming' 1999–2001

In the 1999 season opener Chillicothe set the tone for the entire season in smoking the Springfield Capitals 11-2 and by launching a team-record six home runs (two each by Gator McBride and Scott Pinoni, one each by Mike Horning and rookie Chance Melvin). Early in July a Paints' winning streak reached ten games, and the team might have gone on to compile the best record in the league, but Gator McBride's signing with the Boston Red Sox a week later left a giant hole in the batting order and the team had to content themselves with the second-best finish at 45-38 and a spot in the playoffs.

Armed with what Evansville Otters' manager Greg Taggert called "the best overall pitching staff in the league," the Paints defeated the Otters two games to one in the first round of the playoffs. Andy Lee and Woody Fullenkamp combined on a 2-0 shutout in Game One, while Stephen Byrd and two relievers held down Evansville in the Game-Three clincher (outfielder Eddie Woods' two-run double and Joey Choron's SF accounted for all the Paints' runs in Chillicothe's 3-2 win). The Paints got more solid starting pitching in the finals from Lee and Bob Spears, but no offense, and lost two straight to the Frontier League champion London Werewolves, 2-1 and 4-1. This third loss in the championship round in four years prompted Paints' manager Roger Hanners to say: "I hate losing. But at least, we get to the finals, while most teams do not. Our day is coming."

The Paints put another strong contender on the field in 2000, and Chillicothe entered the All-Star break in first place by half a game with a 22-15 record. Unfortunately, a career-ending injury to the team's best starting pitcher (Josh White) and the loss of the league's two hottest hitters (Mike Cervenak and Joe Colameco, both of whom signed with the New York Yankees) scuttled the team's chances in the second half, and the Paints limped home 42-40, two and a half games out of the playoffs. The worst break of all came near the end of July when a series of heart attacks sidelined longtime Paints' manager Roger Hanners for the rest of the season and led to his decision during the off-season to retire from managing. The two most memorable events of the year: Andy Lee's no-hitter (the first ever by a Paints' pitcher) and former Paint Brian Tollberg becoming the first Frontier League player to graduate to the major leagues.

With new manager Jamie Keefe at the helm (and assisted by coaches Marty Dunn and Gator McBride), the Paints got off to a slow start in 2001, but they moved into first place on June 24 and entered the All-Star break with a two-game lead. Seven straight wins after the break virtually sewed up the pennant, and the Paints coasted home with a league-best record of 51-33.

A very potent Paints' offense was led by four regulars who batted over .300 (Matt McCay, Adam Patterson, Darin Kinsolving, and Joe Colameco) and the power-hitting double play combination of David Daulton (9 HRs) and Kevin Connacher (16 HRs). The starting rotation was anchored by Rick Blanc (13-1) and Sean Boesch (9-4), while Matt Hampton, Kris Buirley, Woody Fullenkamp, and Brian Bogs formed the core of the best bullpen in Chillicothe history.

For the fourth time in six years, the Paints reached the Finals of the Frontier League Playoffs and for the second time in three years they were swept (3-0) in the Finals. The rubber game of the Paints' first-round matchup versus Canton ended in most dramatic fashion when Andrew See's basehit drove in Vinny Cerni with the winning run in the bottom of the tenth inning. Bad defense doomed the Paints in the Finals. Four errors led to an 8-5 loss in the opener in Richmond, while the Roosters' 14-0 pounding of the Paints in Game Two was aided by nine unearned runs in the first inning. Despite home runs by Kinsolving and Connacher (each of whom had also homered in the first game against Canton), the Paints lost Game Three at V.A. Memorial, 6-5, leaving Chillicothe fans in the all-too-familiar position of "waiting for next year."

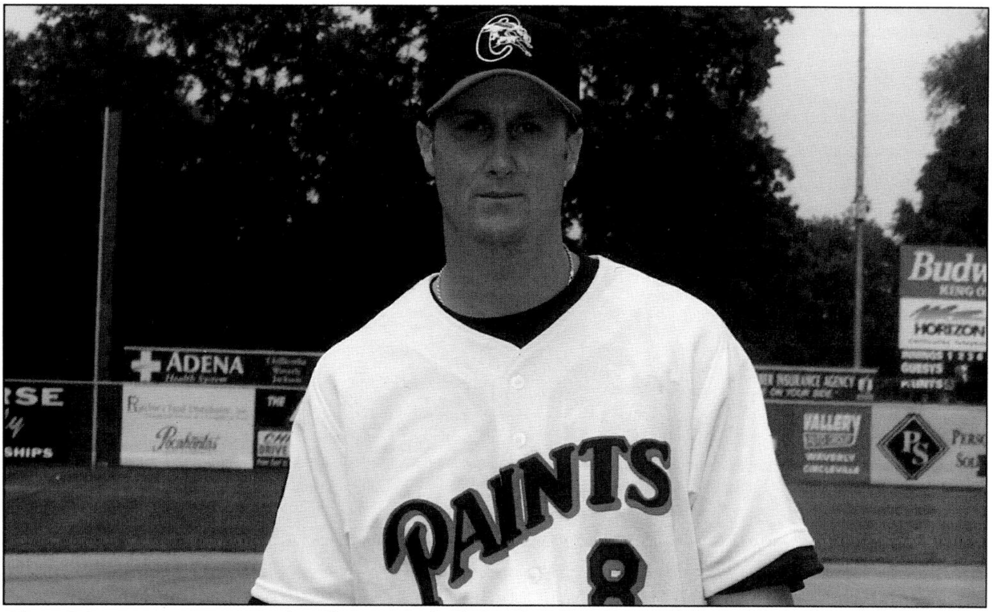

Chris Maness was supposed to have pitched for the Paints in 1998, but he was signed by the Philadelphia Phillies the day before Opening Day. He posted a combined 3-2 record with 49 strikeouts against 16 walks for Martinsville (VA) and Clearwater (FL) but was released at the end of the season and returned to Chillicothe for 1999. Relying on a 90 mph fastball and a good slider, Maness notched eight saves (second best on the team), won two games (against one loss), and fashioned an ERA of 3.19. He made the East Division All-Star team and was nominated for the right-handed reliever position on the Paints' 10th Anniversary Dream Team. Before turning pro Maness played at Elon (NC) College. When he hung up his spikes, he returned to North Carolina to coach high school baseball.

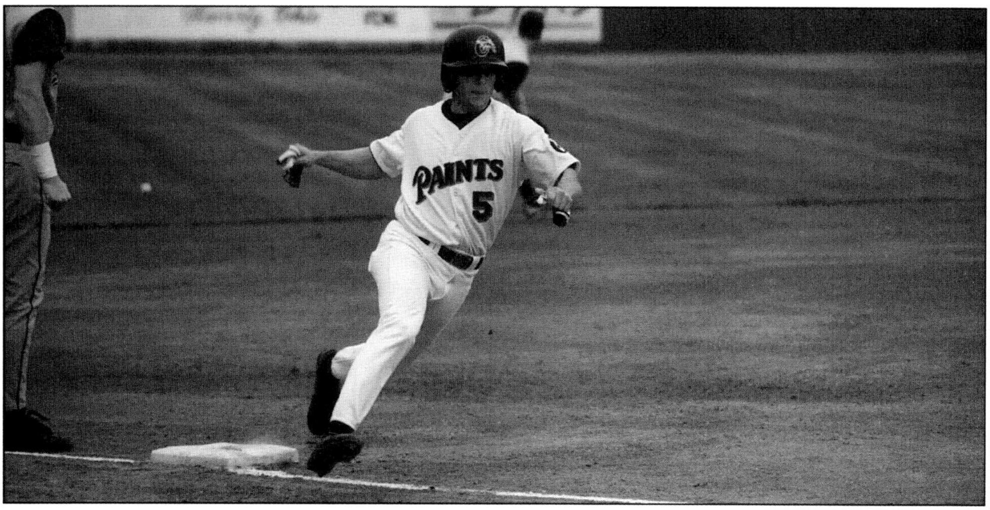

Hustling Mike Horning returned to Chillicothe for 1999 and re-claimed his job as the regular second baseman. The popular Horning, who wore a path in the grass behind his position because he would take three steps back and three steps forward before every pitch, led the team in stolen bases (28) and runs scored (63). He hit .272 with two homers, three triples, and 18 doubles (second on the team).

Two weeks into the 1999 season the Paints signed right-hander Andy Lee who had just completed his senior season at Ohio State University. Andy would tell the *Chillicothe Gazette* that he felt liberated pitching for the Paints. "At Ohio State they were always worried about mechanics; here they let you just go out and pitch," he said. Lee started 14 games for Chillicothe and compiled a 6-5 record with an ERA of 3.88, eleventh best in the league. He also struck out 84 batters in 92.2 innings. Lee was at his toughest in the playoffs. He shut out Evansville for seven innings on four hits to led the Paints to a 2-0 win in Game One of the first round, and he only gave up two runs over 6.2 innings in the Paints' 2-1 loss to London in the opener of the finals.

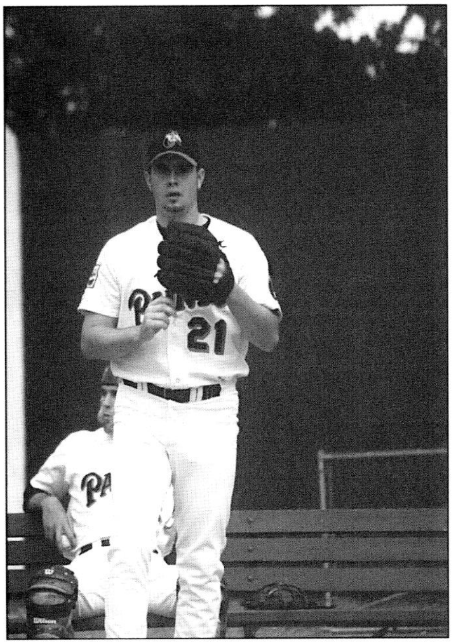

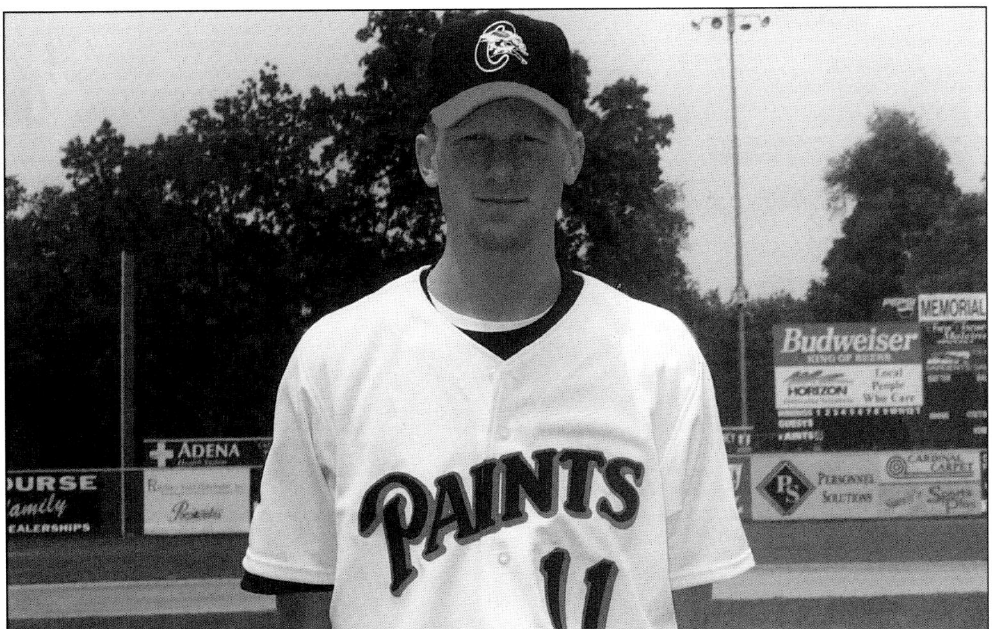

Reportedly, Jamie Tucker hit .500 (with 14 homers and 60 RBI) in the spring of 1999 for the University of Arkansas-Monticello. He did all right as a rookie for the Paints too. He was the second most active outfielder on the team (appearing in 65 games), and he hit .279 with four home runs and 24 RBI. He went 3-3 on June 16 against Canton, and on July 19 he hit a grand slam and drove in five runs as the Paints downed the London Werewolves, 8-5.

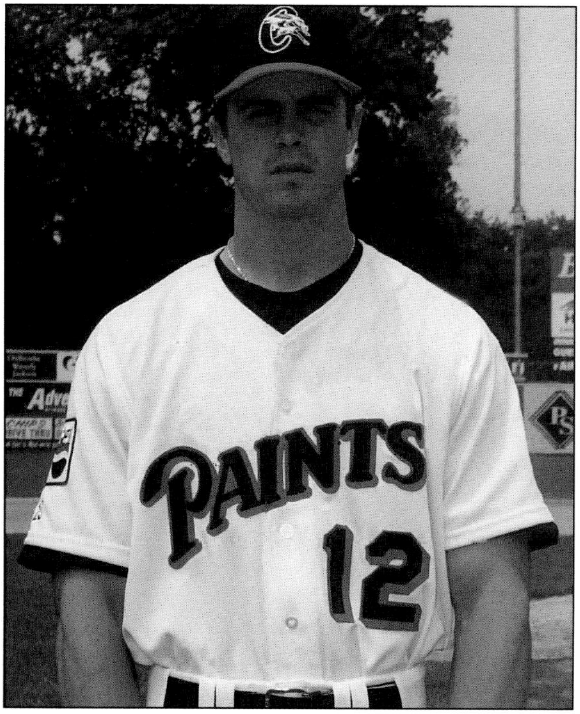

Third baseman Chance Melvin, from Lexington, South Carolina, started his pro baseball career with Chillicothe after turning in a spectacular First-team All-American senior season at the University of West Alabama: .435, 15 HR, 83 RBI, and a slugging percentage of .804. The Paints had high hopes for him, and he didn't disappoint. Melvin hit .299 in 1999, led the team in RBI (76) and doubles (19) and finished second in home runs (11). He introduced himself to the Frontier League by going 2-4 with a home run on Opening Day, and on August 12 he went 5-5 and became the first Paint in history to hit for the cycle. He was voted the third baseman to the Frontier League All-Star Team for 1999.

Gator McBride was on fire right from the start of the 1999 season. He went 3-4 on Opening Day (June 3) with a pair of home runs. Less than a week later he became the first Paint to hit three home runs in a game (a baseball feat more rare than a no-hitter), which gave him seven homers in Chillicothe's first seven games. He had one consecutive-games hitting streak of 13, and a second hitting streak of 17 games, which was stopped not by pitchers but by the Frontier League All-Star Game, after which he did not play again for the Paints. If he had finished the 1999 season in Chillicothe, it is likely that Gator would have set the Frontier League record for highest season batting average.

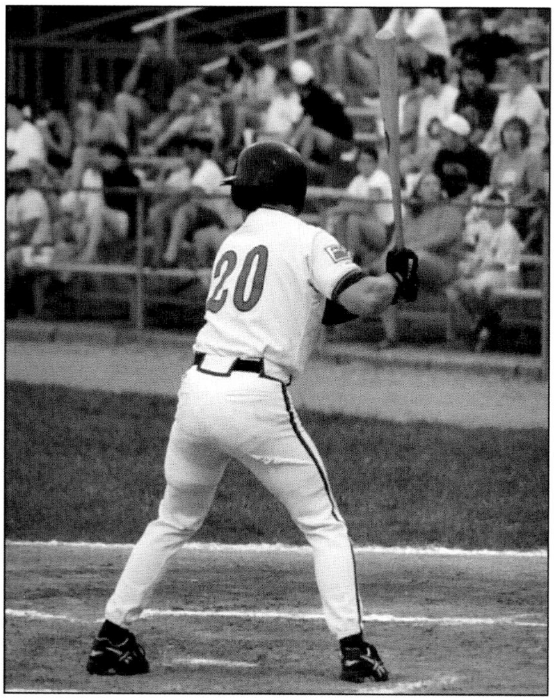

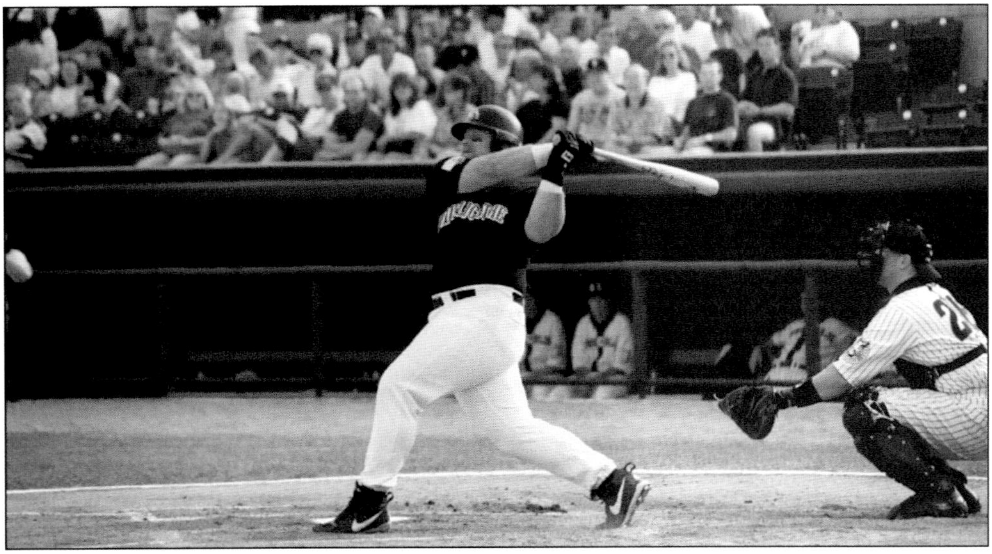

In 1999, Scott Pinoni returned for his third and final season with the Paints. He performed superbly despite being hampered by nagging hamstring injuries, which he jokingly blamed on Gator McBride ("Gator left his injuries in my locker," he said). Pinoni won his second Frontier League batting title with a mark of .377, clubbed a league-second best 22 home runs, and drove in 74 runs. Scott enjoyed a 22-game hitting streak during the season, hit a pair of homers three times, and on July 6 hit his 51st home run as a Chillicothe Paint to break Mitch House's team record. An indication of how terrified of Pinoni league pitchers were came on August 16, when, after he hit an RBI single in the first inning, Springfield pitchers walked him five straight times.

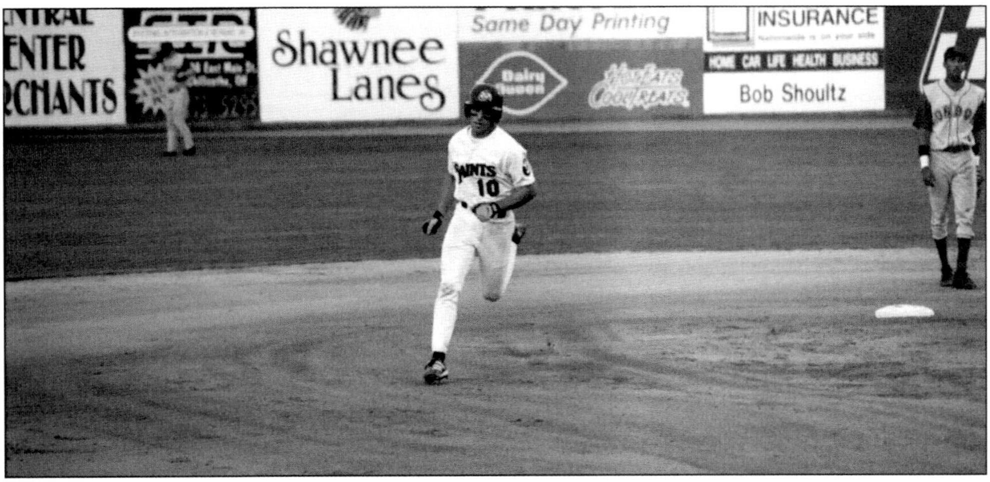

Rookie Mike Cervenak joined with McBride, Pinoni, and fellow rookies Chance Melvin and Joe Colameco to form a Paints' Murderers' Row in 1999. Cervenak joined the team two weeks into the season, having recently ended his college career as the all-time hits leader (284) at the University of Michigan; even so, he wound up with more at bats (301) than anyone else on the team besides Melvin and Mike Horning. A natural third baseman, Cervenak began his Paints' career playing right field, but he took over at shortstop when veteran Jamie Keefe retired. Mike hit .306 with 17 doubles, four triples, three home runs, and 46 RBI. He went 2-3 in the 1999 All-Star Game and homered for the Paints' only run during their 2-1 loss in Game One of the Finals against London.

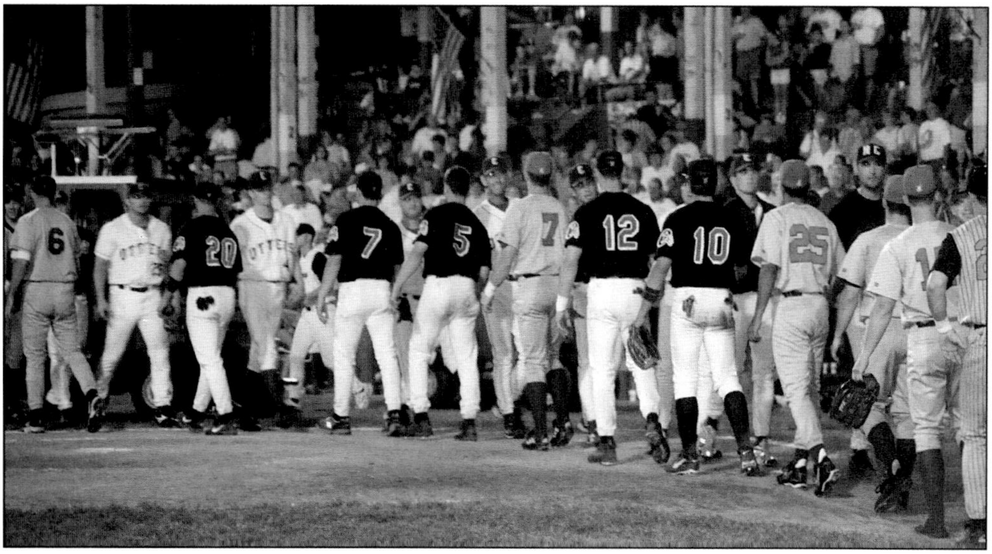

As usual, the Paints were well represented at the 1999 Frontier League All-Star Game, played at Huntingburg, Indiana's League Stadium. In fact, the London Werewolves were the only other team in either division to send as many players to the game as the Paints: seven. The West won the game 4-1. The Paints' All-Stars, wearing the dark blue jerseys and shaking hands with the West All-Stars, pictured from left to right, are Gator McBride (#20), Stephen Byrd (#7), Mike Horning (#5), Chance Melvin (#12), and Mike Cervenak (#10). At the end of the line (not pictured) were Scott Pinoni and Chris Maness.

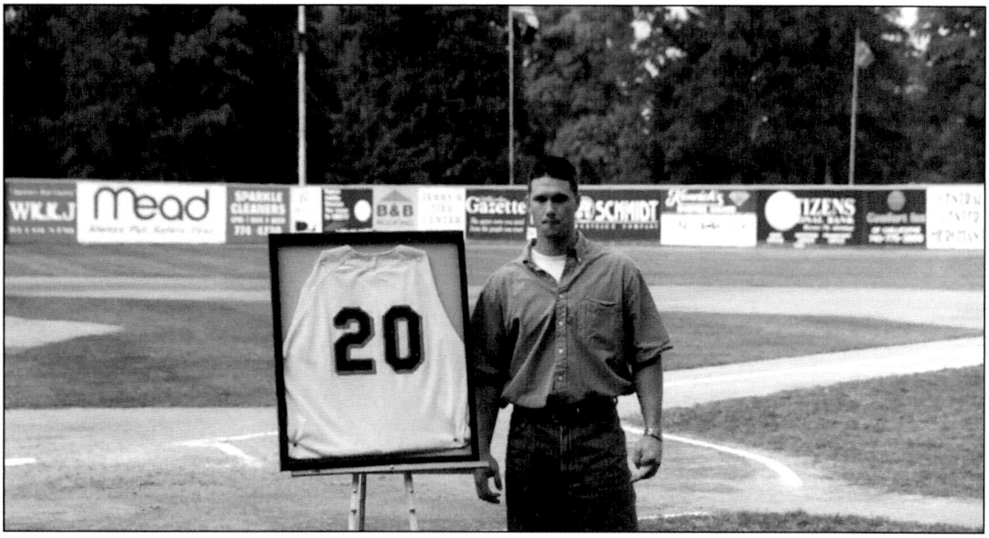

The Paints went right back into action after the All-Star Game, but Gator McBride did not. He sat out the game of July 15, and the next day it was announced that he had been signed by the Boston Red Sox organization, effectively bringing to a close his career with the Chillicothe Paints. On Saturday, July 17, the Paints retired McBride's jersey number. In appreciation for his play in Chillicothe, the members of the Paints' bullpen gave him a most unusual salute. They stood on benches, extended their arms one on top of the other, and then opened and shut their arms repeatedly in imitation gator chomping! At the time of his signing with Boston, McBride was leading the Frontier League in batting average with a .456 mark and home runs with 15.

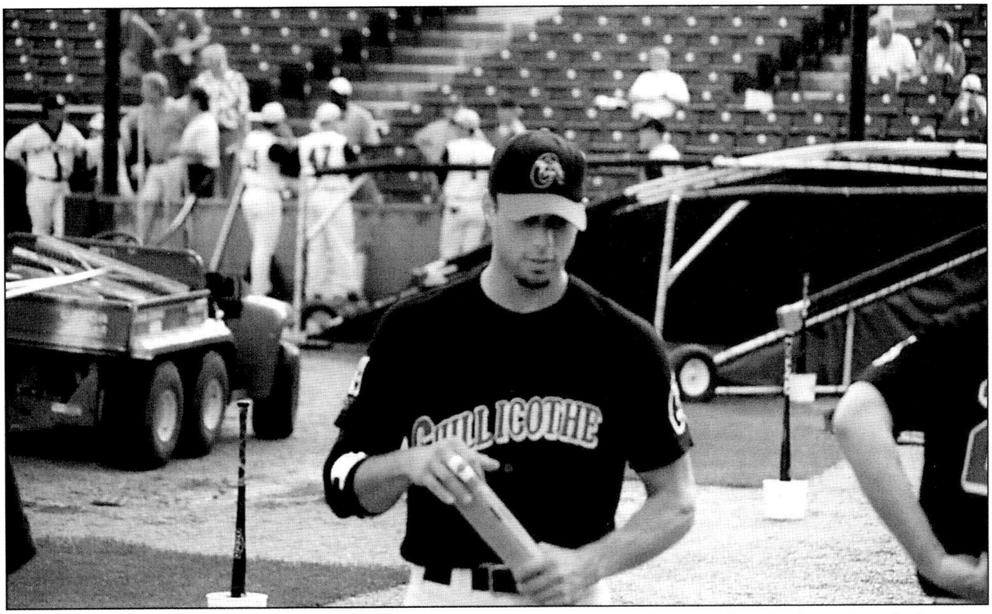

A former teammate of Tony Costantino at Winthrop University in South Carolina, Joe Colameco was a speedy outfielder who could hit for average and power. The Burlington, Ontario native had been the Canadian National Team Player of the Year, and he would have a long and distinguished career with the Paints. In 1999 he batted .280 in 73 games, with 17 doubles, three triples, and four home runs. Joe was also second on the team in stolen bases with 20.

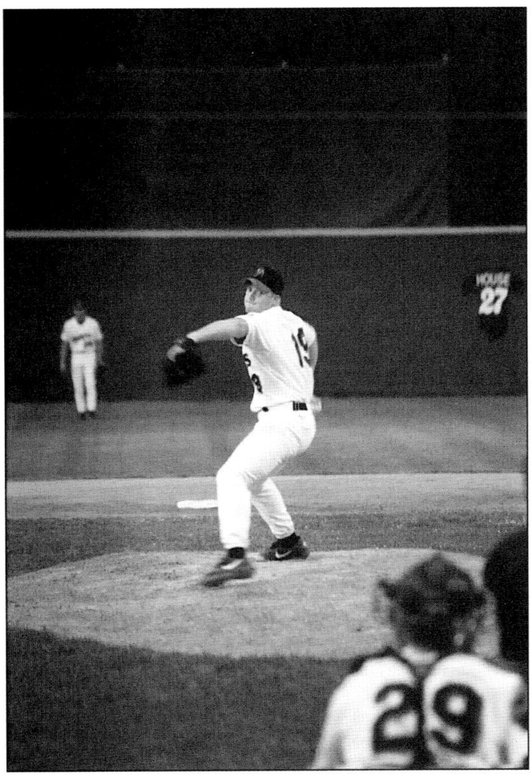

Fastballer Josh White was an Ohio boy (Mt. Vernon) who played collegiately at the University of North Carolina-Asheville. He was signed (along with Andy Lee) two weeks into the 1999 season to help replace released pitchers Greg Sieszputowski, Chris Hughes, and Aaron Sundsmo. White started 13 games and compiled a winning record (4-2) despite an ERA of 6.14. He showed promise, which he fulfilled the following year, by striking out 64 batters in 63 innings. White was the best pitcher in the league in 2000, until an arm injury forced him into retirement. He struck out 73 batters and gave up only 39 hits in 65 innings, finishing the year 5-0 with an ERA of 1.38.

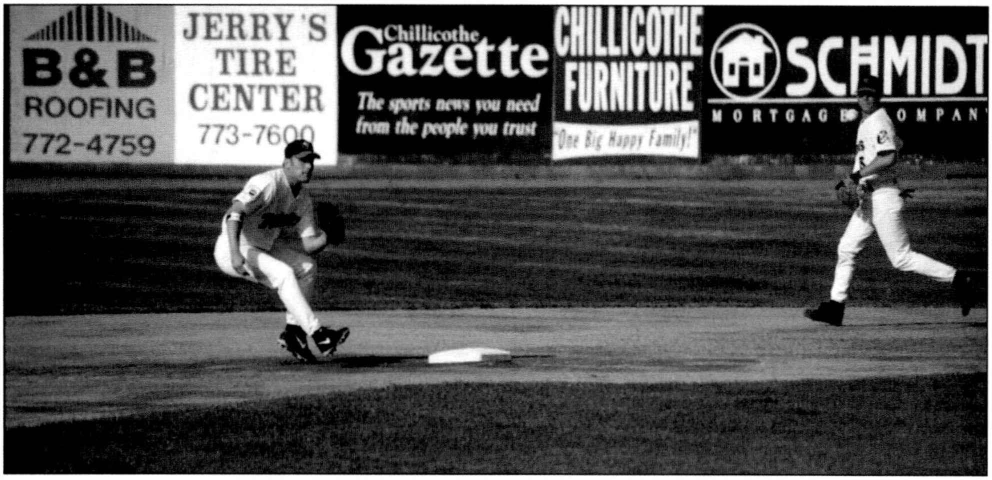

Shortstop Jamie Keefe was the most experienced player on the 1999 Paints, having spent six years in the San Diego and Pittsburgh farm systems and having risen, despite numerous injuries, as high as the AAA level with Las Vegas. Roger Hanners talked the New Hampshire native into giving it one more try on the diamond, but Keefe came to Chillicothe already mentally preparing for a future as a manager. He played the first month of the season ... then graciously stepped aside and became a coach so that the Paints could sign another veteran: pitcher Bob Spears who was returning to Chillicothe from the Taiwan professional league. Jamie was batting .239 at the time of his retirement.

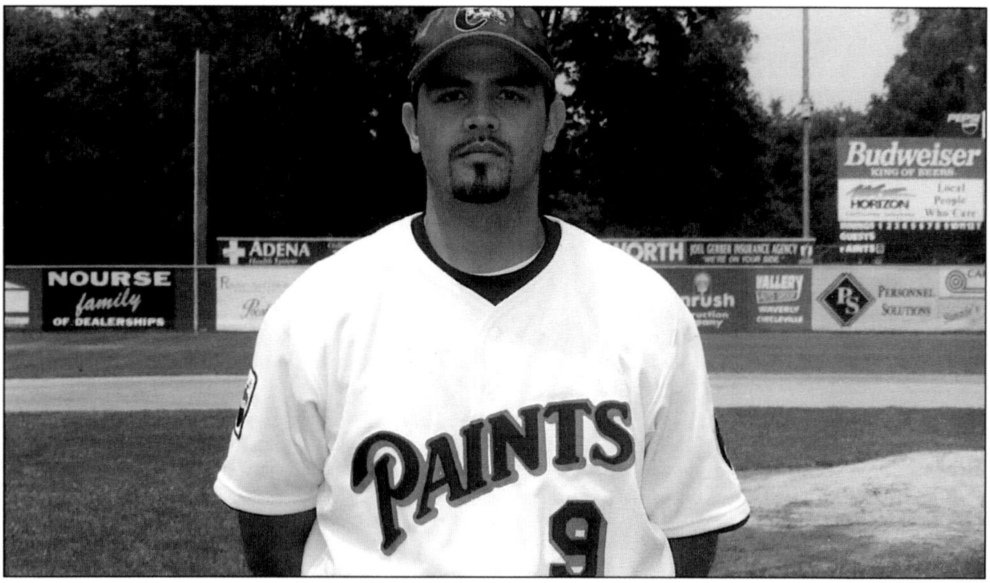

Joey Choron had an All-American season for the University of South Alabama as a junior in 1997, but a knee operation cut short his senior year in 1998. A second baseman by trade, he became a valuable utility infielder for the Paints in 1999. Although he stood only 5-foot-9, Choron had plenty of pop in his bat, and his seven home runs were good for fourth on the team. His 8th-inning grand slam off the scoreboard led the Paints to their third win of the season, and his SF drove in the winning run that clinched the first round of the playoffs for the Paints. In the Game Two loss to London in the Finals, he went 2-4 with a triple. He batted .246 for the year with 39 RBI. In 2000 Choron batted .271 with six homers and 26 RBI.

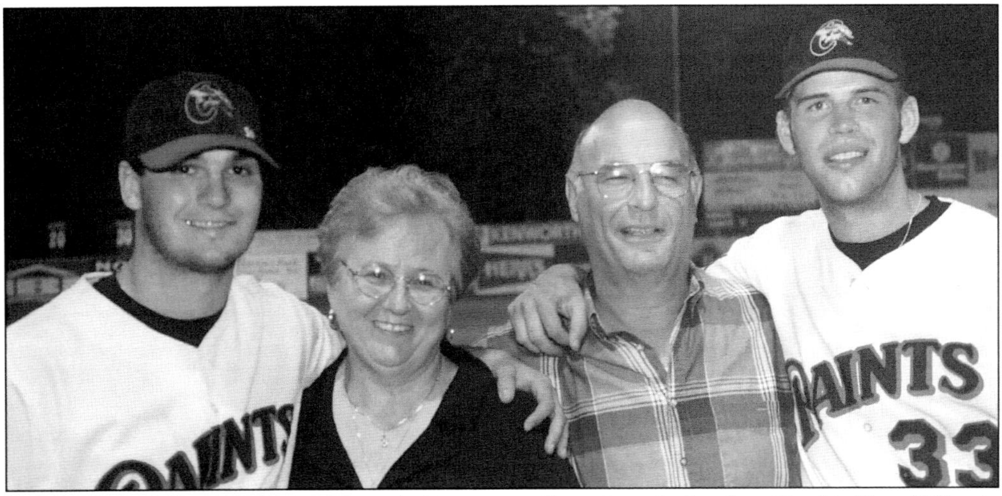

The Paints' pitching staff in 1999 was led by a pair of best friends, Stephen Byrd (#7) and Woody Fullenkamp (#33), posing here with their Chillicothe host parents, Bea and Cliff Beeks. Byrd led the staff in games started (18), innings (110), and strikeouts (92). Those numbers, along with his 9-4 record and 3.60 ERA made him the team's Most Valuable Pitcher. Fullenkamp, another former Ohio State University baseball standout, was the league's best closer. Almost unhittable at times, he went 5-3 on the season with a team-leading 11 saves, 55 strikeouts (in 46.2 innings), and a microscopic ERA of 1.16. Byrd was nominated to the 10th Anniversary Dream Team, and Fullenkamp was voted onto it as the Right-handed Relief Pitcher by the fans of Chillicothe.

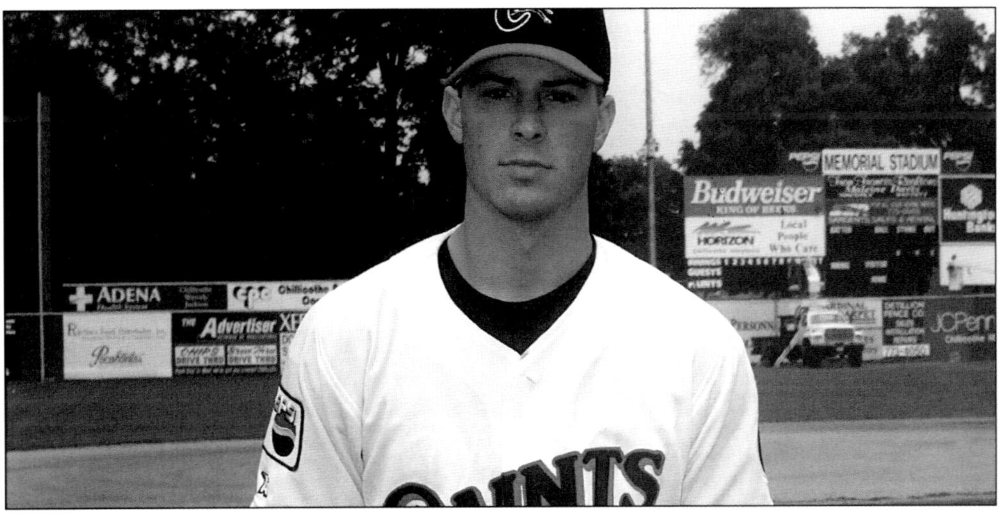

Three days before the start of the 1999 season the Paints obtained left-hander Jamie Blaesing from the River City Rascals in a trade, and Blaesing proved to be a blessing. Working in middle relief he appeared in 31 games and struck out 55 in 41.1 innings, finishing with a 1-1 record. The possessor of an outstanding pickoff move, Blaesing (Quincy, IL) was traded twice in 2000, first to Richmond and then to London. As a Werewolf, he surrendered a single to Canton Crocodiles' coach and former American League Rookie of the Year Joe Charboneau in a Frontier League game at the end of the season. The at-bat by the former Cleveland Indian was mainly a publicity stunt, but it was approved by Frontier League Commissioner Bill Lee and was also an official part of the game.

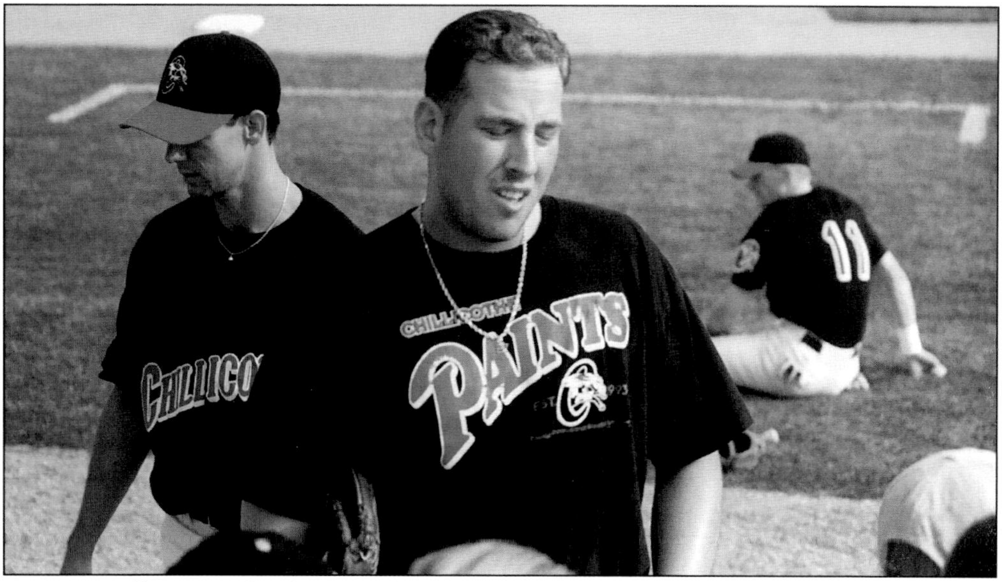

Brian Scarcello returned to the Paints for 1999 after failing to land a job in the Italian professional league. Even with his late start, he became a regular member of the rotation, appearing in 15 games, 13 of them as a starting pitcher. He went 5-2 on the year (giving him a career record of 18-3) with a 3.80 ERA. He pitched the staff's only shutout of the year: a 3-0 one-hitter against Canton on August 21.

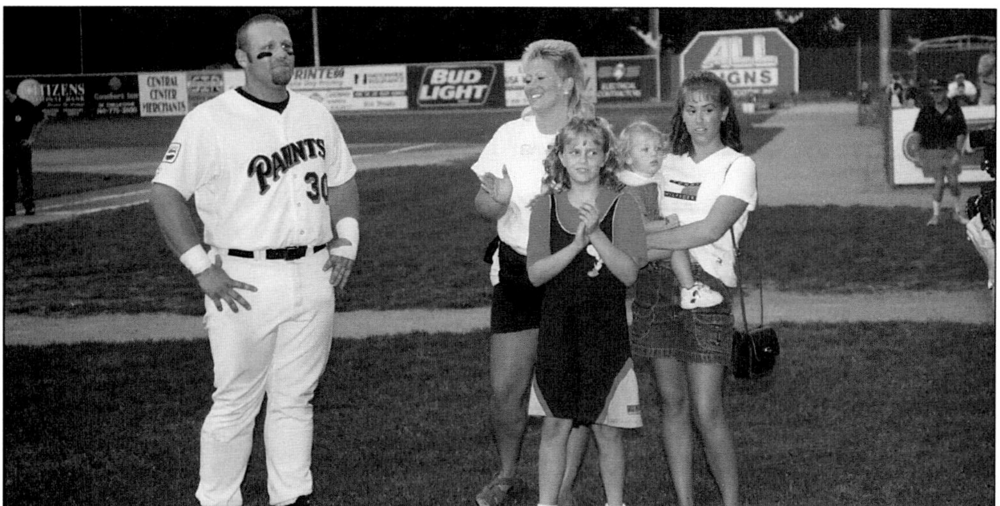

On August 23 the Paints stopped the game against the Richmond Roosters in the fourth inning to have another number-retiring ceremony. This time the honoree was Scott Pinoni, who would finish the 1999 season with another gaudy batting average (.377), 22 home runs, and 74 RBI. Pinoni ended his career in Chillicothe as the Paints' all-time leader in at-bats (850), hits (302), runs (187), doubles (49), home runs (58), and RBI (237). He finished second in batting average (.355) and slugging percentage (.625) to the career marks set by Gator McBride (.423 and .738). Pinoni went 2-4 and homered in the Game Two Finals loss that gave London the 1999 Frontier League championship. Scott was the first baseman voted by the fans to the 10th Anniversary Dream Team.

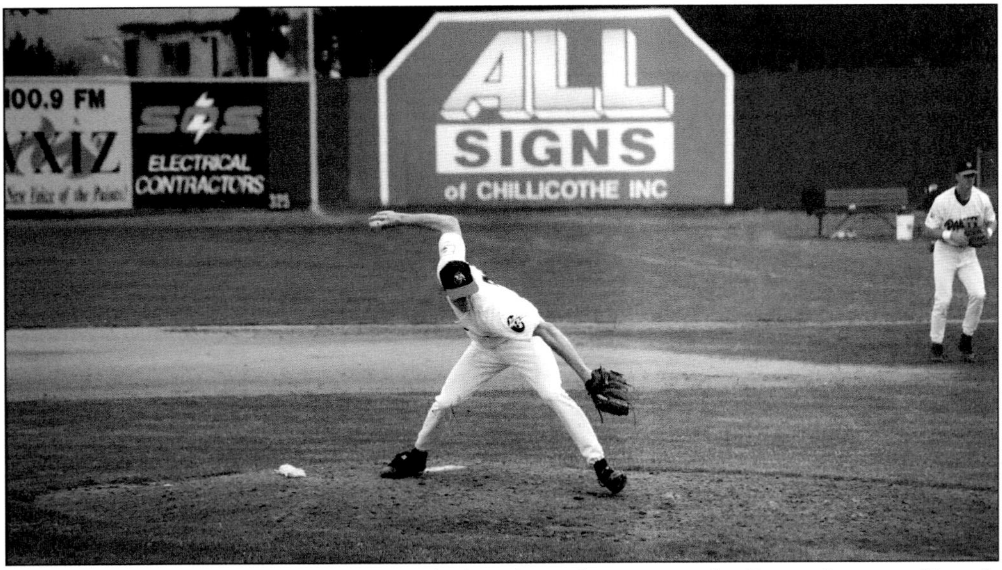

Eric Frodsham was another submarine relief pitcher, who came to the Paints from tiny Friends University (Wichita, Kansas), where he set the career record for saves. Pitching in middle relief, he did not pick up any saves for the Paints, but he led the 2000 staff in appearances with 35 and compiled a 3-3 record with an ERA of 4.88. Nicknamed "Sweats" because of his most common attire, Frodsham was considered to be something of a flake, but the philosophy major and cooking enthusiast was completely dedicated to pitching.

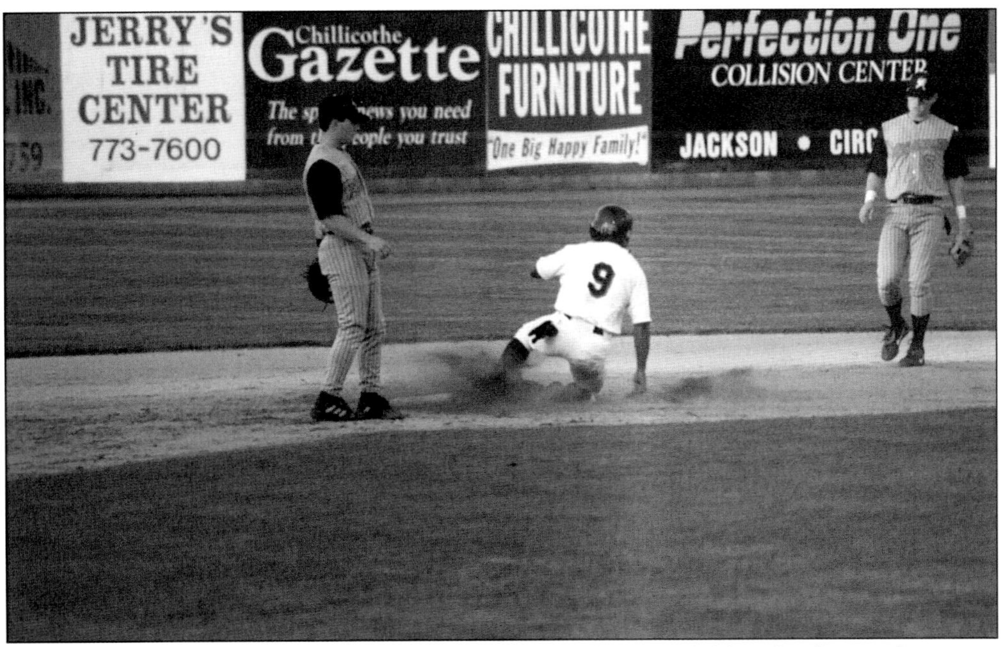

McKenzie, Tennessee native Greg Strickland was a speedy center fielder who'd spent three years in the Atlanta Braves' farm system before playing for Chillicothe in 2000. A left-handed thrower and batter, Strickland led off for the Paints and turned in an outstanding year both on offense and defense. He batted .330 (fourth best in the league) with 18 doubles, four triples, four home runs, and 29 RBI. He also led the team in stolen bases with 20 and on-base percentage (.404).

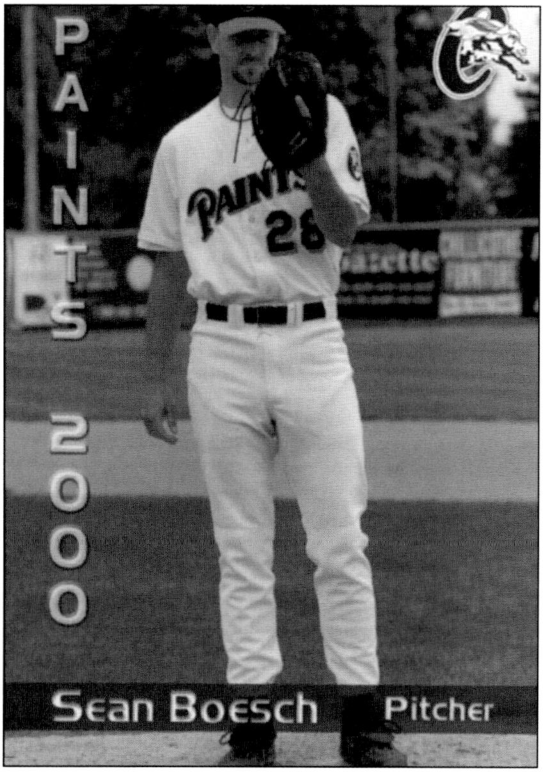

As a senior at Oakland (MI) University where he played for former Paints' catcher Mark Avery, pitcher Sean Boesch (pronounced "Bush") was selected to the All Mid-Continent Tournament Team for 2000. He proved himself to be a real trooper during his rookie season with the Paints, working more innings (107.1) than any other pitcher on the 2000 staff besides Andy Lee. Boesch's record of 7-7 appeared to be mediocre, but his ERA of 3.19, seventh best in the league, was a better indication of the quality of his performance.

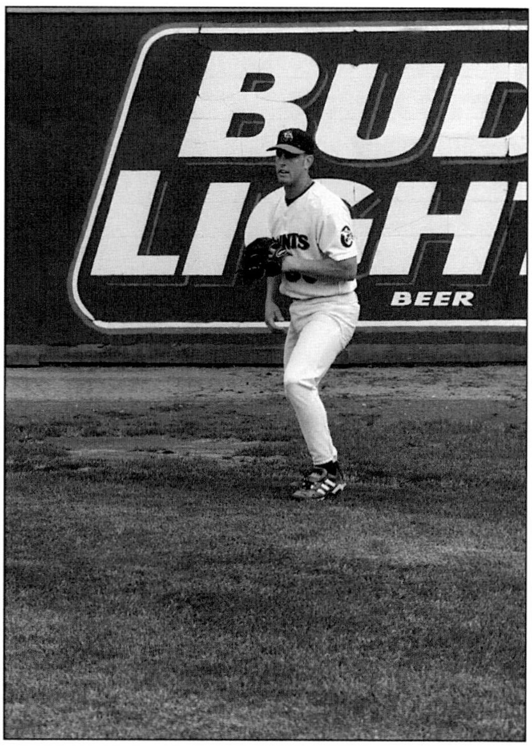

Another important newcomer to the 2000 edition of the Paints was Justin Graham, a 5-foot-10 outfielder out of West Virginia State College (Institute, WV). Justin was the brother of Jason Graham (aka Jess Graham), who had played for Chillicothe in 1997 and would again in 2002. Justin had a super year for the Paints in 2000, batting .312 and tying for the team lead in home runs (6) and RBI (34). He also had a gun in left field, which he showed off when he threw out two Johnstown runners at home in the same series. Justin returned to Chillicothe for the 2001 campaign, but injuries hampered him and he never could get untracked at the plate.

The regular catcher for the Paints in 2000 was Chris Poulsen, who had played the year before in the Braves' system for Jamestown and Danville. Poulsen was an excellent receiver with an accurate throwing arm, and Paints' pitchers loved having him behind the plate. In 2000 he batted .269 with three home runs and 25 RBI in 61 games. Sharing time with Adam Patterson in 2001, Poulsen appeared in 48 games and batted .269. Chris made only three errors in 2000 for a fielding percentage of .993.

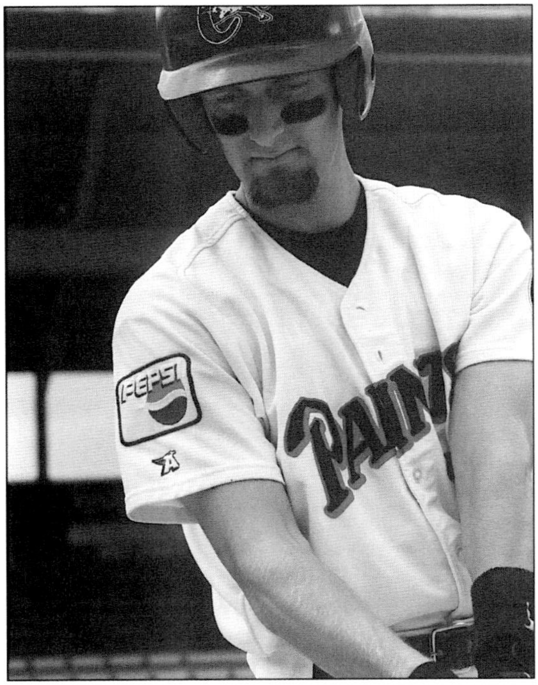

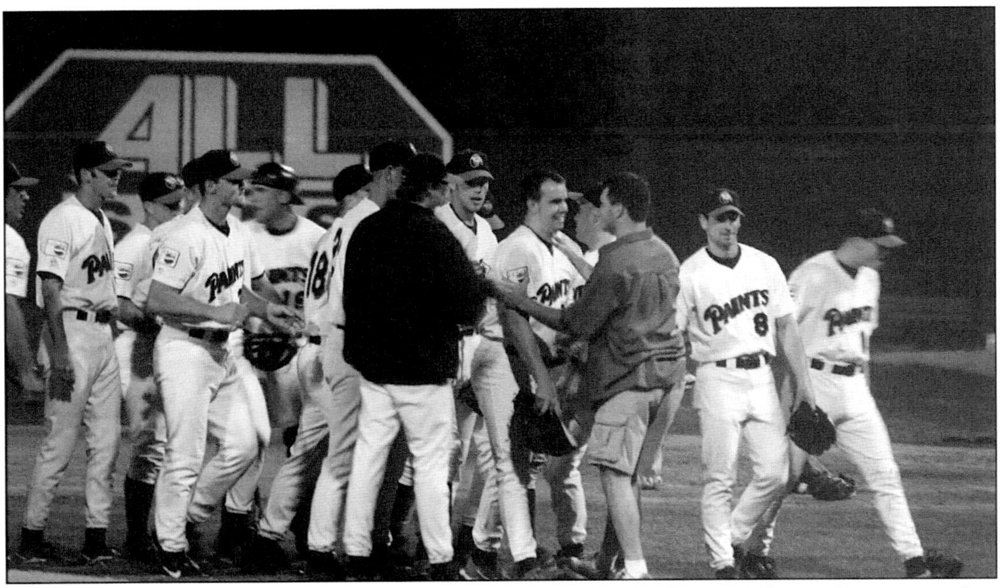

The highlight of an otherwise disappointing season for Paints' fans was the no-hitter turned in by Andy Lee on June 8 against the Richmond Roosters at V.A. Memorial Stadium. Lee managed only a .500 record (5-5) for the season, but he was voted by his teammates as the Most Valuable Pitcher on the team. He led the staff in starts (17), complete games (3), and innings (113.1), and his ERA of 3.10 was fifth best in the league. He also led the league in strikeouts with 126, setting a new team record at the same time. This picture was taken right after the final out of the no-hitter. Moments later, Andy was carried off the field on the shoulders of his teammates.

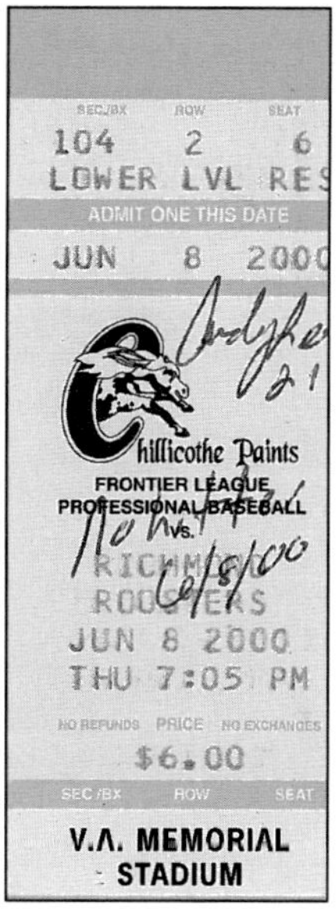

This is a photo of a ticket from Andy Lee's historic game, only the second no-hitter in league history at that point. Lee's gem came exactly three years to the day Richmond's Christian Hess had thrown the first Frontier League no-hitter. Andy Lee signed this full ticket from the game and added his uniform number, the date, and the words "No hitter" to it. Only one walk, an error, and a hit batter kept Lee's no-hitter from being a perfect game. Chris Poulsen caught the game, and Jim Schaly umpired it behind the plate.

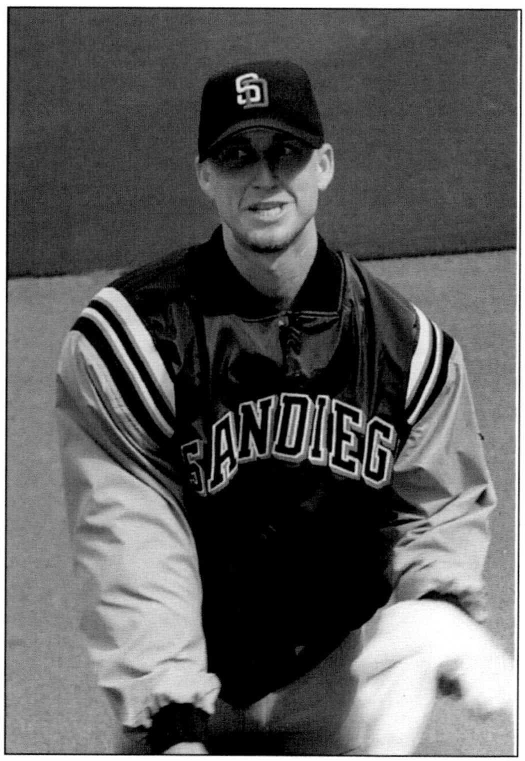

The biggest news around the Frontier League in 2000 was the major league debut of former Paints' pitcher Brian Tollberg with the San Diego Padres on June 20. Frontier League watchers expected Richmond Roosters' legendary hitting machine Morgan Burkhart to be the first alumnus to graduate to the majors, but Tollberg beat out Burkhart (who got the call from the Boston Red Sox) by about a week. Tollberg won his first big league game, going seven innings and limiting the Arizona Diamondbacks to a single hit. He beat the Cincinnati Reds in his next start and was named the National League Pitcher of the Week. Tollberg had several good years with the Padres before arm trouble slowed him down. (Courtesy of Maleine Davis.)

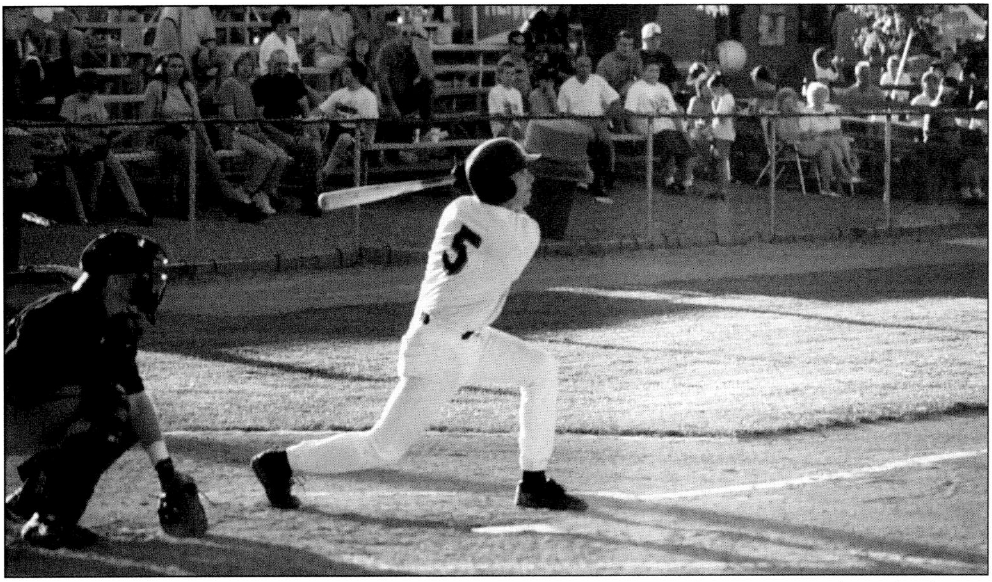

Back for his third go-round with the Paints, second baseman Mike Horning slipped a bit in 2000, statistically speaking, but he played as hard as ever, and his teammates recognized his grit and leadership by voting him the team's Most Valuable Player. Horning hit .252 with four homers and 28 RBI in 2000. Horning left town with his name all over the Paints' record book. He was first in career at-bats (860), first in stolen bases (47), third in hits (229), third in doubles (42), third in runs (152), sixth in RBI (94), and tenth in home runs (8).

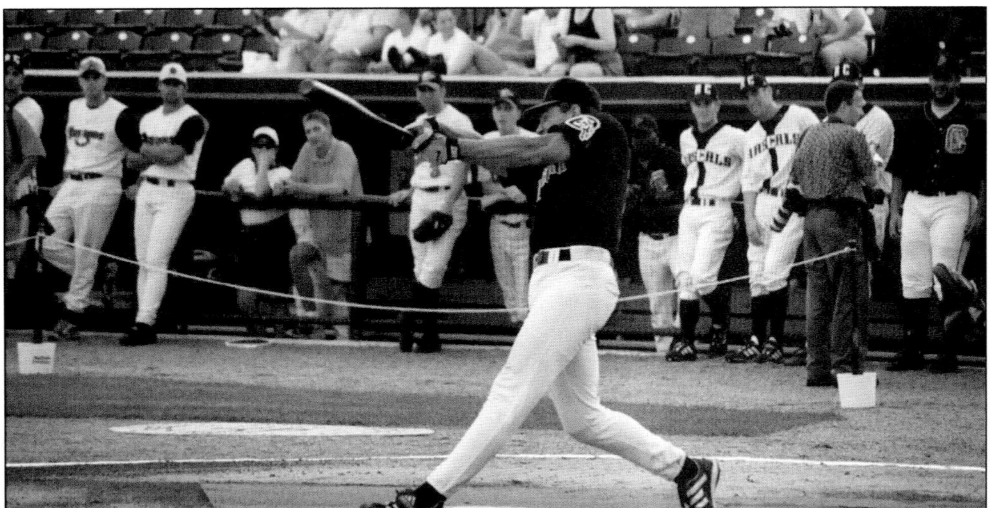

Shortstop Mike Cervenak returned to Chillicothe in 2000 and played like the MVP of the league for the first half of the season. Mike is shown here winning the home run-hitting contest at the All-Star Game which was played in River City. A few days later Cervenak was signed by the New York Yankees. At the time, Cervenak was batting .357 and leading the Frontier League in hits (61), home runs (12), extra-base hits (21), RBI (43), and slugging percentage (.620). His departure effectively derailed the Paints' pennant chances. The San Francisco Giants acquired Cervenak from the Yankees in the minor league Rule V draft, and from 2001 through 2004 Mike played for the Giants' Double A team in the Texas League, the Norwich Navigators.

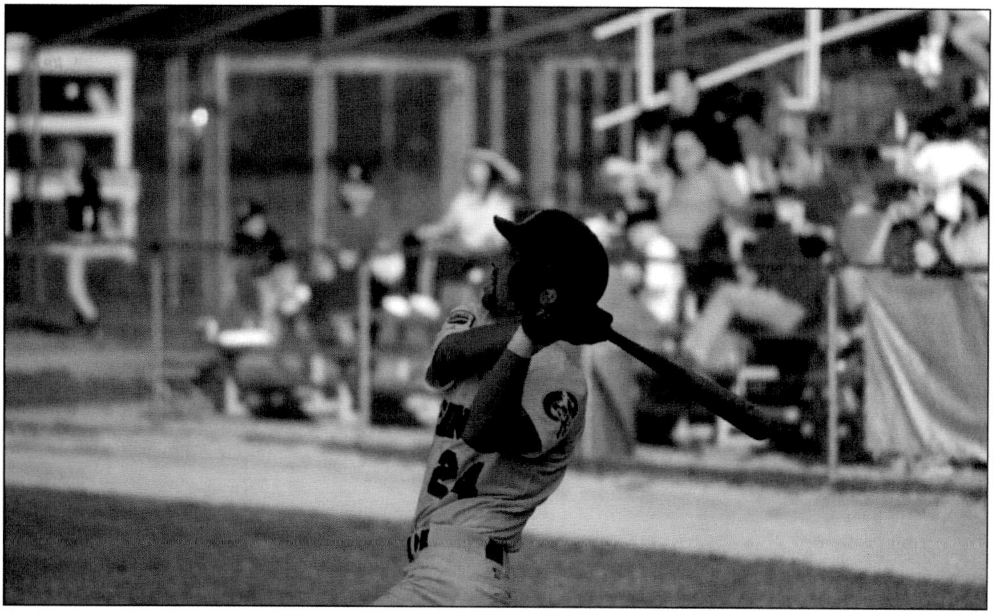

A former star at Division III North Carolina Wesleyan College (Rocky Mount, NC) and the University of North Carolina, Matt McCay made the 2000 Paints' roster as a utility player. He was not expected to play much but became the regular right fielder after Joe Colameco was signed by the New York Yankees. Matt immediately became a hit with Paints' fans for his excellent play, his toughness, and his country charm (for his batting intro music McCay selected the theme to The Dukes of Hazard television show, and he put a little skip in his step on the way to the plate when the song mentioned "two good old boys"). McCay batted .299 in 56 games with three home runs and 24 RBI.

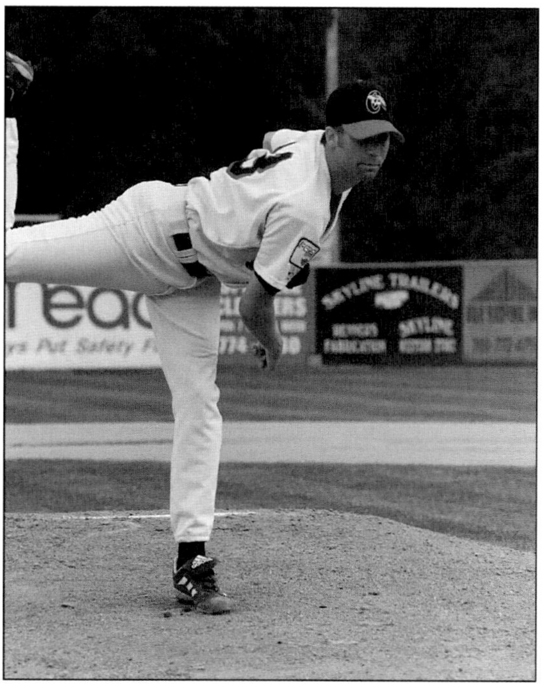

After spending all of 1999 in the Northern League and the first part of 2000 in the Western League, skinny Rick Blanc decided he wanted to return to Chillicothe. Fortunately for the Paints, Rogers Hanners welcomed him back. Blanc started his second tour of duty in Chillicothe in the bullpen, but injuries forced him, uncomplainingly, into the starting rotation. Rick appeared in 18 games and started 12 of them. He compiled a 5-3 record with an ERA of 5.12. The season was a learning experience for Blanc, and it paid off big time the following year.

Rookie Chris Dickerson was a switch-hitting infielder from the same home town as Nolan Ryan (Alvin, Texas). Before signing with the Paints, he played for Blinn College and then for a semi-pro team in the Netherlands. Dickerson played in a total of 66 games in 2000, 37 of them at third base. His 230 at bats were fifth highest on the team, and he batted .278 with three home runs and 30 RBI. He was nominated for the third base position on the Paints' 10th Anniversary Dream Team.

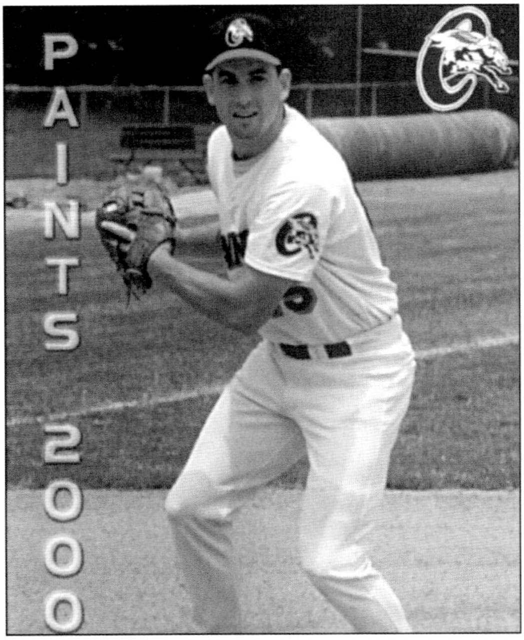

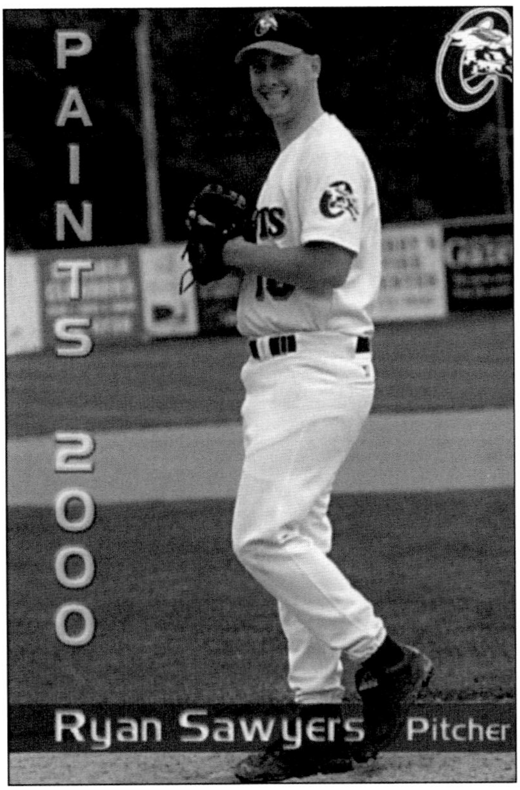

Right-hander Ryan Sawyers was another rookie on the 2000 team. The former collegian at West Virginia Wesleyan, who had been named Conference Pitcher of the Year in 1999, started seven games and relieved in seven others. He pitched a total of 48 innings and posted a record of 4-2 with one save. Ryan went into coaching after 2000. He served as Shepherd College's pitching coach from 2001 to 2003 and as the assistant pitching coach at Purdue University in 2004. He returned to Chillicothe and worked as Jamie Keefe's pitching coach in 2004.

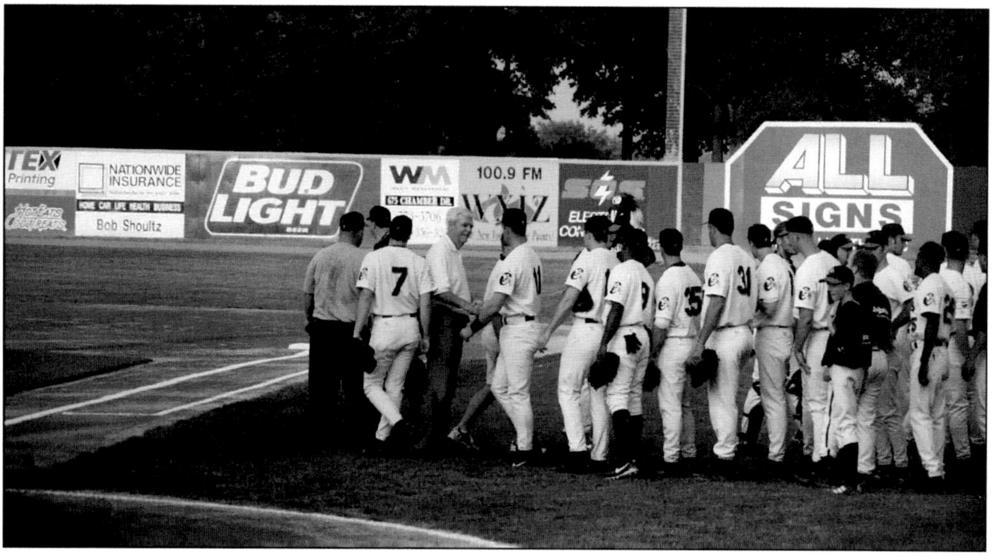

At the end of July 2000 Paints' manager Roger Hanners suffered a heart attack which knocked him out of uniform for the first time since he took the job a couple of weeks into the team's inaugural season of 1993. Long-time assistant coach Marty Dunn filled in for Hanners until his job with Chillicothe High School started, and then coach Jamie Keefe became interim manager. Hanners recovered enough to pay an emotional visit to the team before the start of the last home series of the year. John Wend's announcement that Roger would throw out the ceremonial first pitch drew a standing ovation from a packed house at V.A. Memorial Stadium, and after Hanners delivered the pitch the entire team rushed onto the field to welcome him home and give him a hug.

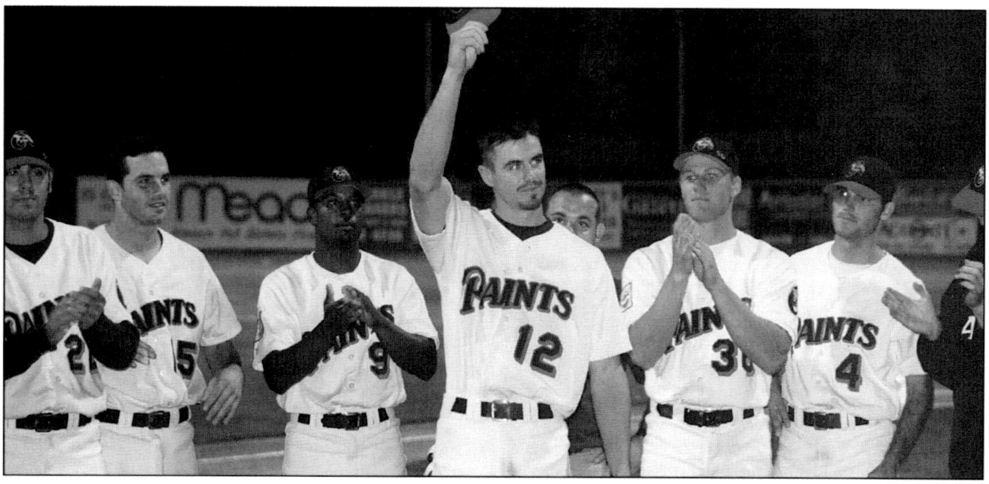

The Paints' organization has a classy tradition of saying goodbye to esteemed players not returning to Chillicothe. At the last home game of the 2000 season third baseman Chance Melvin received such a send-off. Melvin's batting statistics for 2000 (.229, 5 HR, 34 RBI) dropped off considerably from his great rookie season, but he remained a fan favorite and was nominated for the 10th Anniversary Dream Team. After leaving Chillicothe he started a career with the FBI. Standing behind Melvin, from left to right, are pitcher Jason Harrison, infielder Chris Dickerson, center fielder Greg Strickland, trainer Rodger Fleming, outfielfer-first baseman Jason Baker, and utility infielder Nick Dumas.

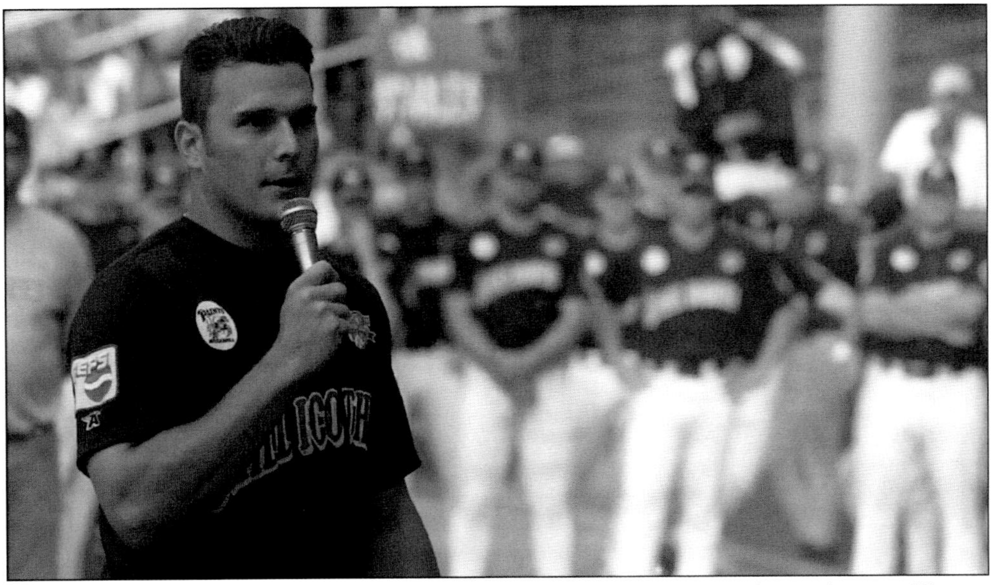

Jamie Keefe began the 2000 season as a full-time coach. He was activated as a player to fill in at short when Mike Cervenak left for affiliated ball but broke his thumb and returned to coaching. He assumed the Paints' managerial reins ahead of schedule, towards the close of the season, after Roger Hanners left the team due to poor health. The 2001 season was Keefe's first full year at the helm, and Jamie proved that the organization's faith in him was justified by leading the team to the best record in the Frontier League. (Courtesy of Scott Osborne.)

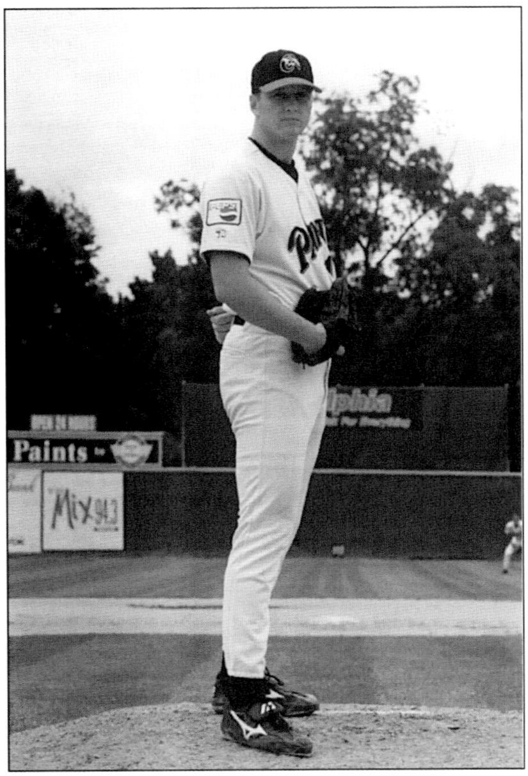

Matt Hampton was a strapping (6'4", 220lbs) left-hander from Wenatchee, Washington with a blazing fastball and a sharp slider. The former University of Washington Huskie was almost unhittable as a rookie in 2001. Hampton gave up only 24 hits in 37 innings over 25 games, and opponents batted only .178 against him. While winning four games and saving eight more (high on the team), he fashioned a microscopic ERA of 1.70. Such dominance didn't go unnoticed, and he was signed by the San Diego Padres after the season. Hampton started the 2004 season with the Padres' AA team in Mobile, Alabama, and he was named, despite his brief time in Chillicothe, as the left-handed reliever to the Paints' 10th Anniversary Dream Team.

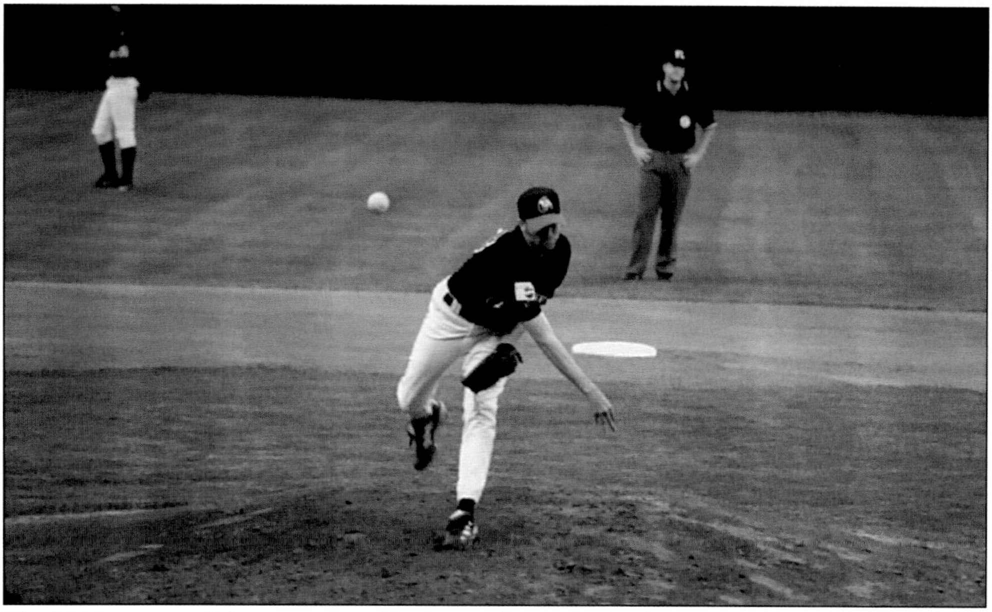

The 2001 season will be remembered by Paints' fans as Rick Blanc's year. After getting bombed on Opening Day, Blanc decided to rely on his sinker, not his average fastball, and he never lost a game the rest of the season. His record of 13-1 tied him with Brian Scarcello for best ever in Frontier League history, and his ERA of 3.24 was eighth best in the league. Rick swept the end-of the-season awards, being voted the Paints' Most Valuable Pitcher, the Starting Pitcher on the Frontier League All-Star Team, and the Frontier League Most Valuable Pitcher. Blanc went 6-8 the following year with an ERA of 4.49, but he was again voted the Paints' Most Valuable Pitcher. Rick was voted onto the 10th Anniversary Dream Team, and in 2003 he served as the Paints' pitching coach.

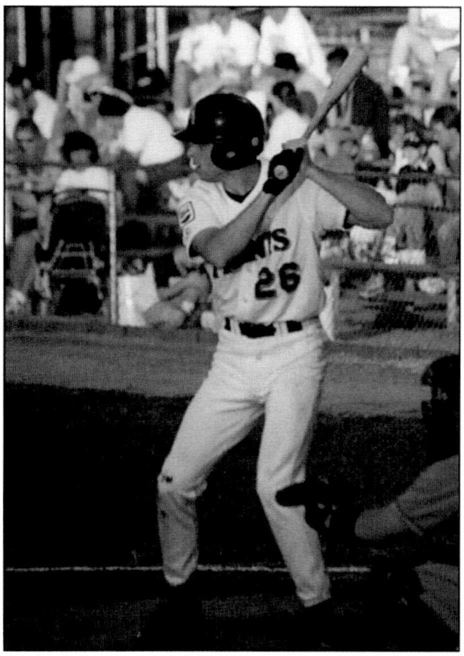

Joe Colameco, the Canadian Comet, came back to Chillicothe for the 2001 season after being released by the New York Yankees and turned in the best year of his professional career. Joe batted .325 (13th best in the league) with ten home runs and 60 RBI. He also swiped seven bases in seven attempts. Colameco played for the Rio Grande Valley White Wings of the independent Central League in 2002, but he returned to Chillicothe for a last hurrah in 2003, as a player-coach. In 82 games he batted .244 with four homers and 30 RBI. Paints' fans paid tribute to his contributions by voting him the center fielder on the 10th Anniversary Dream Team.

Outfielder Matt McCay went from a popular, very good player in 2000 to a bona fide star in 2001. He led the team in hits with 112, and his batting average of .345 was fourth best in the league. Unfortunately for Matt, the three players with better batting averages than him were all outfielders, and the trio (Clay Snellgrove of Canton, Jeremy Coronado of Evansville, and Kirk Taylor of Johnstown) were voted to the three outfield positions on the 2001 Frontier League All-Star Team. (Courtesy of the *Chillicothe Gazette*.)

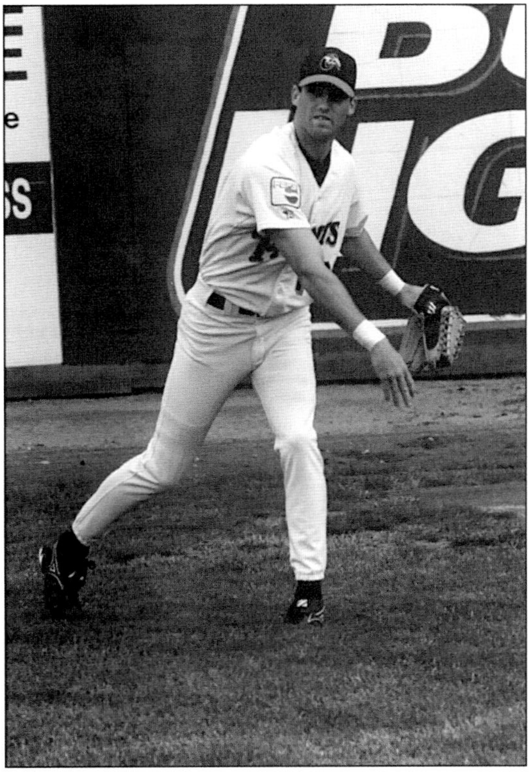

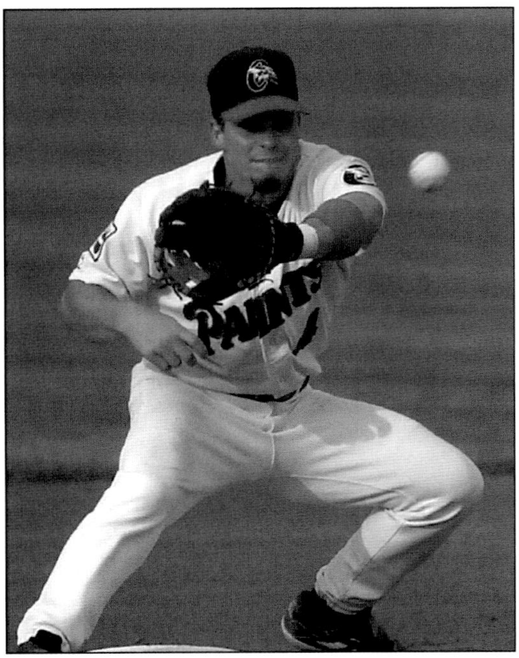

Kevin Connacher may have needed a ladder to change a bulb in a ceiling light fixture, but he did not come up short in his performance with the Paints in 2001. The little second baseman from West Palm Beach, Florida, combined speed and power to make himself the most dangerous lead-off batter in the league. Connacher led the team in home runs with 16 and extra-base hits with 37. He stole 29 bases in 33 attempts, led the team in runs scored with 72, and, amazingly, knocked in 46 runs himself (the fourth highest total on the team). He was named to the Frontier League All-Star Team after the season. Connacher had been playing in the affiliated minors since 1997, and his great year with Chillicothe was his return ticket. He made it to AAA Rochester in the Twins' organization in 2003. (Courtesy of the *Chillicothe Gazette*.)

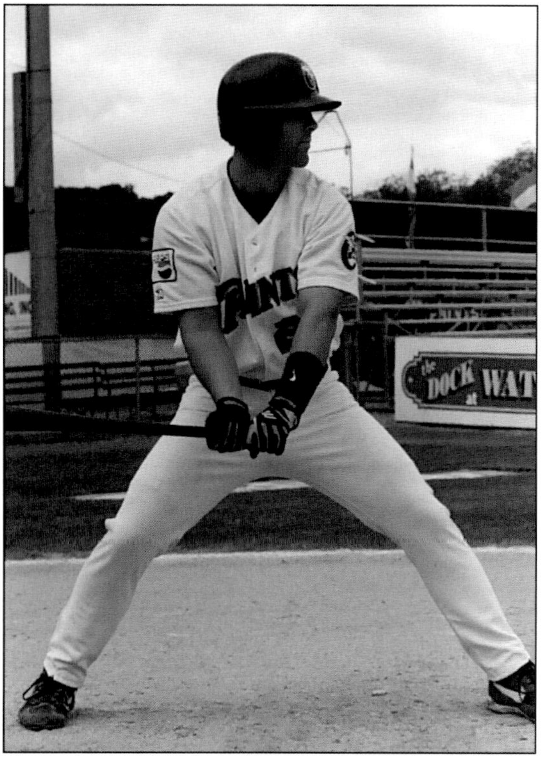

First baseman Darin Kinsolving came to the Paints in the trade that sent Greg Strickland to the River City Rascals. After seeing limited time in his rookie year in 2000, Kinsolving blossomed into a star with the Paints. The Southeast Missouri State University graduate was the only player on the team to play in all 84 games, and he was hot right from the start; as he reached base safely in the first 26 games of the season. For the season he batted .327 with ten home runs and a team-leading 62 RBI.

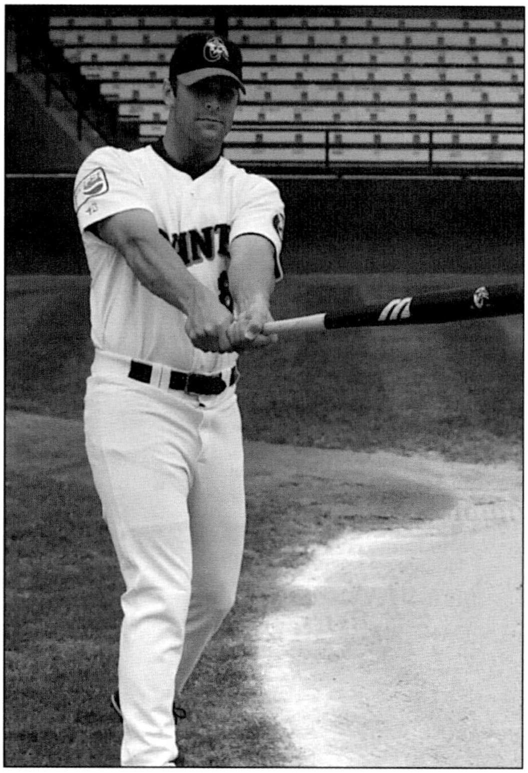

Outfielder Joe Estep made his professional baseball debut in 2000 with the Canton Crocodiles, batting .289 in 49 at bats. The former Shawnee State Bear was signed as a reserve-pinch hitter and saw little playing time in the first part of the 2001 campaign, but he kept himself ready to play and delivered when given his chance. Given a start on August 6 against Johnstown, Estep went 4-4 with a walk. The next night he hit safely in his first two times at bat, to give him streaks of six straight hits and reaching base safely in seven consecutive at bats. For the season he batted .276 in 54 games with one home run and 14 RBI.

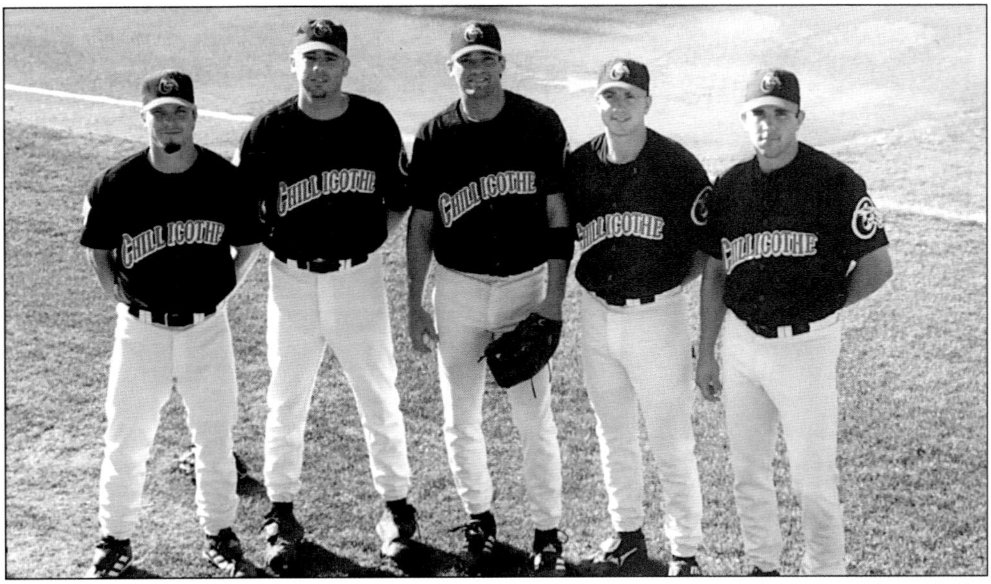

The 2001 Frontier League All-Star Game was played in Chicago at Hawkinson Ford Field, the home of the Cook County Cheetahs. The Paints' delegation of five All-Stars, seen here from left to right, are second baseman Kevin Connacher, starting pitcher Jason Harrison, outfielder Matt McCay, relief pitcher Kris Buirley, and shortstop David Dalton. All five played in the game (won by the East), and four at once. Connacher hit a home run in four at bats, Daulton singled in two tries, and Harrison and Buirley each pitched a scoreless inning. (Courtesy of Maleine Davis.)

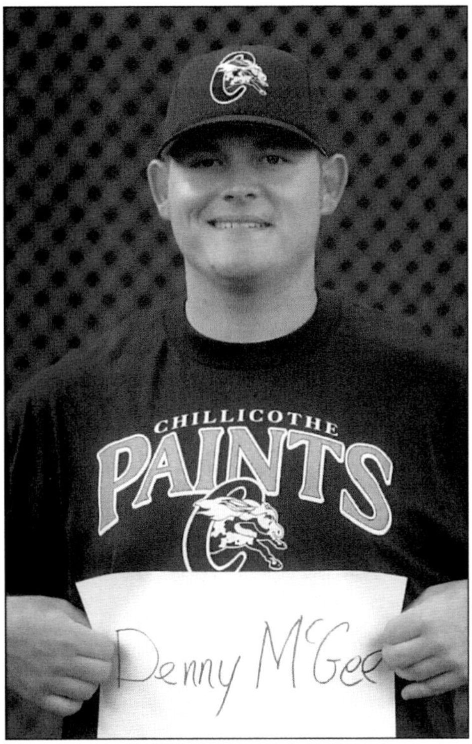

Stocky right-handed pitcher Denny McGee put his name in the Paints' record book in 2001 when he joined Rick Blanc and Sean Boesch in pitching back-to-back-to-back complete-game shutouts against the Kalamazoo Kings (9-0, 4-0, 9-0). McGee appeared in 15 games, nine as a starter, and on the year he went 4-6 with an ERA of 5.26 and one save. He started poorly the following season (0-2, 13.50) and was released after pitching in four games; however, he caught on with the Kings and turned into a different pitcher. He beat the Paints on the day (June 29) the team celebrated its 10th Anniversary, holding his old teammates to one hit over six innings. When he started against the Paints again on August 21 in Kalamazoo, his record with the Kings coming into the game was 6-1 with an ERA of 1.71. This time the Paints knocked him out of the game but still lost, and McGee wound up with a No Decision. (Courtesy of Scott Osborne.)

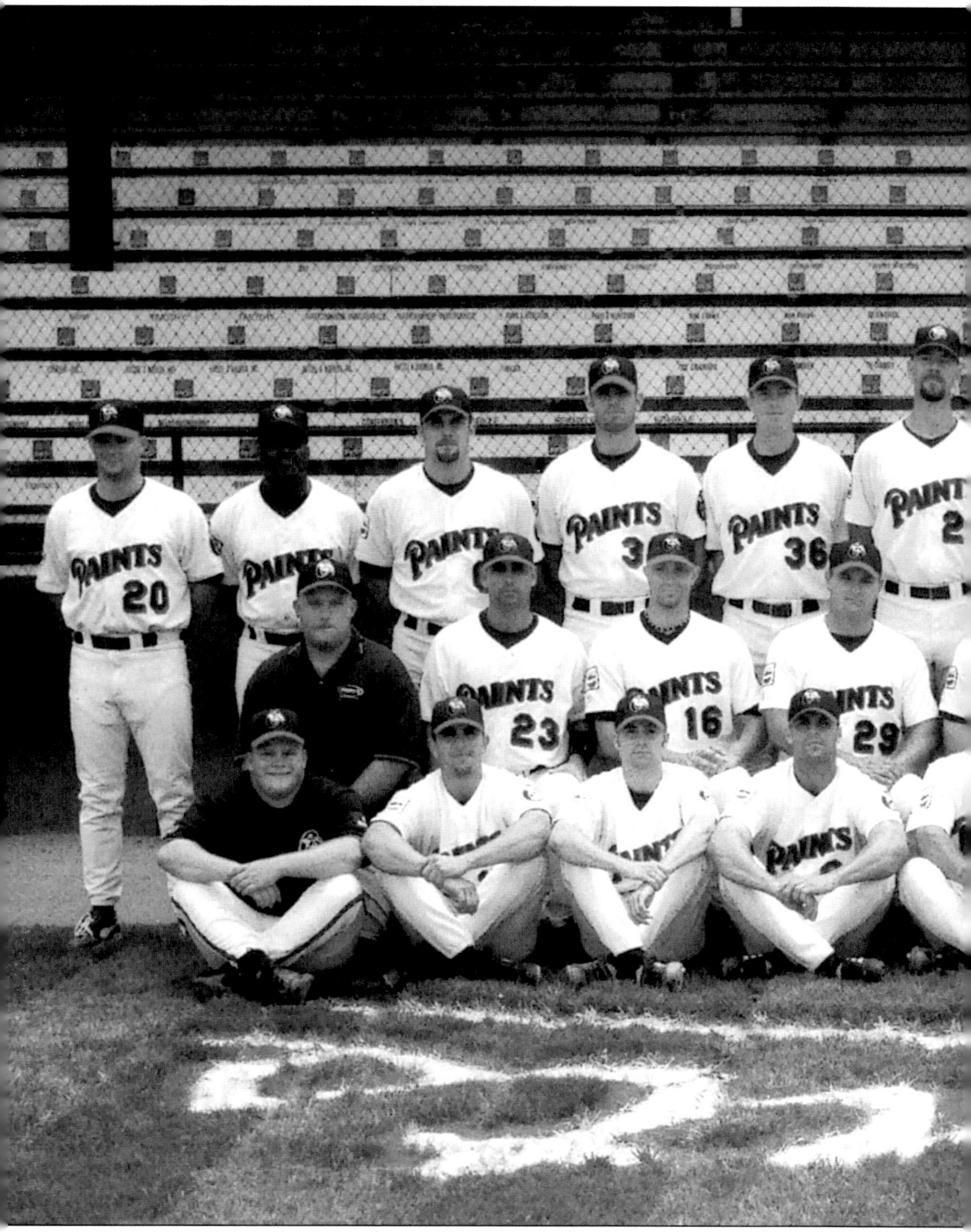

The 2001 Frontier League East Division Champions, pictured from left to right: (front row) Mitch Joseph (bat boy), David Daulton, Rick Blanc, Joe Estep, Rob Annicelli, Vinny Cerni, Kevin Connacher, Justin Graham, Kris Buirley, and Cody Chenault (bat boy); (middle row) Aaron Queen (clubhouse manager), Darin Kinsolving, Andrew See, Rusty Swackhamer, Denny

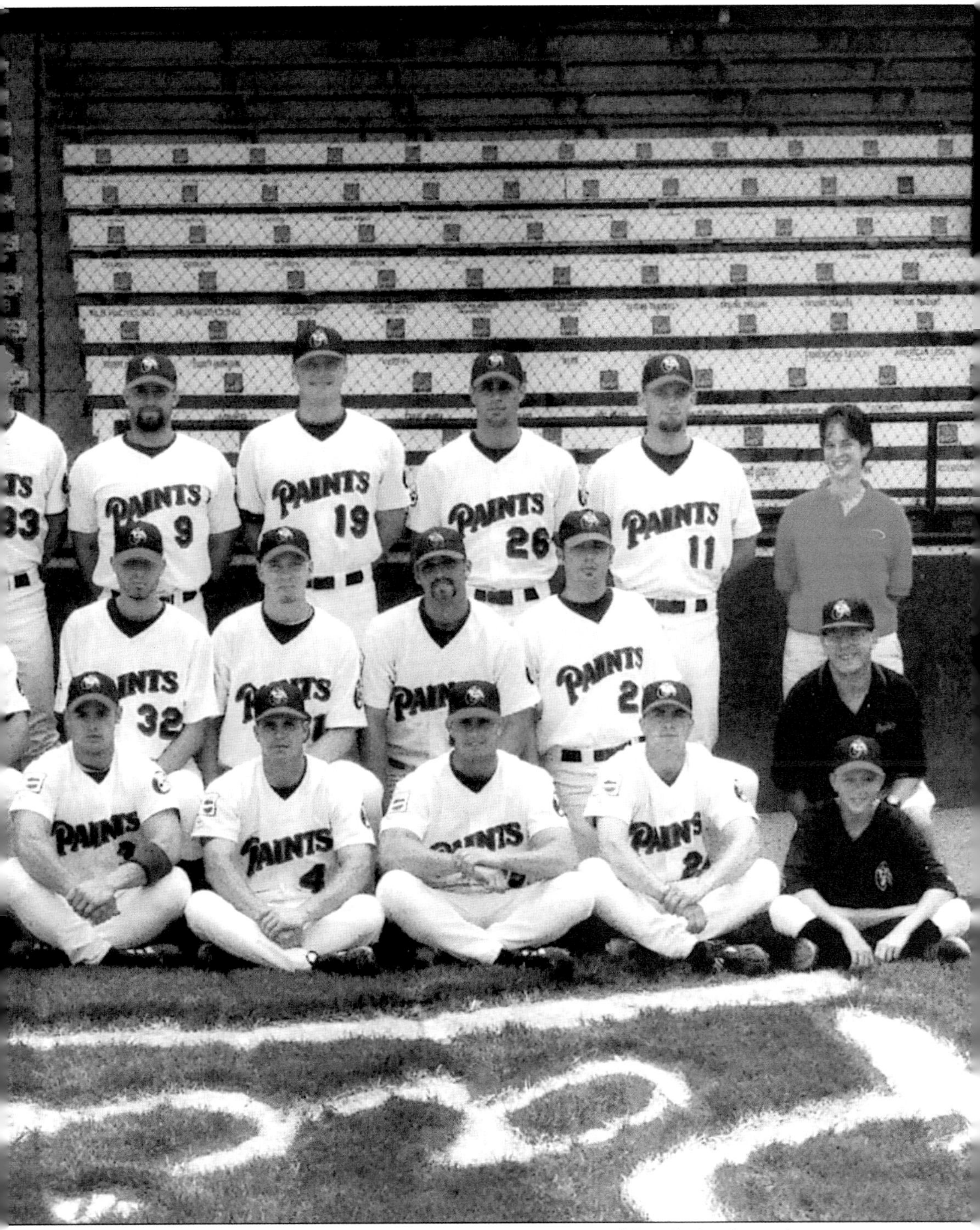

McGee, Greg Kisch, Brian Bogs, Matt McKay, Jason Harrison, and Butch Atteberry (equipment manager); (back row) Gator McBride (coach), Marty Dunn (coach), Jamie Keefe (manager), John Guiseppe, Reed Goemann, Sean Boesch, Woody Fullenkamp, Adam Patterson, Matt Hampton, Joe Colameco, Chris Poulsen, and Julie Hall (trainer).

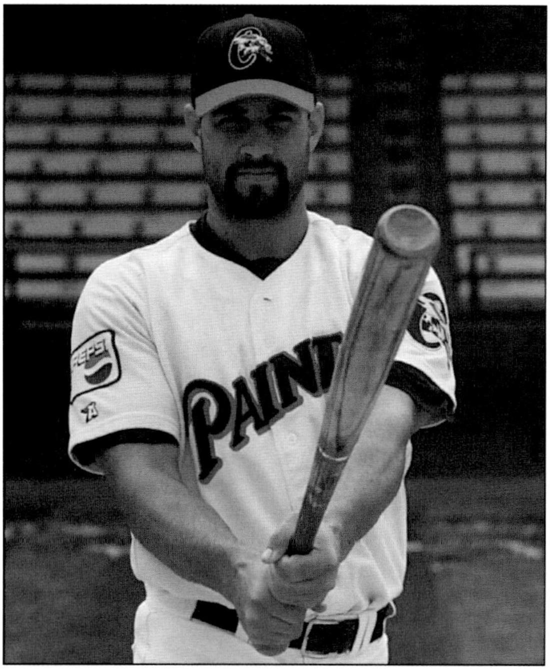

As a rookie with the Dubois County Dragons in 2000, catcher Adam Patterson proved he could hit Frontier League pitching, batting .291 with four homers and 38 RBI in 70 games. He played in 69 games with the Paints in 2001 and posted even better offensive numbers than he did as a rookie. His .328 average was ninth best in the league, and he added five home runs and 33 RBI, stats which earned him a spot on the Frontier League All-Star Team for 2001. He returned to Chillicothe in 2002 and batted .259 with three homers and 17 RBI in 45 games. Adam was nominated for the Paints' 10th Anniversary Dream Team.

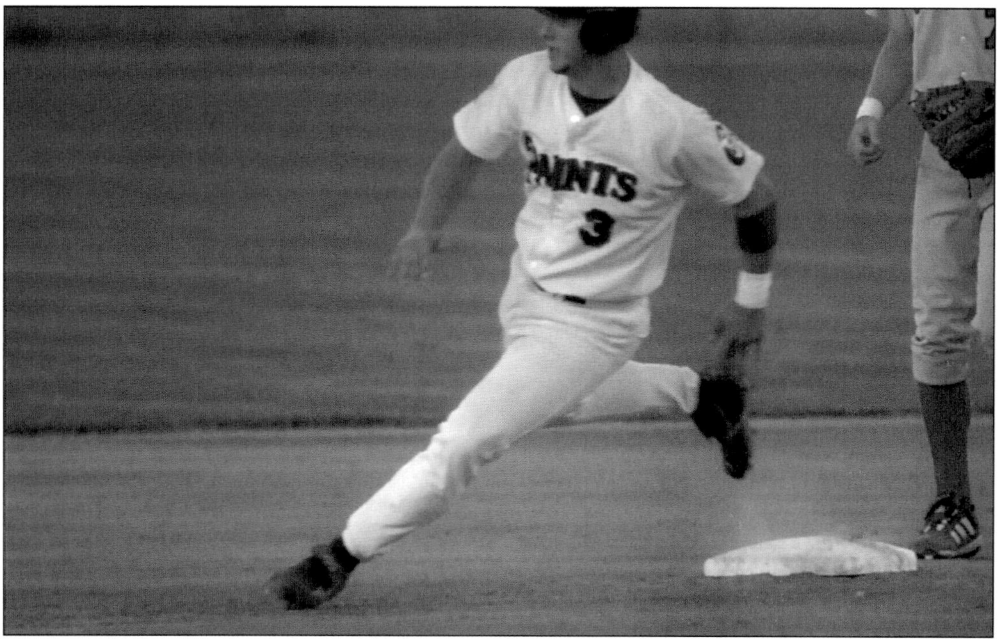

Hustling Vincent Cerni (Canfield, OH) was penciled in as a utility infielder for 2001, but he became the Paints' regular third baseman when Radames Torres did not hit as expected. A product of the University of West Florida, Cerni played in 70 games and batted .264 with 16 doubles, one homer, and 40 RBI. The Paints released Cerni before the start of the 2002 season but re-signed him right after the All-Star break and installed him as the regular second baseman. A torrid hitting streak enabled him to overcome a very slow start at the plate and to finish the year at .258 with three homers and 22 RBI. He was nominated for the Paints' 10th Anniversary Dream Team. (Courtesy of the *Chillicothe Gazette*.)

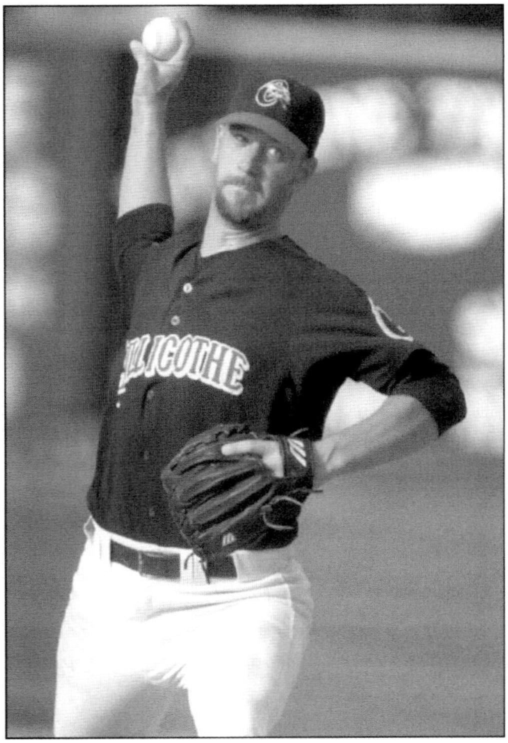

In his second season with the team Sean Boesch teamed with Rick Blanc to give the Paints the best 1-2 punch of any starting rotation in the league. Nicknamed "Bulldog" for his competitiveness and intimidating glare, Boesch started 18 games, pitched four complete games, and compiled a 9-4 record with an ERA of 4.28. When the Frontier League's limitation on veteran players forced Jamie Keefe to cut Boesch and Woody Fullenkamp in the spring of 2002, the Paints' manager paid them both a heartfelt tribute: "These are guys who we think are all-time Paints—it hurts." (Courtesy of the *Chillicothe Gazette*.)

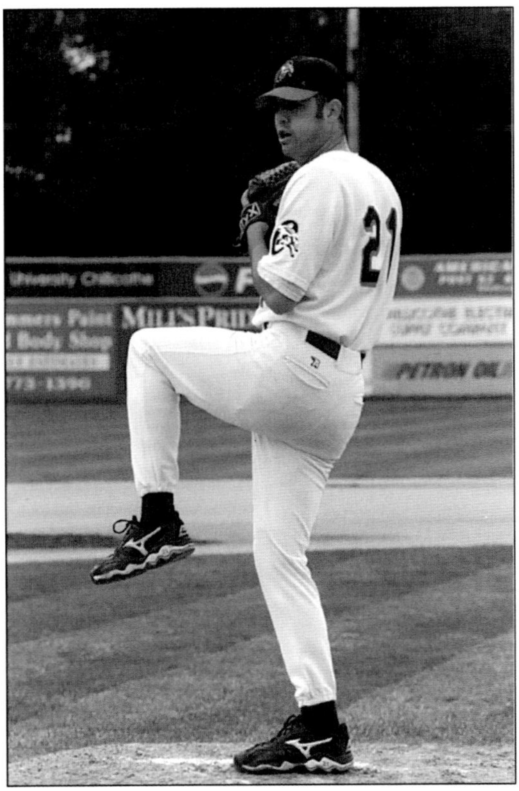

Jason Harrison joined the Paints in mid-season 2000 and pitched well out of the bullpen, recording a 2-0 ledger with a 2.16 ERA in 25.2 innings. The fastballer from Mt. Airy, Maryland, started 17 games in 2001 and finished with a 5-5 record and an ERA of 4.70. His 112 strikeouts led the team. Harrison started Game Three of the first round of the 2001 playoffs against Canton. He went 5 1/3 innings, allowing five hits and two runs, and got a No Decision in the Paints' dramatic extra-inning victory. He also started Game Three of the Finals against Richmond and again wound up with a No Decision.

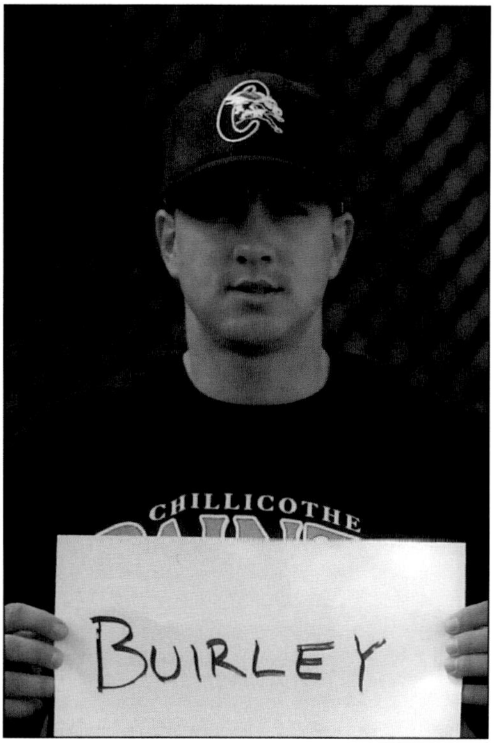

Relief pitcher Kris Buirley was the brother of Matt Buirley, who had pitched briefly and brilliantly for the 2000 Paints before signing with the Cincinnati Reds. Kris did the family name proud with the season he put together in 2001. He finished third on the team in wins with a 7-2 record and turned in a sparkling 2.49 ERA over 32 appearances. The former Marietta College ace added three saves and struck out 57 in 65 innings. Opponents barely batted .200 (.204) against Buirley in 2001. In 2002 Buirley's record slipped to 2-8, but he pitched well as his 3.56 ERA and team-leading 16 saves attested. He became a starting pitcher in 2003 to help the team and went 3-4 with an ERA of 4.39. (Courtesy of Scott Osborne.)

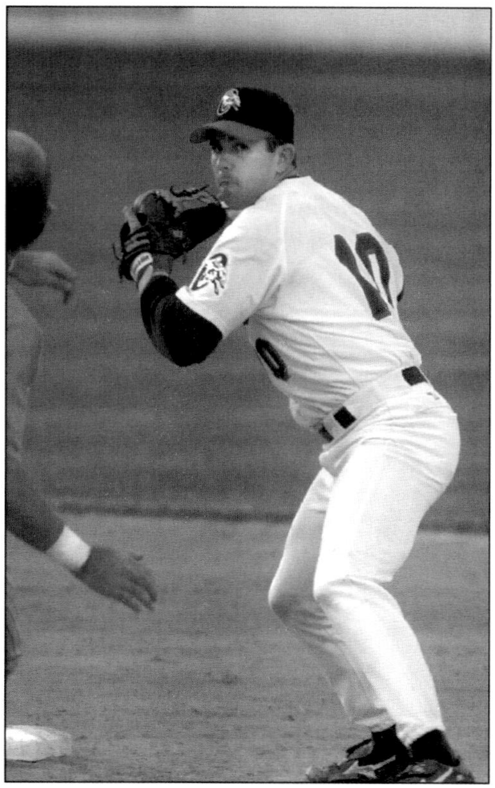

After spending the previous two seasons in the farm system of the Atlanta Braves, shortstop David Daulton returned to Chillicothe in 2001 for his second tour of duty with the Paints. He teamed with Kevin Connacher to form the best offensive and defensive double play combo in team history. Daulton batted .286 on the year with nine home runs and 45 RBI. He had many big days at the plate, including June 29 when he went 4-4 with a two-run homer in an 8-5 win at Richmond. Chillicothe fans voted Daulton onto the Paints' 10th Anniversary Dream Team. (Courtesy of Scott Osborne.)

Six

The Roller Coaster Ride Continues 2002–2004

The year (2002) the Paints celebrated their 10th season opened ominously with the death of Roger Hanners, who died on January 24 of a heart attack at the age of 70. The death was front-page news in the Chillicothe Gazette, and tributes to the former beloved Paints' manager poured in. To honor Hanners Commissioner Bill Lee announced that the Frontier League's Manager of the Year Award would be named after him.

The Paints had high hopes for 2002 with Jason Graham, Rick Blanc, and long-coveted slugger Willie Edwards, acquired in a trade, filling the three "Veteran" slots on the roster; but injuries, inconsistency, and atrocious defense did the team in. The Paints were eliminated from the playoffs with 12 games to go and finished with a 35-49 record. Nevertheless, 2002 did produce some highlights, such as Adam Patterson's hitting the 500th home run in Paints' history, the ceremonies which honored the members of the 10th Anniversary Dream Team, Blanc's team career record 300th strikeout and 25th win, and Eric Rossy's basehit which scored Vincent Cerni with the run that won a 17-inning marathon at V.A. Memorial against Richmond.

The Paints were right back on top in 2003, as they compiled not only the best record (54-31) in the league, but also the best record in team history. The team was led on offense by a trio of stars enjoying their last hurrah in Chillicothe—Darin Kinsolving, Matt McCay, and Rusty Swackhamer—and by another trio of newcomers: Tony Cosentino, Adrian Gascon, and Doug Dreher. While not dominating, the pitching was solid from top to bottom, with the most consistent contributions coming from starter Jeff Hunter and relievers Jeremy Durkee, Mike Gits, Ramon Royce, and Mark Skrukrud. Unfortunately, the Paints, once again, could not finish the job. They lost the opening round of the playoffs to the Evansville Otters two games to one, marking Chillicothe's sixth trip in eleven seasons to post-season play without bringing home the coveted Frontier League Cup.

The roller coaster ride that Paints' fans have been on for so long went back down in 2004, as Chillicothe finished out of the playoffs in fourth place in the East Division, 14 games behind the first-place Washington Wild Things. The Paints' playoff aspirations were severely damaged when ace starting pitcher Mark Hamilton was signed by the Milwaukee Brewers halfway through the season, but the team had already demonstrated that its streakiness would be its downfall. After winning six of the year's first seven games, the Paints lost nine of ten a week later. Then, after losing eight of nine right before the All-Star break, the team won eleven of 14. The team just never could hit its stride and had to rally with four wins in the last six games to finish at .500 (48-48) for the year. Returning stars Adrian Gascon, Tony Cosentino, and Doug Dreher all had fine years at bat, as did power-hitting newcomers Beau Blacken and Dustin Brisson. Starting pitchers Perry Cunningham and Josh Rahrer each won seven games, while Ramon Royce with 17 saves and Mike Gits with a 6-3 record and a 3.11 ERA provided effective pitching out of the bullpen. If history is any guide, the Chillicothe Paints will bounce back strong in 2005.

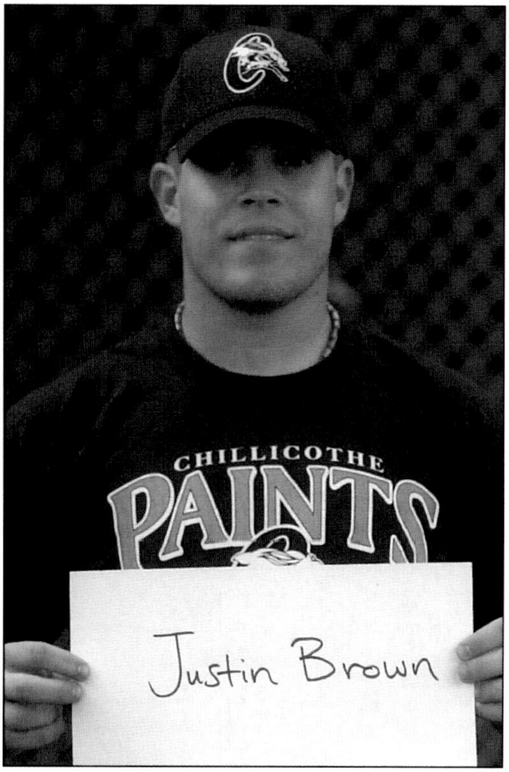

Infielder Justin Brown was a former Chillicothe High School standout whom the Paints discovered in Kalamazoo, Michigan, at the 2002 Frontier League tryouts. After going 3-5 on June 10, Brown was batting .389 (14-36), but he wasn't able to keep up that pace and finished the year at .233 with no homers and seven RBI in 49 games. Justin played college ball for Division III Urbana (OH) University and ended his career there ranked in the top five of most batting categories. (Courtesy of Scott Osborne.)

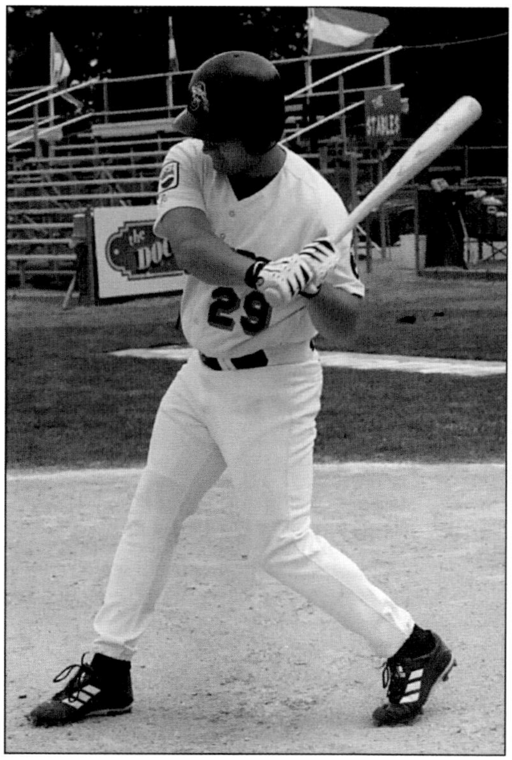

Rusty Swackhamer was a slugging outfielder-first baseman-DH with the most onomatopoetic name in Paints' history. A native of nearby Hillsboro, Ohio, who played college ball at East Tennessee State University, "Swack" debuted with the Paints in 2001. He appeared in 37 games and batted .245 with six home runs and 15 RBI. In 2002 Rusty played in 65 games and batted .275 with five homers and 41 RBI. On June 8 Swackhamer hit a pinch-hit grand slam against the Richmond Roosters. He did even better in back-to-back games in late July, collecting seven straight hits and reaching base safely eight straight times.

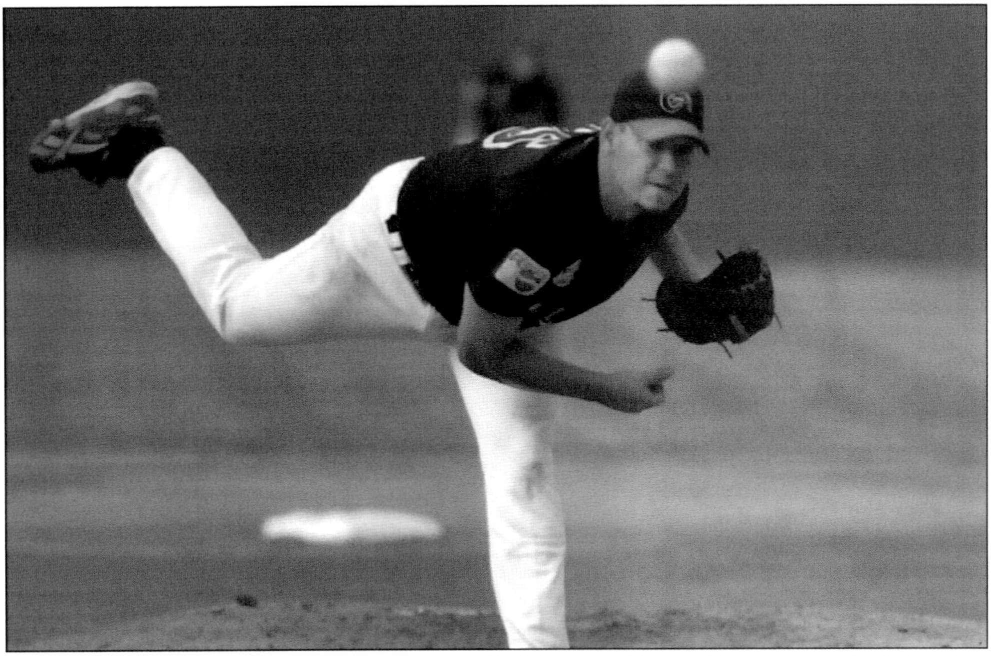

After a great high school career, Sciotoville (OH) native Dustin Sampson pitched for Kent State University where he compiled a 42-23 career record in 227 innings. The Paints signed him after he displayed a good fastball and a sharp breaking ball in a preseason tryout camp. Sampson started 14 games in 2002 but his effectiveness was limited by elbow problems. He went 5-5 with a 5.60 ERA. (Courtesy of Scott Osborne.)

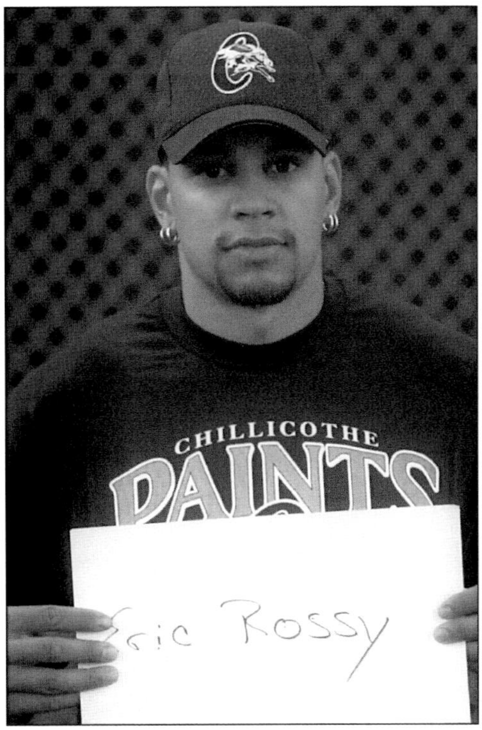

Eric Rossy looked more like a linebacker (6'2", 200 lbs.) than a middle infielder, but the Paints liked him after he showed in tryouts that he had all the tools. Rossy spent 2001 in the independent Northern League with the New Jersey Jackals, where he hit .246 with one homer and 14 RBI in 52 games. Nagging injuries kept Rossy from performing at his peak, and he finished the 2002 season batting .235 with five homers and 25 RBI in 59 games. Prior to turning pro, Eric had played at Downing College in New York, where he was named NCAA Division II Player of the Year in 2000. (Courtesy of Scott Osborne.)

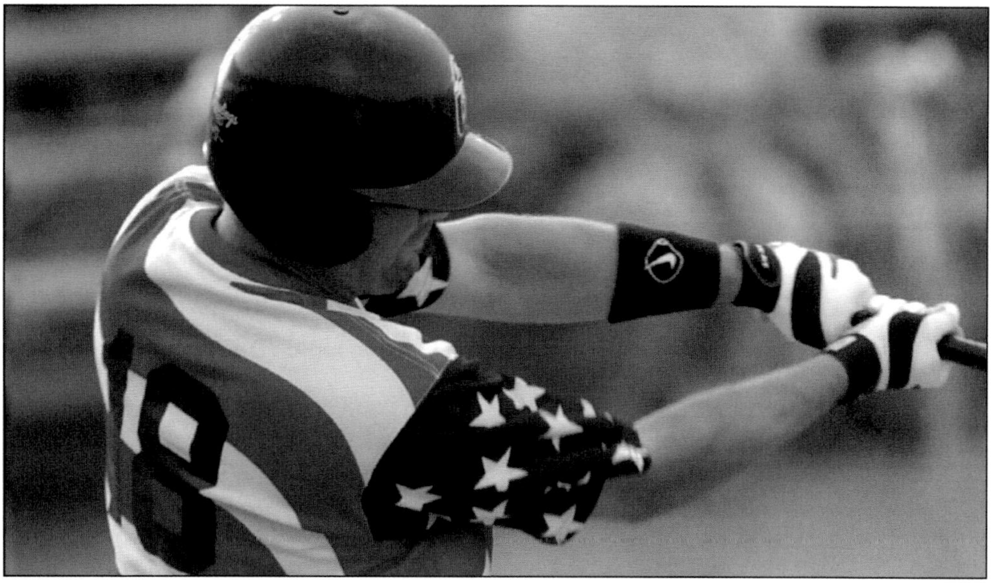

For the second year in a row Matt McCay collected more than 100 hits (105) and compiled the Paints' highest batting average: a mark of .322, which was 17th best in the Frontier League for 2002. McCay also improved his power numbers, swatting seven home runs (second best on the team) and driving in 50 runs. The Hillsborough, North Carolina native was voted co-winner of the Paints' Most Valuable Player Award with Darin Kinsolving. When informed of the vote, the humble McCay expressed astonishment that his teammates regarded him so highly. (Courtesy of the *Chillicothe Gazette*.)

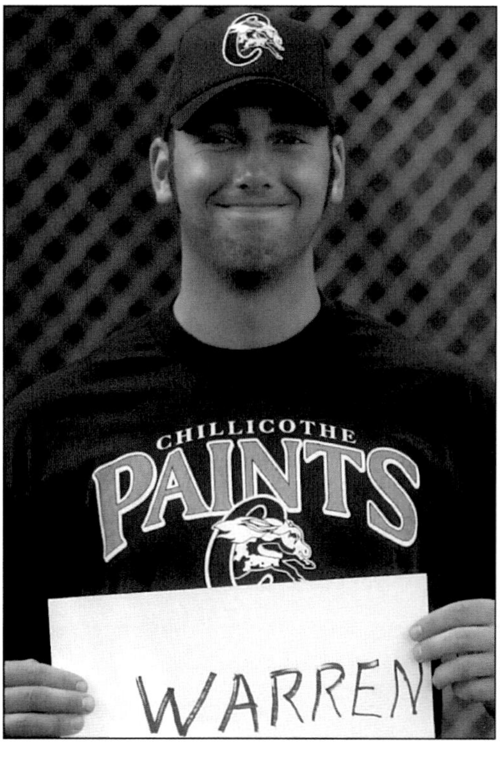

After Phil Warren made his successful debut in the second half of 2000 (.317, 5 HR, 20 RBI in 32 games), Paints' fans were expecting big things of the graduate of Southeast Missouri State University. Injuries limited Warren to 18 games (and a .224 batting average) in 2001, but in 2002 he made good on his potential. He played in 67 games and batted .314 with three home runs and 41 RBI. In a July 31 9-7 win over the River City Rascals in O'Fallon, Missouri, Phil hit a grand slam and knocked in six runs. Warren moved on to the Gateway Grizzlies and put together two great years; especially in 2004 when he led the league in home runs and extra-base hits and was named to the Frontier League All-Star Team. (Courtesy of Scott Osborne.)

Jason (aka Jess) was the original Graham brother to play for Chillicothe, signing with the Paints out of Ohio University towards the end of June 1997. Jason had an outstanding professional debut in 1997 (.349, 3 HR, 17 RBI) and signed with the Boston Red Sox. He returned to the Paints in 2002 and was counted on heavily to provide offensive production but had difficulty getting untracked. In 62 games he batted .217 with one homer and 17 RBI. (Courtesy of Scott Osborne.)

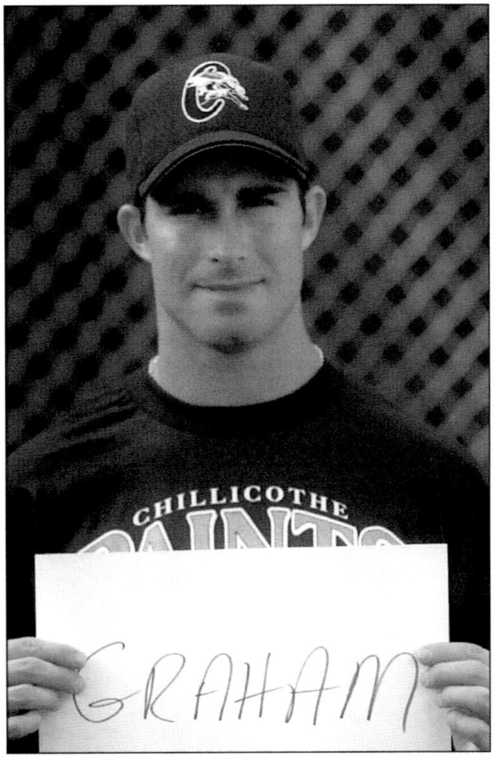

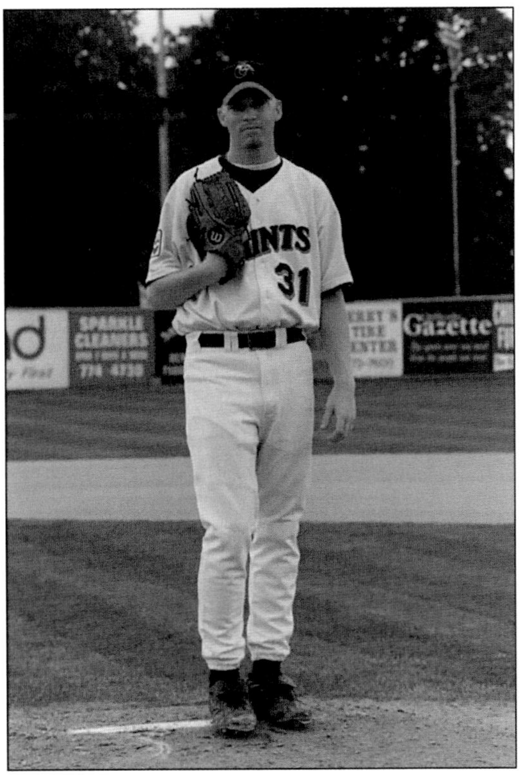

Manager Jamie Keefe called Brian Bogs "one of the top two left-handed relievers we've ever had here." Armed with a "Bugs Bunny Slider," Bogs was usually called on to retire tough left-handed hitters in clutch situations. In 2001 Bogs pitched 52.1 innings over 30 games and had a 2-0 record with one save and a 4.13 ERA. The following year the former Indiana University-Purdue University Mastodon pitched 43.2 innings and set a Paints' record by appearing in 50 games. His record in 2002 was 2-2 with four saves and an ERA of 3.30. Bogs was nominated for the Paints' 10th Anniversary Dream Team.

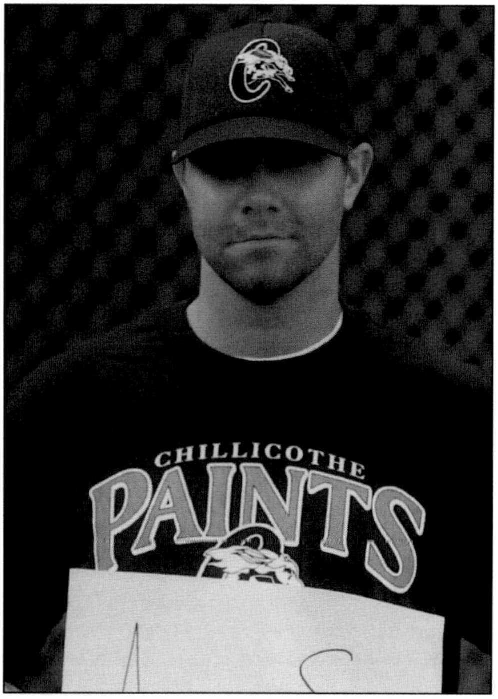

Andrew See was Mr. Versatility for the Paints during his three-year career in Chillicothe, at one time or another catching, pitching, DH-ing, pinch hitting, and playing third and the outfield. Although he batted only .242 in 91 at bats in 2001, he got more than his share of clutch hits. For example, on August 19 he was called out of the bullpen to pinch hit and delivered a two-out, two-run, game-winning single against London. He struck out 15 batters in 12.2 innings in 2001 and became more of a pitcher in 2002 and especially in 2003. He went 3-3 with one save in 19 games in 2002, and in 2003 he posted a 2-1 record with a 4.26 ERA and a team-leading eight saves. See was from Adrian, Michigan, and attended Ohio University where he twice earned All-MAC honors. (Courtesy of Scott Osborne.)

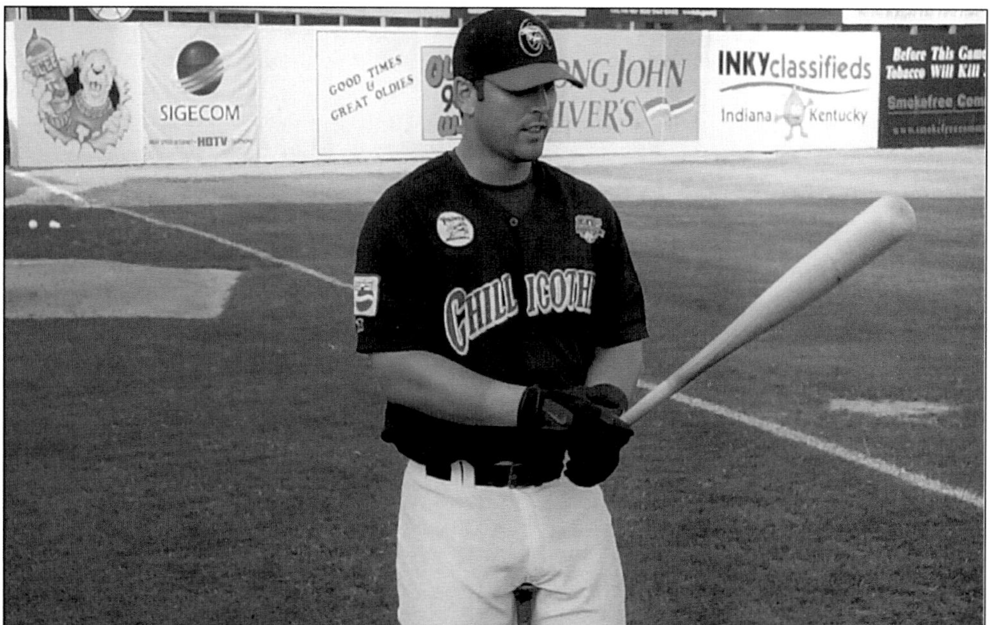

Darin Kinsolving returned to Chillicothe in 2002 and proved that his success the year before was no fluke. He batted .295 in 76 games and lead the team in home runs with 15 and RBI with 58. He hit a pair of two-run home runs in the third game of the season and was named to the East Division All-Star team. At the end of the season his teammates voted him the co-winner (with Matt McKay) of the team Most Valuable Player Award. (Courtesy of Tim Reiter.)

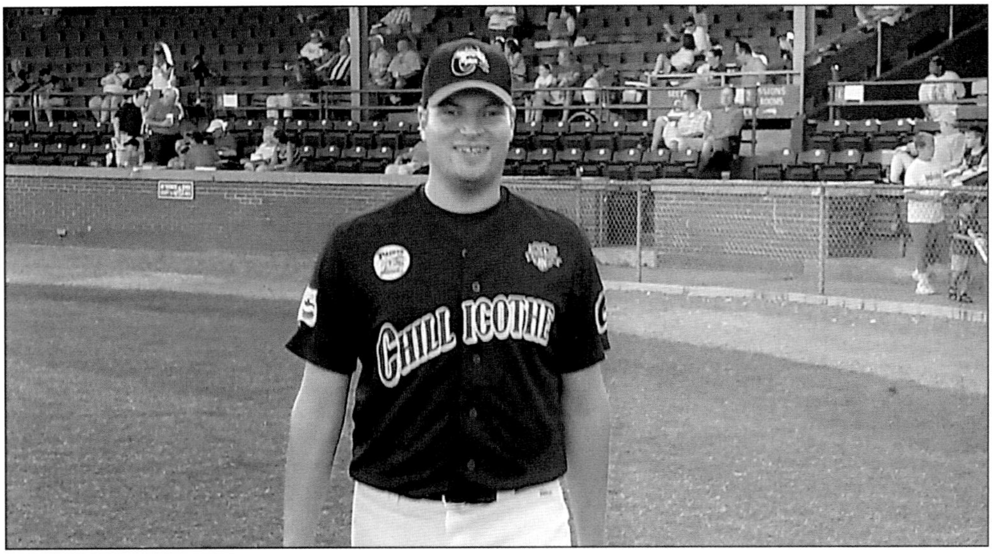

Tony Schiml was a big (6'3", 220 lbs.) left-handed starting pitcher from Dayton, Ohio, who ate up a lot of innings for the Paints in his two seasons (2002–03) in Chillicothe. Schiml threw 105 innings in 2002 (second most on the team) and won a team-high seven games (against five losses) with an ERA of 4.80. He upped his workload to 109 innings in 2003 (tops on the team), while lowering his ERA to 4.21 and winning five games in 11 decisions. The former Ohio University Bobcat also pitched one shutout in each of his seasons in Paints' navy and white. (Courtesy of Tim Reiter.)

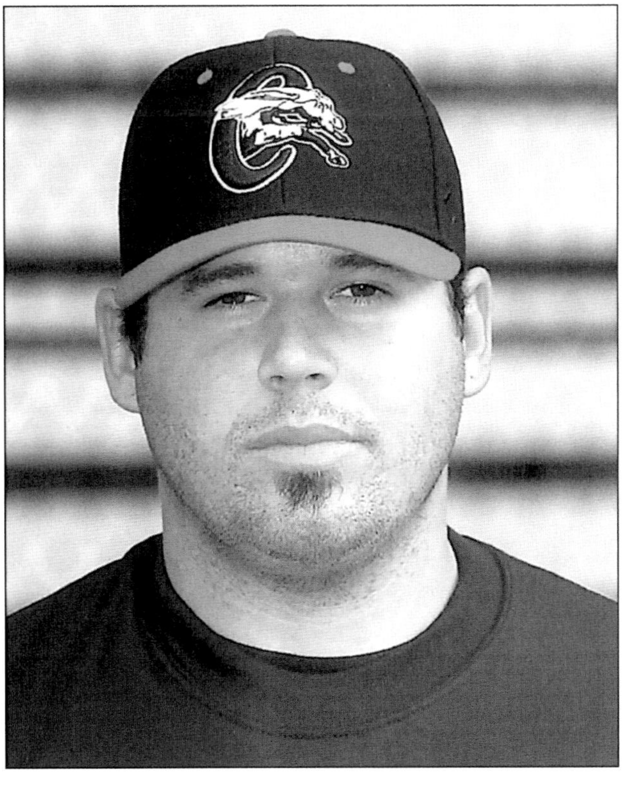

The Paints were so worried about the catching position that the organization looked at ten prospective catchers during the spring training of 2003. Luckily for Chillicothe, stocky Tony Cosentino from Torrance, California, was one of those candidates. An eight-year veteran of professional baseball who'd spent five years in the Padres' farm system, Cosentino was an excellent receiver with a good arm and an ability to swing the bat. He batted .287 with three home runs and 41 RBI.

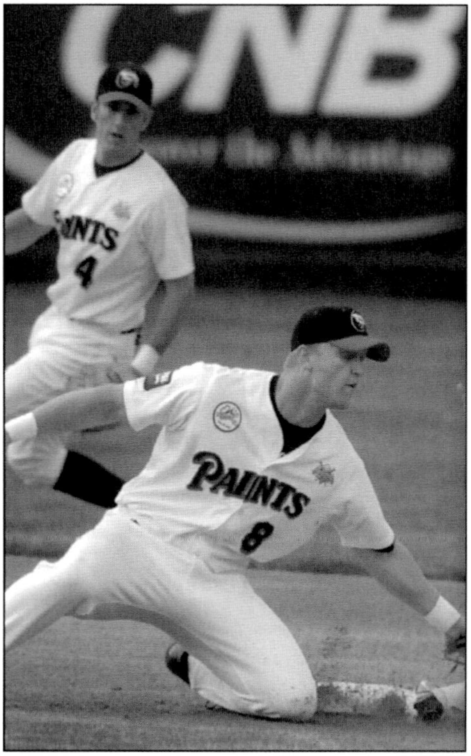

Shortstop Nick Elrod (foreground) and second baseman Corey Loomis (background) had been teammates and an outstanding double-play combination at Bowling Green (OH) State University. Elrod batted .293 in 16 games for the Paints in 2002 before he broke his collarbone and nose in a collision with a runner at second base. He played in 44 games in 2003, batting .231 with two homers and 19 RBI. The Paints' regular second sacker in 2003, Loomis batted .237 in 74 games with four homers and 30 RBI. (Courtesy of the *Chillicothe Gazette*.)

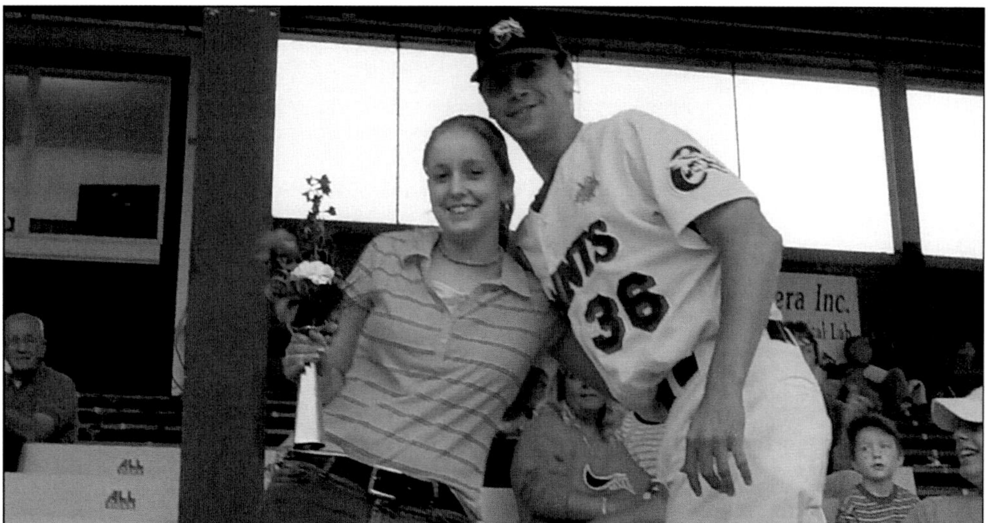

After spending two years in the farm system of the Seattle Mariners, relief pitcher Ramon Royce brought his live arm and colorful personality to Chillicothe halfway through the 2003 season. Royce usually resisted conventional camera poses, and refused to look at the camera for team pictures. He was also once seen sprinting down the streets of downtown Chillicothe at midnight, his explanation being that scavenging raccoons had been chasing him. Despite his quirkiness, Ramon had a big heart and was always ready to help his fellow man. He could also pitch. In 2003 he went 5-1 with six saves, a sparkling ERA of 0.65, and 30 strikeouts in 27.2 innings. In 2004 Ramon led the team in saves with 17. (Courtesy of Tim Reiter.)

Paints' manager Jamie Keefe acquired the services of right-handed pitcher Mike Gits by trading Jason Biddlestone to the Kalamazoo Kings. Keefe knew what he was doing, as the rubber-armed set-up man with the deceiving submarine delivery turned in a year that earned him the team's Most Valuable Pitcher Award for 2003. The Portland, Oregon native who'd played at Western Oregon University won seven games in 2003 (second best on the team), saved three others, and posted a 3.16 ERA.

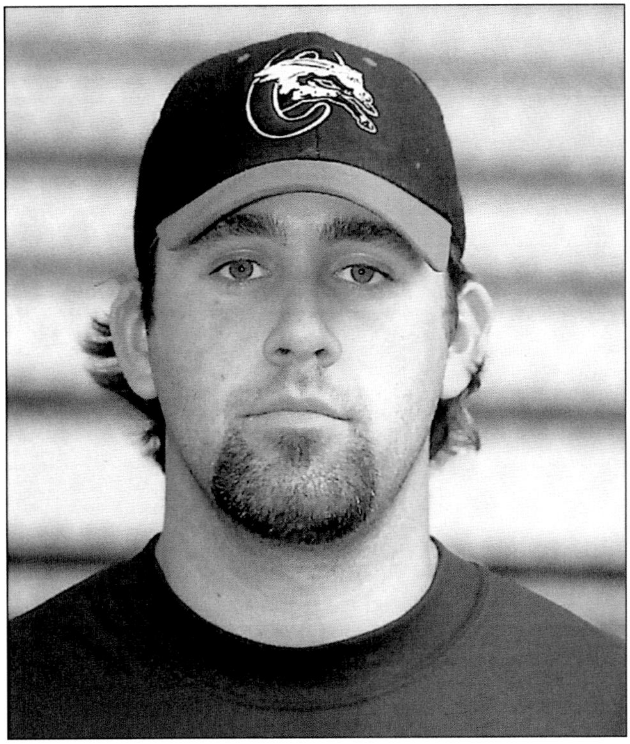

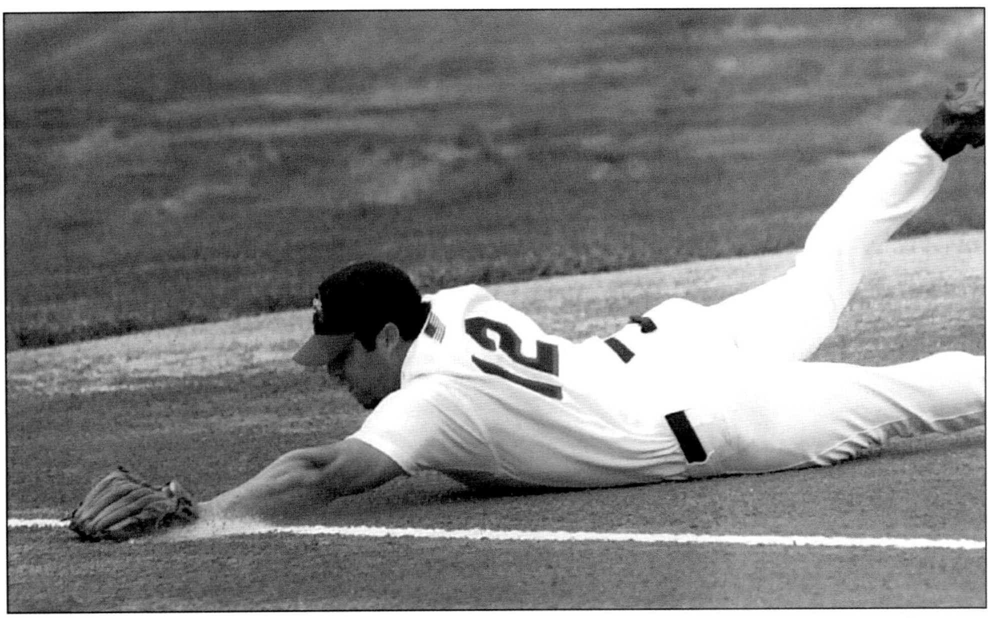

A native of Bayamon, Puerto Rico, Miguel "Mickey" Hernandez was the best Latin player in Paints' history. After playing at Seminole State College and Lamar University, Hernandez joined the Paints in 2002 and batted .298 with one homer and 21 RBI in 46 games. In August of 2003 he carried the team when a lot of players were banged up, and he finished the year batting .265 with nine homers and 37 RBI. Miguel was also a fine defensive third baseman. (Courtesy of the *Chillicothe Gazette*.)

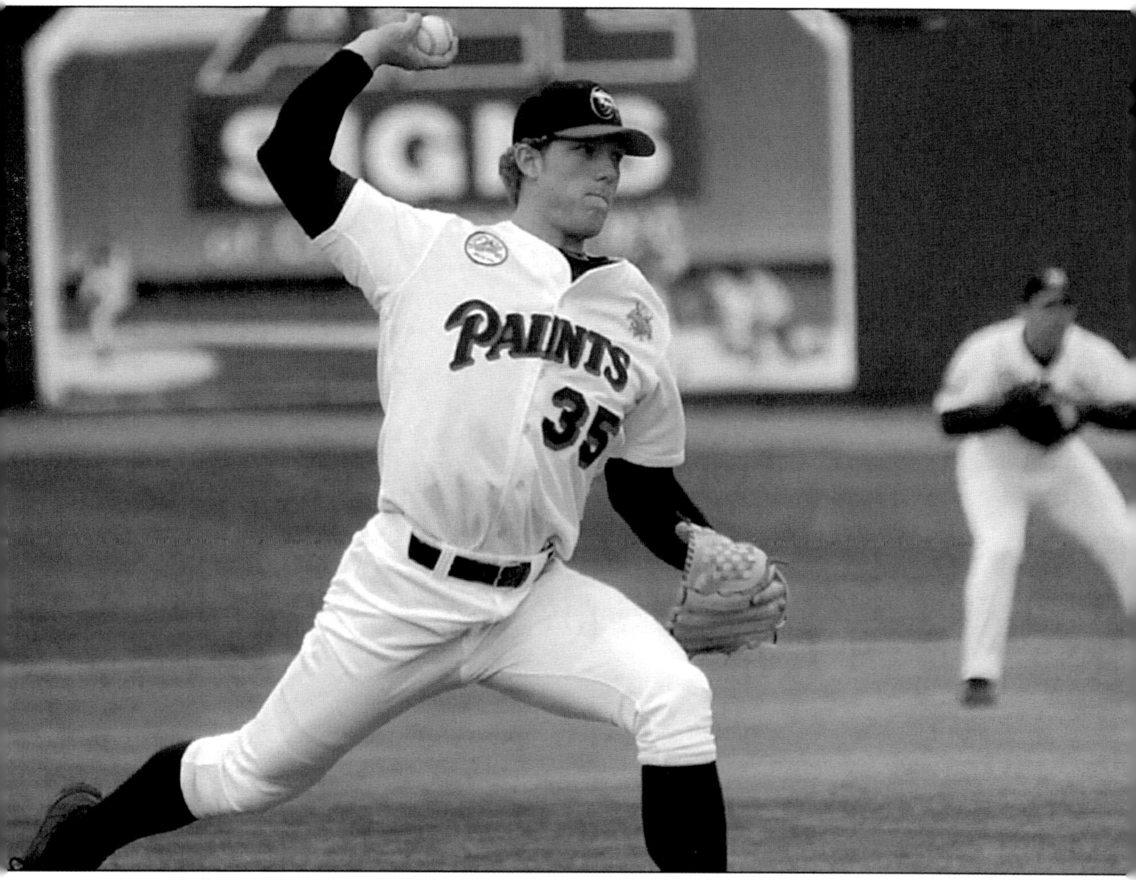

An eighth-round draft pick of the Texas Rangers, Josh Rahrer (from Emmitt, ID) went into pro baseball right out of high school. After being released by Texas, he went 4-7 in 2002, his first year in Chillicothe. In 2003 Josh went 8-3 with a 4.30 ERA, and in 2004 he went 7-4 with a 4.62 ERA. Over the three-year period Rahrer appeared in 46 games for the Paints, all of them as a starting pitcher. (Courtesy of the *Chillicothe Gazette*.)

"He's no bigger than a minute, but he'd run through the scoreboard for you," said Jamie Keefe about one of the coaching staff's favorite players: 5-foot-7 Doug Dreher of Hays, Kansas. Acquired from the Sioux Falls Canaries of the Northern League and signed as a utility man, Dreher became a regular in the Paints' outfield and appeared in 79 games in 2003. He hit .280 with one homer and 36 RBI, while leading the team in doubles with 21. Dreher became the regular second baseman in 2004 and had an even better year at the plate; hitting .324 with two home runs and 51 RBI. He also led the team in hits (120) and doubles (28). Doug showed off his versatility by playing every position on the field, an inning at a time, during the last game of the 2004 season.

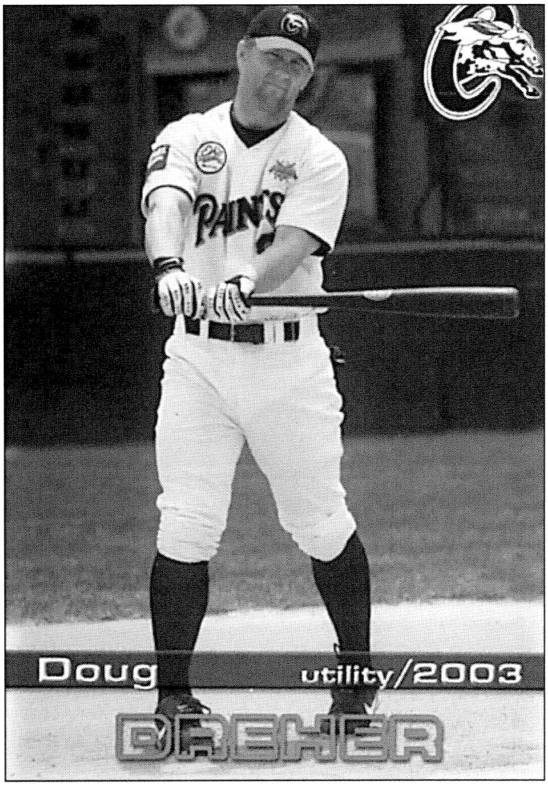

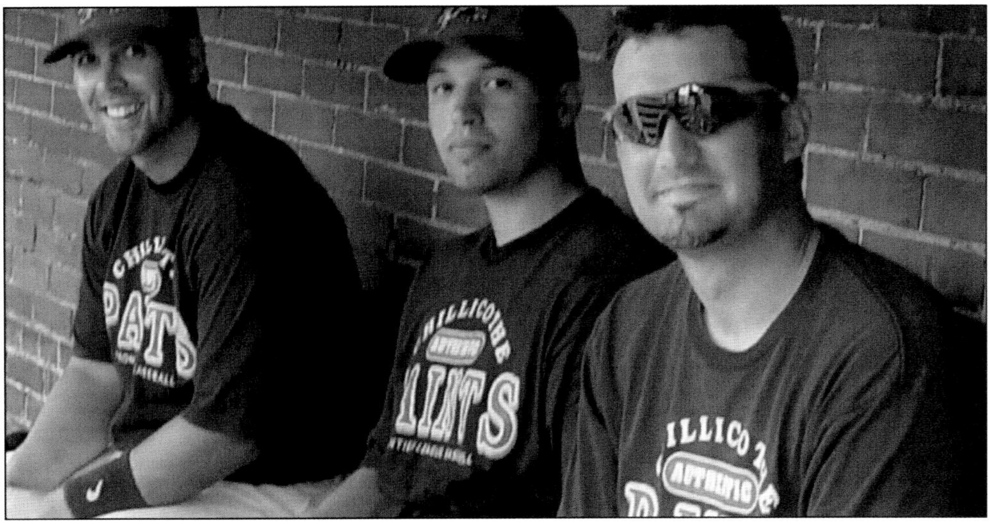

Pictured at the 2003 Frontier League All-Star Game played at Evansville's Bosse Field, from left to right, are Darin Kinsolving, rookie Adrian Gascon, and Matt McCay. Kinsolving made his final season the best of his career; batting .336 with 15 homers and 76 RBI. He won the Paints' MVP Award for the second year in a row and was named to the year-end Frontier League All-Star Team. Gascon (from Oxnard, California) began the season playing third base but moved to short after Nick Elrod's injury. Adrian finished the year batting .301 (ninth best in the league), with eight homers and 51 RBI. He was the shortstop voted onto the FL All-Star Team. (Courtesy of Tim Reiter.)

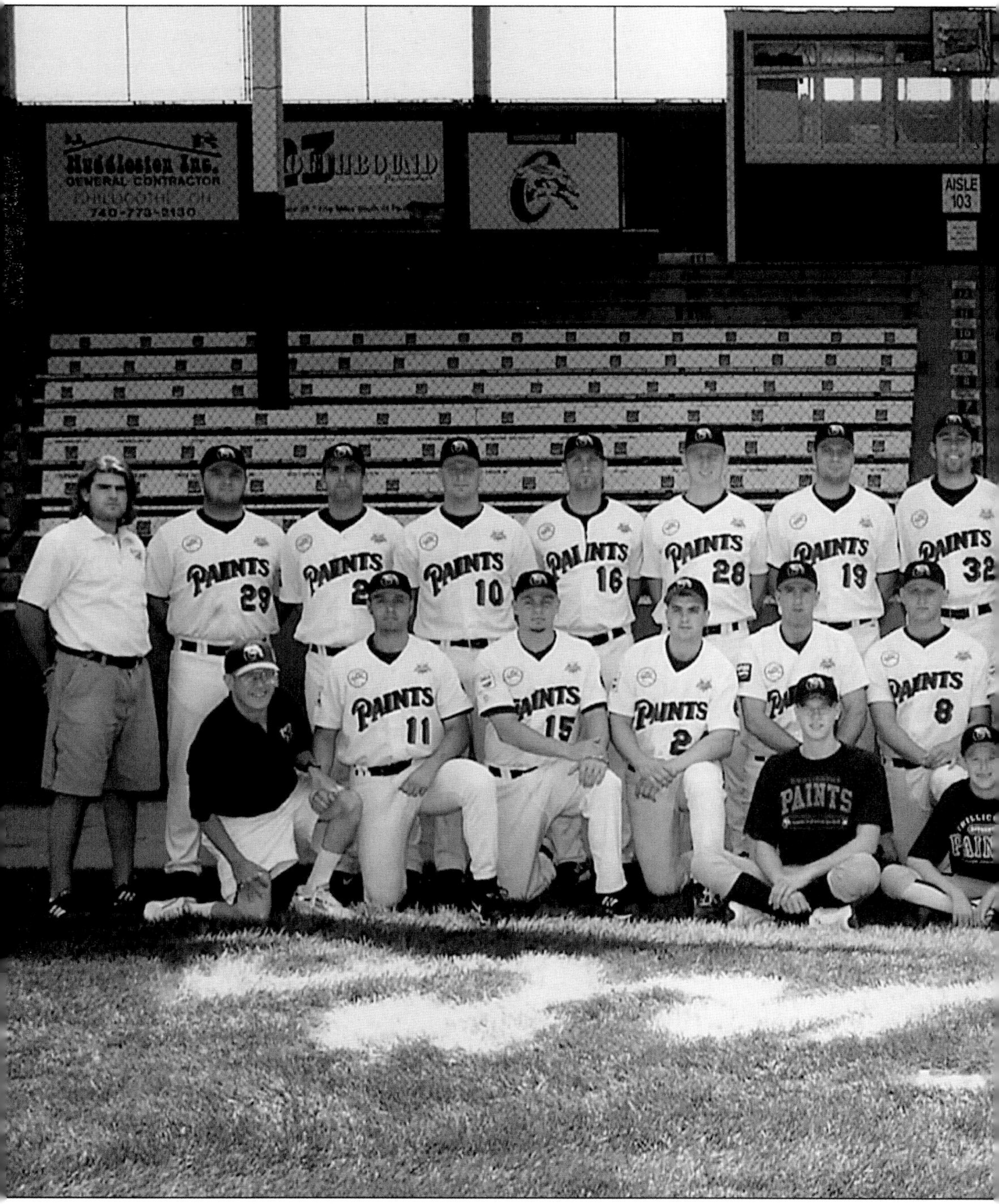

This is the official team photo of the 2003 Paints, who won the most games (54) in the history of the ballclub, finishing 23 games over .500. Pictured from left to right are: (front row) batboys Eric Kimsey, Alex Kimsey, Cody Chenault, and Danny Sneddon; (middle row) Butch Atteberry (equipment manager), Adrian Gascon (11), Mickey O'Quinn (15), Kris Buirley (24), Cory Loomis (4), Nick Elrod (8), Scott Pickens (33), Doug Dreher (9), Tony Cosentino (37), Mark

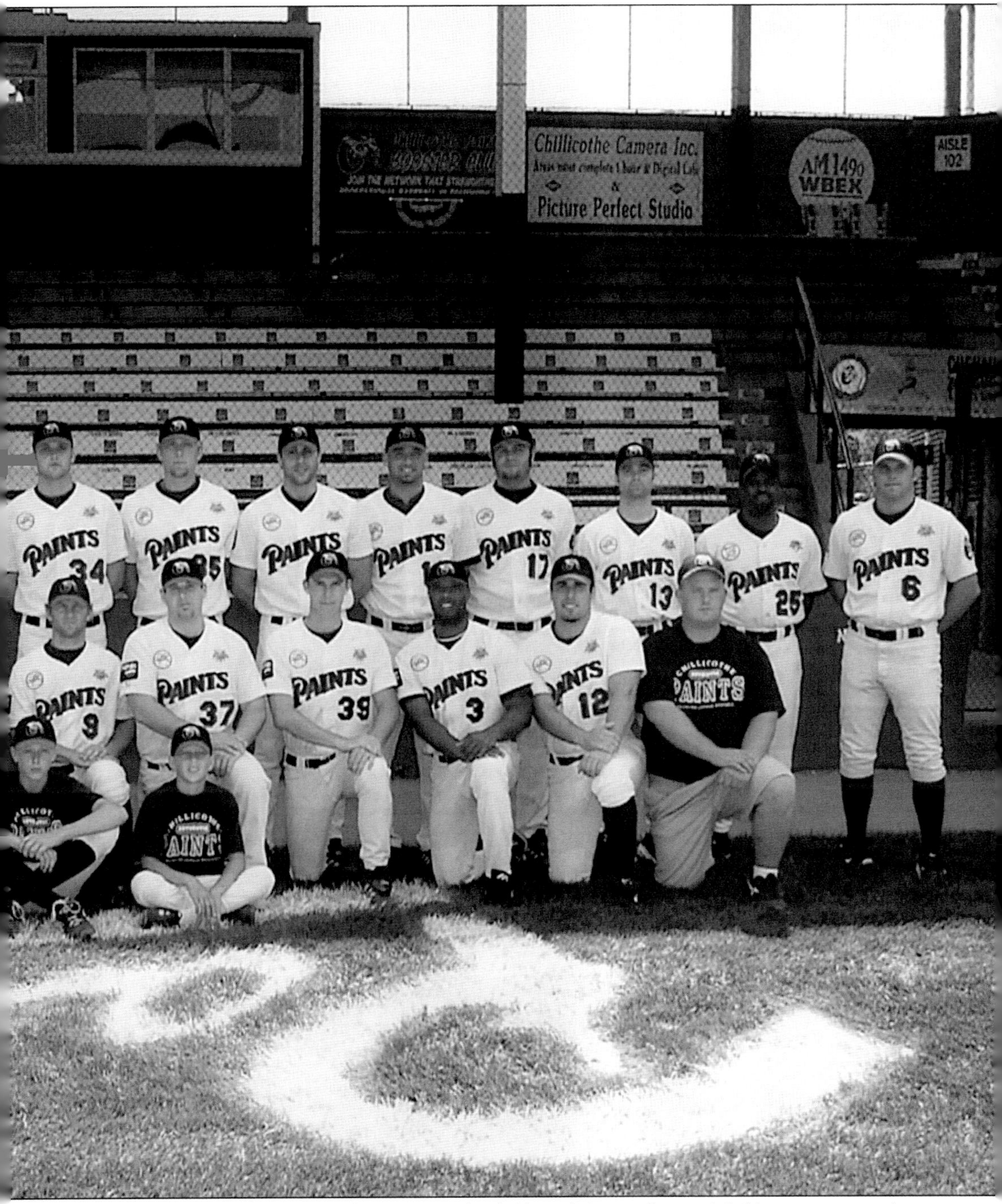

Skrukrud (39), J.R. Revere (3), Mickey Hernandez (12), and Aaron Queen (clubhouse manager); (back row) Aaron Schreiner (trainer), Rusty Swackhamer (26), Darin Kinsolving (23), Brian Epke (10), Andrew See (16), Jeremy Durkee (28), Tony Schiml (19), Mike Gits (32), Ramon Royce (36), Jeff Hunter (34), Josh Rahrer (35), Joe Colameco (26), Matt McCay (18), Michael Kesten (17), Rick Blanc (Coach), Marty Dunn (coach), and Jamie Keefe (manager).

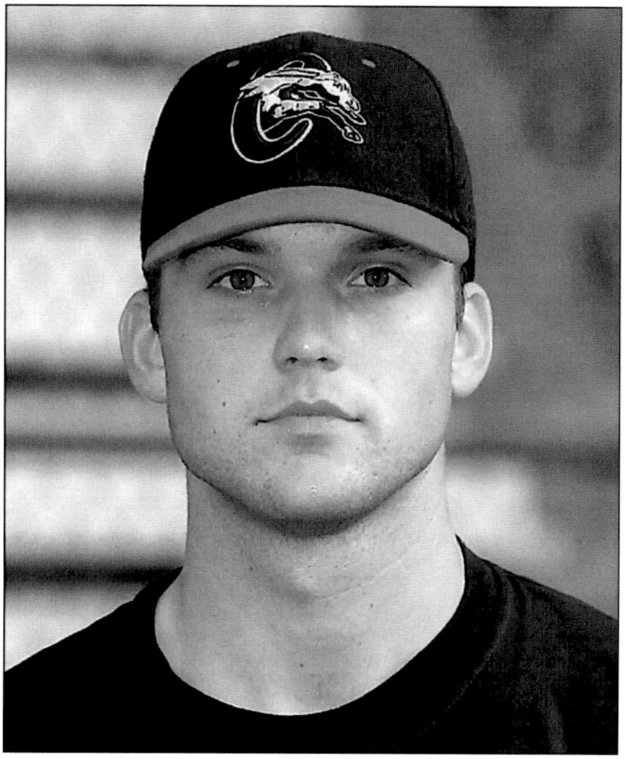

Mississippi native (Columbus, MS) Jeff Hunter started his pro baseball career in Chillicothe in 2003 after having pitched for Meridian Community College and Mississippi State University. Jeff posted a 5-3 record, an ERA of 3.15, and an outstanding 61 to 11 strikeout-to-walk ratio in his rookie season. The fastball/changeup pitcher began the 2004 campaign as the Paints' number one starter, but a shoulder injury contributed to his 0-3 start and landed him on Injured Reserve for three weeks. Hunter returned to action throwing well enough to boost his final record to 4-4 with an ERA of 4.20.

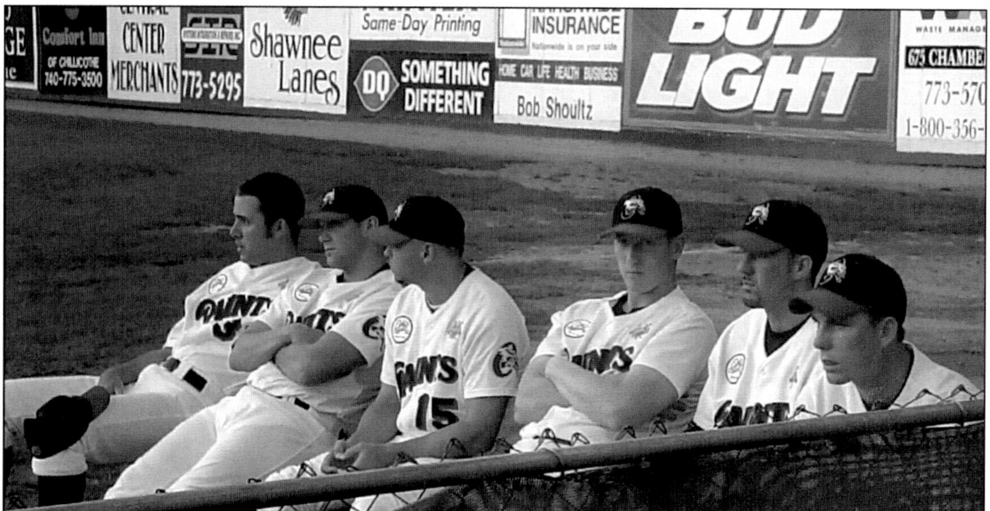

Unneeded for the moment, the Paints' bullpen for 2003 play the role of spectators. Pictured from left to right are Mike Gits, Andrew See, Mickey O'Quinn, Jeremy Durkee, James Callahan, and Mark Skrukrud. See appeared in 22 games and posted a 2-1 record with a team-leading eight saves and a 4.26 ERA. O'Quinn, a former Central League player (San Angelo Colts), took the mound 26 times and put together a 5-3 record with a 4.26 ERA. Callahan pitched only 6.1 innings (over seven games), while the left-handed Skrukrud started eight games and relieved in eight others. A rookie out of Northern Illinois, Skrukrud turned in the third-lowest ERA on the team (2.94) and a record of 4-3 over 67.1 innings. (Courtesy of Tim Reiter.)

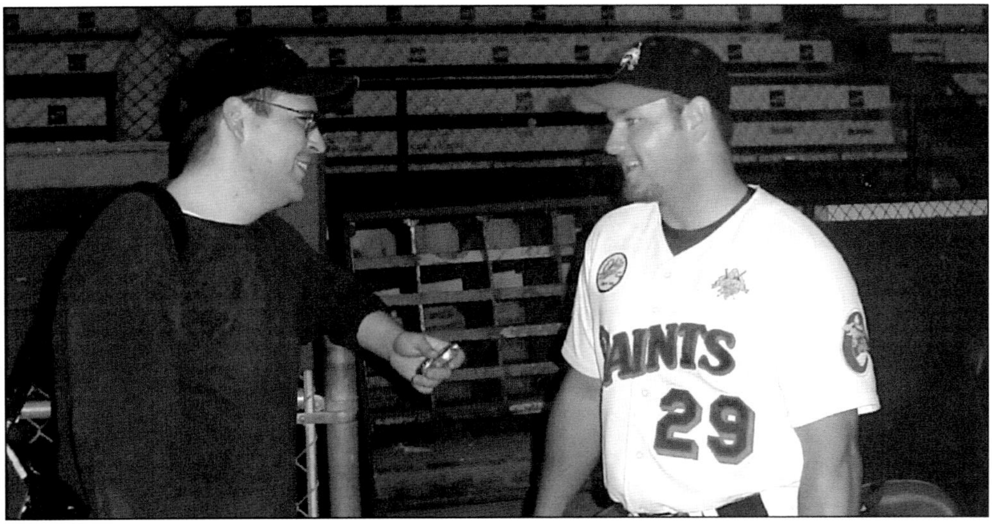

Designated hitter Rusty Swackhamer, the all-time Paints' leader in pinch-hit home runs, is shown here being interviewed by *Chillicothe Gazette* beat writer Phil Gray. His batting average dropped a bit in 2003 (.259) from the previous year, but "Swack" was an important run producer, slugging 12 homers and knocking in 47 runs, the second-highest totals on the team in both categories. A native of Jodie, West Virginia and a graduate of West Virginia University, Gray began covering the Paints in 2000. His writing, insightful and empathetic, continues the Gazette's tradition of providing outstanding coverage of the team. (Courtesy of Tim Reiter.)

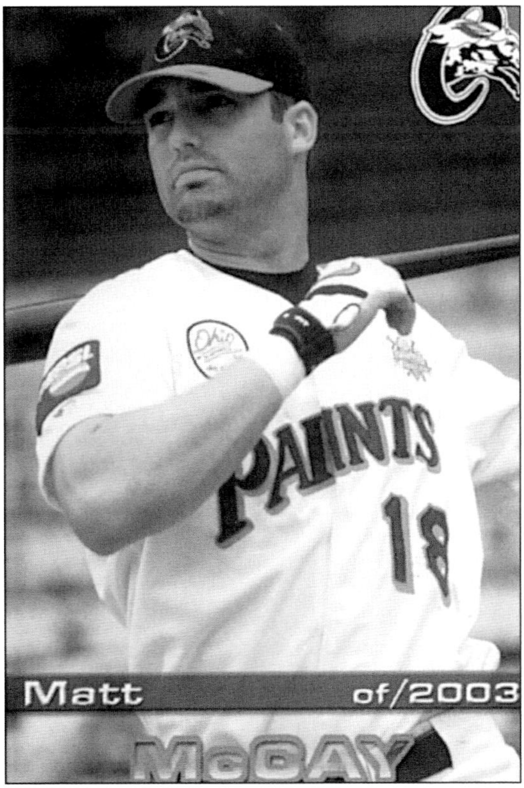

Matt McCay played one final season in Chillicothe in 2003 before moving on to the Northern League. Matt's batting statistics slipped a little from the previous season (.295, 6 HR , 35 RBI), but he was still an integral part of Chillicothe's pennant-winning ballclub. July 1, 2003, was a special day in Paints' history, as McCay collected his 303rd hit (a double against the Florence Freedom) in a Paints' uniform, making him the team's all-time hit leader and dropping Scott Pinoni into second place. McCay finished the season with 90 hits to raise his career-high hit total to 363. Paints' fans showed their appreciation of McCay by voting him onto the Paints' 10th Anniversary Dream Team as the right fielder, and local sportswriters did the same by naming him the 2003 Chillicothe Gazette Sportsperson of the Year.

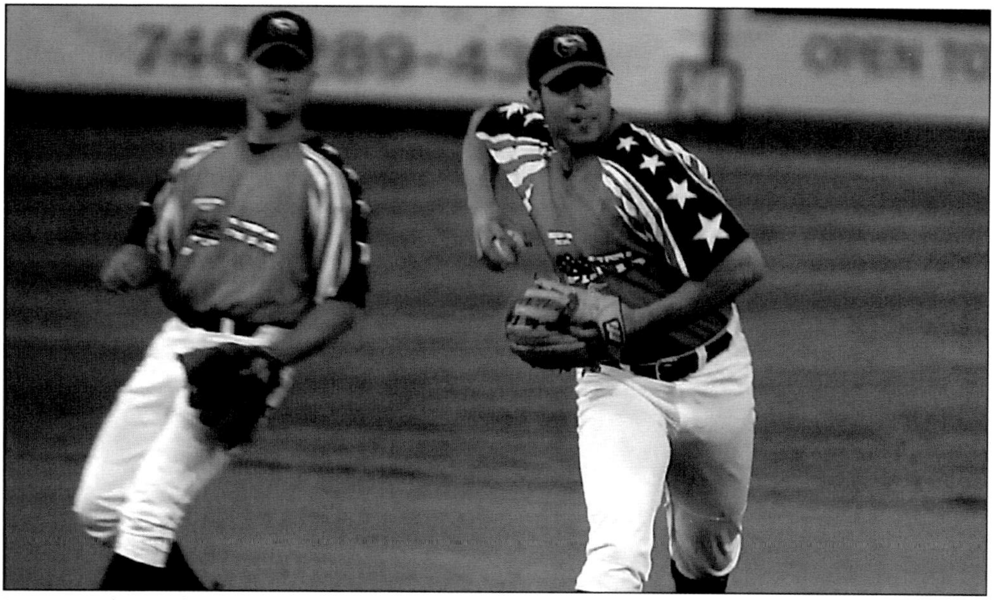

Ignoring the sophomore jinx, shortstop Adrian Gascon played so well in 2004 that he was voted onto the Frontier League All-Star Team for the second year in a row. Gascon, who played collegiately for Oklahoma Baptist University, batted .309, while leading the team in RBI (66) and collecting the second-most hits (116). Adrian had a 5-5 day against the Washington Wild Things on June 15. (Courtesy of Scott Osborne.)

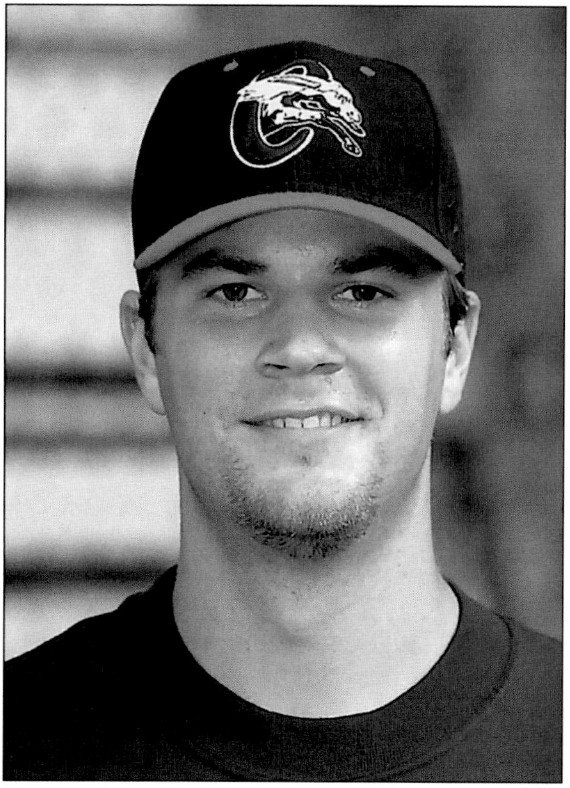

Picked up a week before the start of the 2004 season when OF James Shanks signed with the Florida Marlins, pitcher-outfielder Mark Hamilton turned out to be, in Jamie Keefe's words, "the best player on the team." A former 23rd round draftee out of Texas Christian University, Hamilton had spent four years in the Houston Astros' farm system, and he performed so well with the Paints that the Milwaukee Brewers purchased his contract half way through the season. At the time of his departure Hamilton was batting .323 (ninth best in the league) with three homers and 31 RBI. On the mound he was even more impressive. Despite a 4-5 record, he led the league in complete games with seven, and he became the first pitcher in Paints' history to throw back-to-back shutouts. He struck out 95 in 88 innings, and his ERA was a sparkling 2.25 (fourth best in the league).

As the Paints' third string catcher in 2003, Scott Pickens played in 12 games and batted .188. He started 2004 as the second string backstop but improved so much as a receiver that he played more and more as the season progressed. The former Central Michigan University Chippewa batted .240 in 51 games with two home runs and 13 RBI.

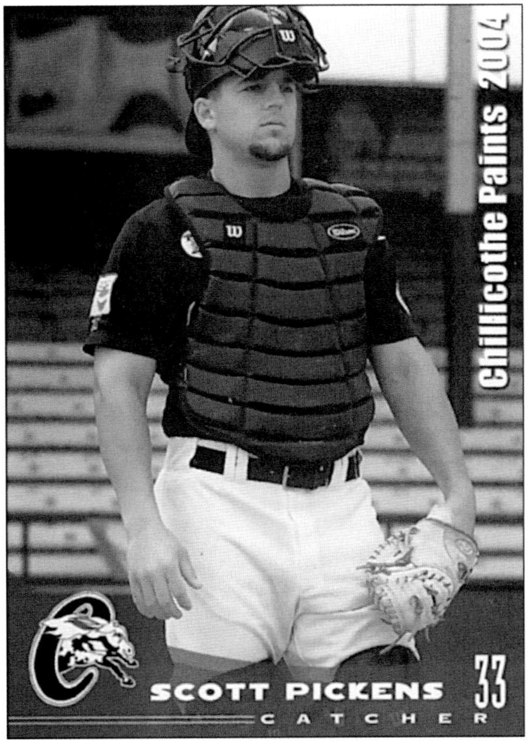

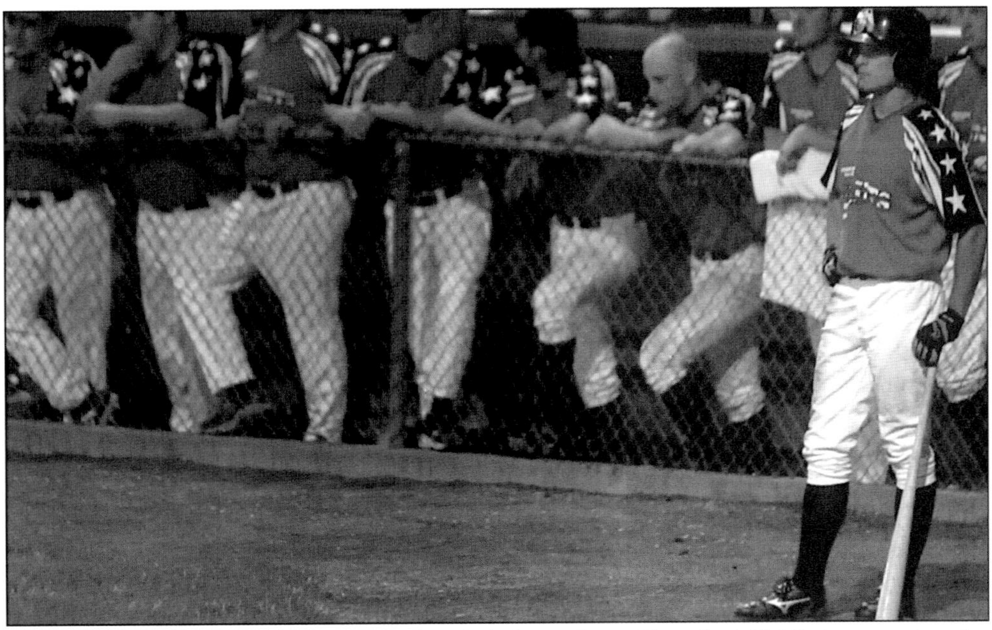

Wearing jerseys designed to honor America's Independence Day, the 2004 Paints stand at the fence in front of their dugout, trying to will a game-winning rally against the Kalamazoo Kings into being. Standing at the right is outfielder Chris Tuttle (hometown: Lagrange, Ohio) who, as a sophomore at Wright State University, won the 2001 NCAA Division I batting title with a .478 average. The Paints acquired Tuttle from the Richmond Roosters in late June, and Tuttle went on to hit .270 for Chillicothe in 47 games. (Courtesy of Scott Osborne.)

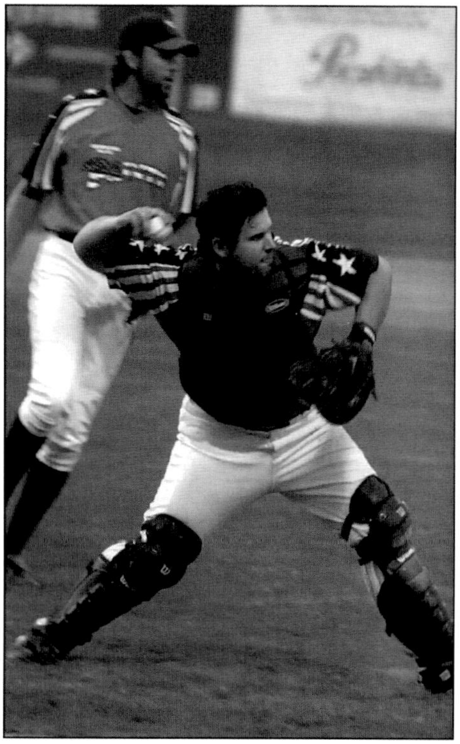

The recognized leader of the ballclub, catcher Tony Cosentino had an even better season in 2004 than he did the previous year; batting .294 with four home runs and 51 RBI. He went 5-5 on Opening Day and was voted onto the Frontier League All-Star Team at the end of the season. Relief pitcher Mike "Gitsy" Gits (background) looks toward first to see how close the play will be. (Courtesy of Scott Osborne.)

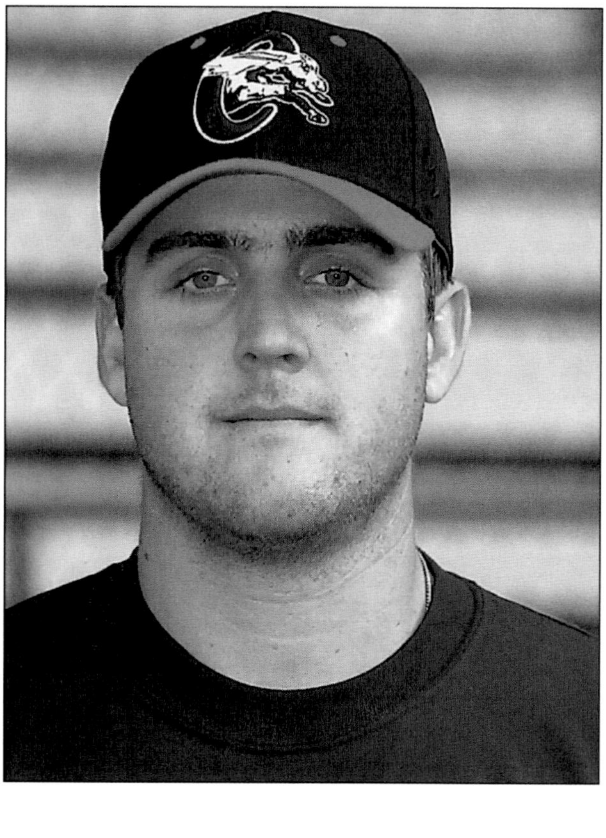

Left-handed Dustin Brisson was the big stick in the 2004 Paints' batting order. He batted a team-high .330, led the Paints in extra-base hits (42), and finished second in home runs (14) and RBI (65). Dustin's best day probably came on May 23 in Richmond when he hit two home runs and knocked in five runs to lead the Paints to a 10-9 victory over the Roosters. Once traded for major leaguer Dustin Hermanson, Brisson came to Chillicothe after playing three seasons in the Boston Red Sox farm system. The Wellington, Florida native starred at the University of Central Florida where he ranks second all-time in home runs.

A former Seattle Mariner's farm hand who pitched briefly (6.1 innings) for Chillicothe in 2003, Michael Kesten became the left-handed ace of the Paints' starting rotation in 2004. The Bellflower, California wild child was almost unhittable early in the season, sporting a 1.71 ERA after his first eight starts. He cooled off in the second half, but still turned in an impressive record, which could have been much better with more run support. Kesten finished 7-8 with an ERA of 3.02. He went the distance on the mound six times and pitched two three-hitters and one four-hitter. He struck out ten or more batters four times with a high of 15 (on August 11 versus Florence) and led the team in strikeouts with 125 in 113 innings.

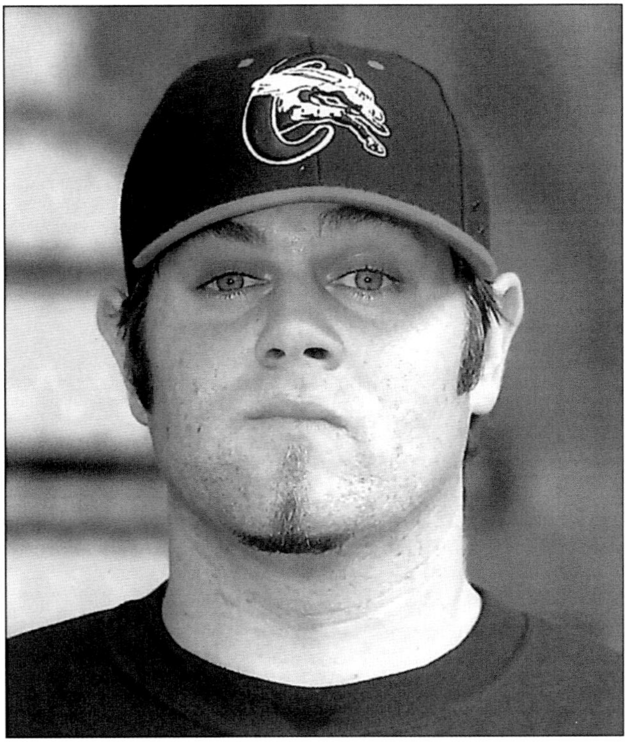

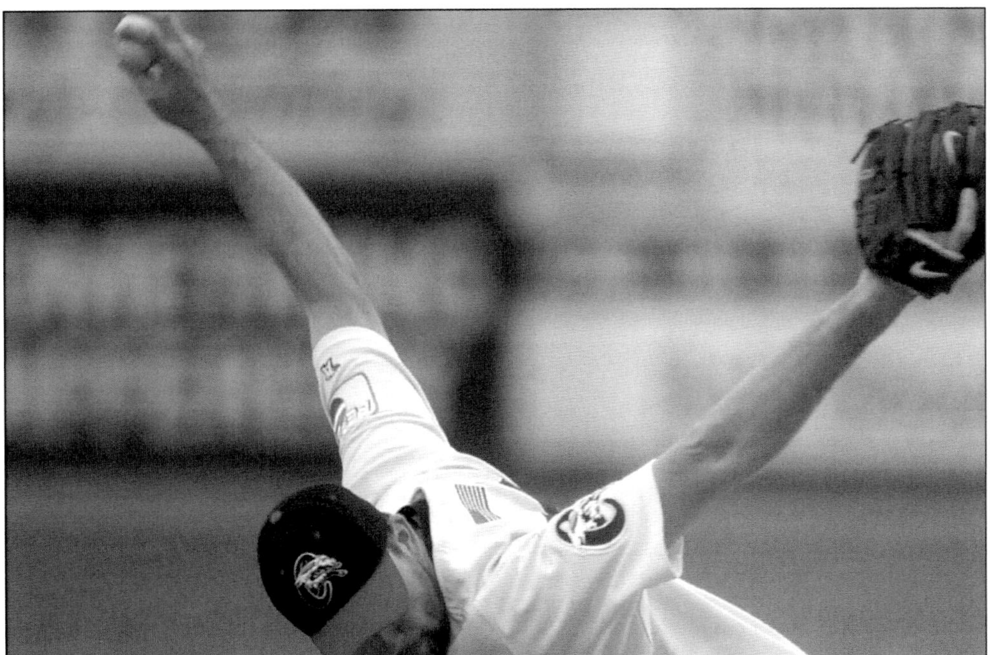

Mike Gits again led the Paints' pitchers in appearances in 2004 (47), while lowering his ERA to a team-best 3.11. Gits finished the season with a 6-3 record and two saves, and his teammates voted him the Most Valuable Pitcher Award for the second straight year. (Courtesy of the *Chillicothe Gazette*.)

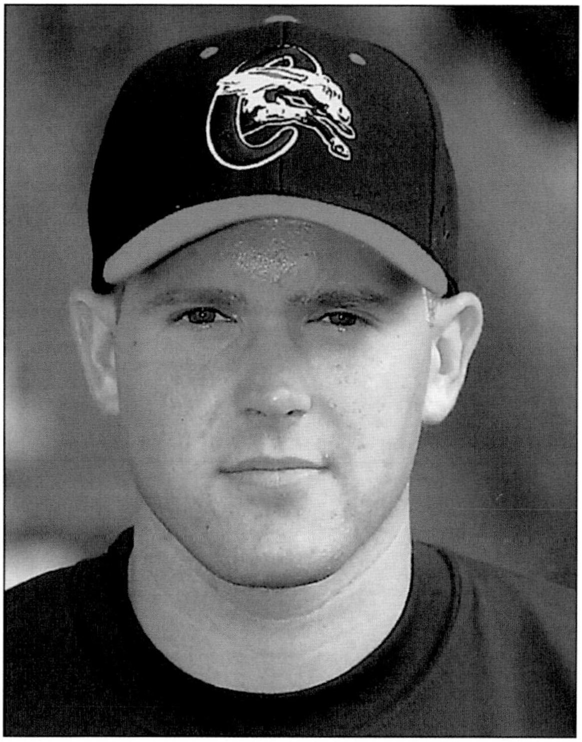

A native of Steubenville, Ohio, Perry Cunningham got his feet wet in pro ball in 2003, pitching briefly for the Allentown Ambassadors of the Northeast League. The big (6'3", 215 lbs.) right-hander was an important member of the Paints' rotation in 2004, starting 16 games and compiling a 7-4 record with a 3.98 ERA. He was third on the team in strikeouts with 74. Perry was all-conference for three seasons at Davis and Elkins College (Elkins, West Virginia).

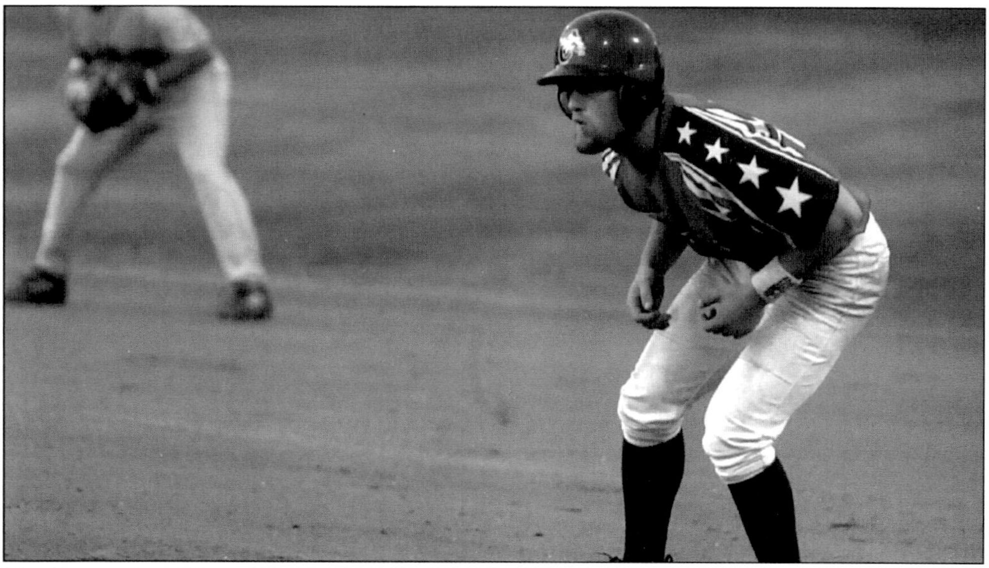

The Paints found Beau Blacken at a San Diego Padres tryout camp in Phoenix, Arizona, and signed him because of the tremendous raw power he displayed as a batter. Although Blacken had been a catcher at New Mexico State University (where he set the school record for throwing out baserunners attempting to steal), he played third and the outfield for the Paints in 2004 because of Tony Cosentino's hold on the Paints' catching job. Blacken, who also got quite a few of his 321 at bats as the DH, had an excellent rookie year, hitting .271 and leading the Paints in home runs with 17. He added 21 doubles (giving him the second most extra-base hits on the team) and 58 RBI. (Courtesy of Scott Osborne.)